Roald Dahl's Marvellous Medicine

About the Author

Professor Tom Solomon studied medicine at Oxford, did a PhD in Vietnam and postgraduate virology in the United States, before training as a neurologist. He is Director of the University of Liverpool's Institute of Infection and Global Health, and Professor of Neurology at the Walton Centre NHS Foundation Trust. He studies emerging viral infections, particularly those that affect the brain, has published more than 200 scientific papers, and was awarded the Royal College of Physicians Triennial Moxon medal in 2014. His science communication work includes a highly acclaimed TEDx talk, many radio and television appearances, a Guinness World Record for creating the 'World's Biggest Brain', and another for running the fastest marathon dressed as a doctor.

Twitter @RunningMadProf

www.tomsolomon.co.uk

Roald Dahl's Marvellous Medicine

Tom Solomon

LIVERPOOL UNIVERSITY PRESS

First published in 2016 by
Liverpool University Press
4 Cambridge Street
Liverpool L69 7ZU
UK
www.liverpooluniversitypress.co.uk
@LivUniPress

British Library Cataloguing-in-Publication data
A British Library CIP record is available

print ISBN 978-1-78138-339-1 paperback

Typeset by Carnegie Book Production, Lancaster
Printed and bound by CPI Group (UK) Ltd, Croydon

Front Cover: Tom Solomon and Lucy Frontani; Photo: Stephen Umpleby, Outside Studios/ Roald Dahl Nominee Ltd. Courtesy of The Roald Dahl Museum and Story Centre.

Dedicated to Rachel,
and to all the patients who have shared
their stories with me over the years

Contents

PART FOUR: GOBBLEFUNKING

PART FIVE: NO BOOK EVER ENDS

Introduction

Most people know Roald Dahl as a famous writer of children's books and adult short stories, but few are aware of his fascination with medicine. Right from his earliest days to the end of his life, Dahl was intrigued by what doctors do, and why they do it. During his lifetime, he and his family suffered some terrible medical tragedies: Dahl nearly died when his fighter plane went down in World War II, his son had severe brain injury in an accident and his daughter died from measles infection of the brain. But he also had some medical triumphs: he dragged himself back to health after the plane crash, despite terrible facial and back injuries; he was responsible for inventing a medical device (the Wade-Dahl-Till valve) to treat his son's hydrocephalus; and he taught his first wife, Patricia, to talk again after a devastating stroke, his passion and persistence leading ultimately to the formation of the Stroke Association.

Dahl always said that if he weren't a writer, he would have liked to have been a doctor. His fascination for medicine came through in much of his literature, from the detailed anatomical dissection of the brain in his macabre story 'William and Mary', to the explosive potions in *George's Marvellous Medicine*. Some of Dahl's own medical encounters featured in his writing. He loved nothing better than describing a gruesome operation, with no anaesthetic, performed on the nursery table. Sometimes the influences were more subtle – who would have thought 'Gobblefunk', the strange mixed-up language of the BFG, had its origins in a family illness?

In this unique combination of popular science, biography and memoir, Professor Tom Solomon, who looked after Dahl towards the end of his life, examines Dahl's life and literature from a new perspective. With examples from Dahl's writing as well as Solomon's own casebook, the volume uses Dahl's medical interactions as a starting point to explore some extraordinary areas of medical science, and shows how Dahl's inventive streak extended beyond his storytelling to help him lead some amazing medical advances. During their time together, the trust, honesty and understanding between the doctor and patient grew. Dahl's late-night hospital discussions with Solomon give new insights into this remarkable man's thinking as his life came to an end. Dahl could be proud and boastful when it came to his literary achievements, but he was surprisingly modest about his scientific endeavours. It seems that – despite his childhood dreams of being a great innovator who saves lives around the world – when this was actually realised, he somehow did not recognise his own marvellous medicine.

Prologue

According to the family stories, my great-grandfather Moses Solomon landed in Cardiff as a boy at the end of the nineteenth century, escaping the pogroms of Lithuania. His name was not Solomon when he left his home country, but the immigration officer could not understand his eastern European accent and they chose the new name together. I was visiting Cardiff for the first time in May 2014 for a conference, and with Moses in mind felt I ought to go and look around the docks, though quite what I hoped to find I do not know. As I passed the great shiny glass-and-steel structure of the Welsh National Assembly, I noticed a rather peculiar little church with white slatted wooden sides and a grey roof. It was perched incongruously on the edge of the bay, as if it had perhaps just been dropped there temporarily. It reminded me of the innocent works of the Swedish painter Carl Larsson, which had adorned the walls of my childhood home.

I entered the café, which had taken over the ground floor of the church, and discovered that my instincts had been right. It was indeed a Scandinavian church, built originally as a temporary structure that could be moved if needed. It had been erected in the middle of the nineteenth century by the Norwegians as a seamen's mission; Cardiff had been a major port, and the Norwegian merchant fleet one of the largest in the world. With the decline in the shipping trade, the church had eventually closed, been dismantled and then resurrected nearby as the Norwegian Church Arts Centre.

'You might like to see the exhibition space upstairs,' the lady serving coffee suggested. I was due back at the conference but thought it would be impolite not to take a quick peek. As I climbed the narrow staircase, I looked up and got a shock. There, smiling down at me, was a picture of my old friend Roald Dahl.

What are you doing here? I thought. I soon discovered that the room I was entering was the Roald Dahl Gallery; he had been the first president of the trust that had restored the church. It all came back to me, then: Dahl's Norwegian father had landed here in Cardiff around the turn of the century, and set up a business supplying his compatriots working in the ship industry. His family were regular attendees at this very chapel, and Dahl had been baptised here.

No wonder he had wanted to restore it. In the gallery I found the Dahls' Silver Christening Bowl and a few wall panels outlining his biography, but there was not much detail.

Never mind, I thought. I had been listening to a BBC Radio Four 'Great Lives' podcast that morning; *I'll download the programme on Dahl and listen on the train home.* The problem was there did not seem to be a programme on Dahl. I wrote indignantly to the BBC questioning why this was the case, and listing all the reasons why he should be included in the series.

A few months later, I found myself sitting opposite Matthew Parris in a small studio at Broadcasting House making a Great Lives programme on Dahl. His was a great life, I argued, not just because of his fantastic literature, but because of the extraordinary way he had dealt with adversity, particularly all the medical challenges he and his family had faced. We were joined on the programme by Dahl's official biographer, Donald Sturrock.

'You can't cover much in forty minutes,' I complained to Donald afterwards over a drink.

'I know,' he sympathised, 'that's radio, I'm afraid.'

'We barely scratched the surface of Dahl's medical work. There's so much more to say.'

'Well, why don't you write a book on it ... ?'

PART ONE

A TOWERING GIANT

Chapter 1

The Witching Hour

In 1990 I was a junior doctor at the John Radcliffe Hospital in Oxford. I had just finished all my training as a medical student, and was starting my first year working on the wards. Roald Dahl was one of the patients. He was in his seventies, and had been in and out of hospital in the preceding few months with anaemia. He was being cared for by my boss, one of the country's most distinguished haematologists, Professor Sir David Weatherall. Dahl was becoming increasingly frail as the summer progressed, and Weatherall was doing all he could to determine the cause of the anaemia. I can remember the night I first met Dahl. I was on call that evening, and was told in the handover that the 'great author' had just been admitted for tests. As the doctor on call, I had to stay in the hospital overnight to complete any jobs left over from the day, give the night-time drugs and deal with any new problems that arose.

That night I had finished examining the patients, talking to relatives and taking blood samples. Things had quietened down. Rather than go and rest in the on-call room, I settled in front of the ward computer, and was busy writing up some research I had been doing the previous summer when as a medical student I went to study malaria in Africa. It must have been nearly midnight, and the lights were all down low when I became aware of this large figure wandering slowly up the ward, casting a great big shadow. I carried on tapping away at the keyboard, concentrating on my data. The restless patient walked past the nurses' station where I was working, and a few moments later wandered back again. He must have come past three or four times, each time a little bit slower, peering over my shoulder, trying to see what I found so absorbing. Eventually he stopped.

'What are you doing?'

It was a deep, booming voice. I looked up to see an enormous giant of a man towering over me. He was wearing a silk nightshirt, and was wrapped in a huge dressing gown. He had large ears, and twinkling inquisitive eyes. It almost felt as if the BFG were peering down at me. But it wasn't the BFG. It was the author of *The BFG*, Roald Dahl himself.

We started chatting. I think Dahl was intrigued. Being a world-famous author he was used to people fussing and fawning over him, yet here was someone who seemed to be paying him no attention at all, and was much more interested in something else. Rather than dismiss me, however, Dahl wanted to know all about the research I was doing on malaria. He had lived and worked in Africa, and loved it there. He'd also been struck down by malaria, so had a personal interest.

'And have you read any of my books?' he asked after a while.

'Well,' I said, and paused. 'I have not *read* any, but I loved the film of *The Jungle Book.'*

The Jungle Book, as you probably know, is a wonderful film based on a fabulous book, but it is not by Roald Dahl at all, it is by another great British author, Rudyard Kipling. Dahl looked at me curiously for a moment or two, trying to decide whether I was completely ignorant, or just teasing him. Suddenly, having decided that this was a great joke, he roared with laughter. We became good friends after that.

As a junior doctor, or house officer as it was known back then, I was on call covering the wards every third night. So once all the jobs were done I would head to the haematology ward, which is full of patients with leukaemia and other blood diseases. Here I would chat with Dahl in his side room. We would talk late into the night. I think he found it difficult to sleep, especially in this unfamiliar environment.

The hospital at night is a very special place. The hurly burly of the day has passed, and there is a quiet, intimate atmosphere. It is not completely silent. There is the gentle hum of medical equipment, the subtle hiss of oxygen masks and the soft footsteps of nurses down the corridor. Occasionally someone calls out in their sleep; you might hear the sobs of those who have just lost a loved one, or even the distant cry of a newborn baby. If patients are awake in the middle of the night, they often want to hear some comforting words. As Dahl knew only too well, this is the witching hour when, if you're not careful, your worst fears can creep up on you.

The witching hour, somebody had once whispered to her, was a special moment in the middle of the night when every child and every grown-up was in a deep deep sleep, and all the dark things came out from hiding and had the world all to themselves

– The BFG

It was in these wee small hours, in the semi-darkness, when all was hushed, that Dahl and I would chat. What did we talk about? Just about everything.

People, places, literature, love, music, marriage ... and medicine. He told me all about his life, and especially his fascinating, and often tragic, encounters with the medical world.

A Majestic and Drunken Arrival

Dahl loved talking with doctors. He was full of admiration for them, or I should say for *most* of them, because if a doctor were pompous or incompetent, he'd be quick to spot it. In *Boy: Tales from Childhood*, he described what happened to his father, Harald, who broke his elbow, aged fourteen, falling off a roof.

> *Somebody ran to fetch the doctor, and half an hour later this gentleman made a majestic and drunken arrival in his horse-drawn buggy. He was so drunk that he mistook the fractured elbow for a dislocated shoulder.*
>
> *'We'll soon put this back into place!' he cried out, and two men were called off the street to help with the pulling. They were instructed to hold my father by the waist while the doctor grabbed him by the wrist of the broken arm and shouted, 'Pull, men, pull! Pull as hard as you can!'*
>
> *The pain must have been excruciating. The victim screamed, and his mother, who was watching the performance in horror, shouted, 'Stop!' But by then the pullers had done so much damage that a splinter of bone was sticking out through the skin of the forearm.*
>
> *This was in 1877 and orthopaedic surgery was not what it is today. So they simply amputated the arm at the elbow, and for the rest of his life my father had to manage with one arm.*

Dahl was not there when all this happened. He hadn't even been born. The account is based on the story passed down through the family, and is a wonderful example of Dahl's literary style. He draws you in, with vivid imagery of the sights and sounds; every time you think things can't get any worse, they do, until Dahl's father loses his arm altogether. It would be comic if it were not so tragic. Indeed, Dahl felt as long as you made things funny, you could get away with murder, and in several of his stories people most certainly did.

He was a great storyteller and was not averse to stretching things a little if it made for a better tale. He often made events that were absolutely dreadful sound hilarious. His childhood memoir, *Boy*, is full of such medical encounters; there are more than thirty references to doctors, illness and medicine, in just twenty-five chapters. It is a fabulous book that everyone should read, if only just to realise how lucky schoolchildren are now, compared to back then.

The manoeuvre the drunken doctor was using to replace the supposedly dislocated shoulder is one of several rather vicious techniques that are still used in casualty departments today. Dahl was curious to hear every brutal detail. The Kocher technique involves the doctor gripping the arm tightly and rotating it inwards, so the head of the humerus pops back into place. With the traction-countertraction approach, the doctor pulls the arm one way, whilst the body is pulled in the opposite direction – this is what was being attempted on Harald Dahl. In using the Hippocratic method, the doctor's foot is placed in the armpit to help lever the joint back into position.

As you may surmise, doctors have been replacing dislocated shoulders for a long time; a wall painting in the Egyptian tomb of Ipay appears to show someone trying it three thousand years ago.

When I was in casualty, the approach I preferred was Stimson's method. You lay the patient face down on a trolley with their injured arm dangling down towards the floor. Then you give them an empty bucket to hold, and gradually over half an hour add water to slowly increase the weight. This gently pulls the arm down until suddenly, *clonk*, the shoulder pops back into its socket. Dahl and I agreed this was the one we would want, if either of us dislocated a shoulder in the future.

'But why is shoulder dislocation so common?' he asked me.

'Well, it's the most mobile joint,' I explained, 'so it comes out more easily than any other.'

Some scientists believe this flexibility reflects the fact that our ancestor might have been a brachiate, a primate that swings from tree to tree like an orang-utan. If you watch a child on the monkey bars in a park, you will see that we still have the basic neural software in place. Later, as humans became bipedal and walked upright, our shoulders lost much of their muscle strength and bulk. This design fault has left us vulnerable to shoulder dislocation, which is rare in the primates that still swing in the trees.

Moans and Groans

Dahl was a keen observer of any illnesses in his family members. When he was about nine, his 'ancient half-sister', twelve-year-old Ellen, had appendicitis. Dahl delighted in watching her every moan and groan, taking careful note of how she behaved as the doctor examined her. But he was not allowed to watch as she had her appendix removed in the nursery.

... we stood there spellbound, listening to the soft medical murmurs coming from behind the locked door and picturing the patient with her stomach sliced open like a lump of beef. We could even smell the sickly fumes of ether filtering through the crack under the door.

The next day Dahl was allowed to inspect the appendix, 'a longish black wormy-looking thing', in a glass bottle. He asked his nanny what made an appendix go bad like this.

'Toothbrush bristles,' she answered.

'Toothbrush bristles?' I cried. 'How can toothbrush bristles make your appendix go bad?' Nanny, who in my eyes was filled with more wisdom than Solomon, replied, 'Whenever a bristle comes out of your toothbrush and you swallow it, it sticks in your appendix and turns rotten. In the war,' she went on, 'the German spies used to sneak box loads of loose-bristled toothbrushes into our shops and millions of our soldiers got appendicitis.'

'Honestly, Nanny?' I cried. 'Is that honestly true?'

'I never lie to you, child,' she answered. 'So let that be a lesson to you never to use an old toothbrush.'

For years afterwards Dahl used to get nervous whenever he found a toothbrush bristle on his tongue. He eventually had appendicitis as an adult; 'they got it just in time and it was a very inflamed thing, which was going to burst,' he wrote to his mother. My own grandma Spooner, who was born around the same time as Dahl, used to tell me and my siblings that appendicitis was caused by a grape pip getting stuck in the appendix. She said we must always spit out pips, or risk getting sick. But this wasn't true either.

'So what does cause appendicitis?' Dahl asked me.

'In most cases we think it gets blocked up with a faecalith, which is lump of hard faeces,' I explained. 'Occasionally it is a foreign body, but I don't think a toothbrush bristle or grape pip can cause it. Once it is blocked, the appendix swells up and becomes inflamed and necrotic, with black dying tissue.'

'And is it true we still don't know what the appendix is for?'

'Yes, though there are several theories ...'

Pocket of Bacteria

For many years people used to think that in humans the appendix served no function at all.

Darwin proposed this small blind-ending tube, which comes off the side of the intestine, was a vestigial organ, a remnant no longer needed, from a time when our primate ancestors ate much more vegetable matter. Supporting this was the fact that rabbits, horses and other herbivores have a much larger appendix than we do. The appendix was thought to house bacteria specifically to help digest the tough cellulose in vegetation. The fact that the inflamed human appendix could apparently be removed with no harm done appeared to support the notion that it no longer serves a purpose.

In recent years, however, ideas have changed. Professor Bill Parker at Duke University in the United States thinks the appendix holds essential bacteria, not so we can digest cellulose, but to act as a reservoir for repopulating the bowel with 'helpful' bacteria after an episode of severe diarrhoea.

Bacteria play a key role in digestion, especially in the large bowel where they make up about fifty per cent of faeces, and produce large quantities of vitamins. Parker hypothesised that after someone has had an attack of severe diarrhoea, for example due to cholera, much of the bacterial population is washed away, and the blind-ending appendix would be the source of vital replacement bacteria.

There is some evidence supporting this idea. *Clostridium difficile*, or *C. diff*, is one of the nasty superbugs that people can get in hospital. It is often present in the human bowel in small harmless amounts, and is kept in check by the large numbers of friendly bacteria. But courses of antibiotics can wipe out these helpful bacteria, allowing *C. diff* to take hold. A study published in 2011 found people who have had their appendix removed have more problems with recurrent *C. diff* than those who have not. Parker argues this is because if you still have your appendix your bowel will quickly be replenished by the good bacteria, but if you do not *C. diff* can take hold once again. He doesn't say whether he thinks horses evolved a larger appendix because they get more diarrhoea.

C. diff is a major killer around the world. In the UK there are now more than 1,500 deaths annually, and in the USA it is closer to 15,000. Traditionally *C. diff* has been treated with more, and stronger, antibiotics, but you can see there is a logical flaw in treating a problem caused by antibiotics with yet more antibiotics. However, if you think carefully about Parker's hypothesis, you can take this approach one step further: if the natural bacteria in the appendix make *C. diff* less likely to recur, then why rely on this small pocket of bacteria to recolonise the gut? Why not replace the bacteria wholesale? And this is the way modern treatment of *C. diff* is going. The thousands of different bacteria that make up the large bowel community, or microbiota, are reintroduced into the gut using a faecal transplant.

Dahl would have loved to hear how this is achieved: faeces is taken from a healthy volunteer, often a relative or friend, blended in a liquidiser, and then inserted into the colon of the patient. A number of methods are used. Some patients, taking a DIY approach, simply squirt it in using an enema. Because this doesn't get the faecal matter high up into the colon, however, gastrointestinal surgeons use a colonoscopy. Alternatively, it can be inserted at the top end via a gastric tube into the stomach. In America and Australia, faecal matter is now being delivered via capsules – 'crapsules' they have been called, or 'pooh in a pill'.

Although these approaches are being used increasingly they are not actually new. Faecal transplantation was first employed by American surgeons in 1958, and an Australian clinic has been offering the treatment routinely since the 1990s, long before Parker's hypothesis about the appendix. In fact, the earliest references to treating diarrhoeal disease by consuming faeces are found in ancient Chinese texts, and the Bedouin have for many years recommended ingesting fresh warm camel faeces as treatment for dysentery.

Bounce and Splat

Like many patients in hospital, Dahl got bunged up at times. Indeed he was rather obsessed with his bowels from his childhood onwards.

'Thanks awfully for the figs & biscuits etc.,' he wrote in one of his weekly letters home to his mother from boarding school. 'Those figs will keep me going in more sense than one for quite a long time.' In another he described how the news that his mother had bought him a motorbike 'acted on me like a squitter pill acts on a constipated man'. Over the years Dahl tried all sorts of conventional and alternative treatments. These included *Superdophilus*, available from food suppliers, that according to the manufacturer contained 'billions of micro-organisms (chiefly *Lactobacillus acidophilus*) per gram to restore the microorganisms in the bowel'. Curiously enough, this was not all that far from the new treatments being used today. Dahl was keen to learn from me what is happening when someone is constipated.

'You have to really know how the whole digestive tract works to understand that,' I explained. The basic function of the gastrointestinal tract is to get nutrients out of the food we eat. So whether it's a delicious two-penny chocolate bar, as beloved by Dahl and his fictional creations Charlie and Mr Wonka, or some stinky cabbage that has been stewing for hours, the essential process is the same. In the mouth, food gets chewed up with saliva to make a soft ball that is easy to swallow; the saliva also contains enzymes to get the digestive process started.

At medical school they taught us a simple experiment to prove this: put a piece of white bread in your mouth and, rather than swallow it, just let it rest on your tongue. After five minutes, as your mouth salivates, you'll notice that the bread starts to taste much sweeter because the carbohydrates within it are breaking down into sugar; it is the enzymes in your saliva that are responsible for this initial stage of digestion.

Digestion begins in earnest in the stomach and small intestine, also known as the small bowel. Here carbohydrates, fats and proteins are broken down into their constituent building blocks: the sugars, lipids and amino acids. Your food thus becomes a soup of tiny molecules that can then be absorbed through the wall of the small intestine into the bloodstream, which delivers all the nourishment to the rest of the body. Once all the goodness has been absorbed from it, the soup, more of a thin stock at this stage, passes down into the large intestine, or large bowel. Here the body absorbs much of the water in it, so that it becomes thicker, and thicker, until it eventually it is more like a soft wet cake mix, which is expelled as faeces.

However, if it takes too long travelling through the large bowel, then too much water is absorbed. The cake mix becomes drier and harder, more like a rock cake, which is much more difficult to expel. This is essentially what happens when someone is constipated. The slow transit through the large bowel might be because someone is lying in bed in hospital rather than being up and about, or because they are taking painkillers, which slow the bowels motility, or for a whole range of other reasons.

Dahl was quite comfortable discussing all this. Indeed he seemed to relish this conversation with someone he had only just met. He did not shy away from such subject matter in his writing. For example, in *My Uncle Oswald*, we are told, for no particular reason than the sheer delight of the fact, that a tompion 'is a small pellet made out of mud and saliva which a bear inserts into his anus before hibernating for the winter'. This is thought to be to keep ants out.

In *My Uncle Oswald*, Dahl ascribed this pearl of wisdom to A. R. Worseley, a chemistry tutor at Cambridge, but I discovered later that he actually learned it from Ian Fleming.

'You writers should know these things,' Fleming teased Dahl. 'You should have a wider vocabulary.'

In *Boy*, Dahl described how he filled the pipe of his 'ancient' half-sister's fiancé with a little heap of dried goat droppings. The fiancé was an English doctor and rather unpopular with the Dahl family at the time, and the novel tobacco had the desired effect: '... all of a sudden the manly lover let out a piercing scream and his whole body shot four feet into the air'.

Later in the same book we learn about Corkers, Dahl's teacher at Repton, who:

> ...would stop suddenly in mid-sentence and a look of intense pain would cloud his ancient countenance. Then his head would come up and his great nose would begin to sniff the air and he would cry aloud, 'By God! This is too much! This is going too far! This is intolerable!'
>
> We knew exactly what was coming next, but we always played along with him. 'What's the matter, sir? Are you feeling ill?'
>
> Up went the great nose once again, and the head would move slowly from side to side and the nose would sniff the air delicately as though searching for a leak of gas or the smell of something burning. 'This is not to be tolerated!' he would cry. 'This is unbearable!'
>
> 'But what's the matter, sir?'
>
> 'I'll tell you what's the matter,' Corkers would shout. 'Somebody's farted!'

The school was full of such characters, including Captain Hardcastle, who 'was never still. His orange head twitched and jerked perpetually from side to side in the most alarming fashion, and each twitch was accompanied by a little grunt that came out of the nostrils'. The boys thought he had shell shock, but it is almost certain that Dahl was describing Tourette's syndrome, without realising it.

It was at Repton that Dahl developed his love of chocolate. The school was not too far from the great chocolate manufacturers Cadbury's, and every now and again the company would send boxes of their new products for the schoolboys to assess. They would grade each bar from one to ten, comparing against an old favourite like the Coffee Cream Bar, which was included as a 'control'. The boys could also write comments: 'Too subtle for the common palate,' Dahl wrote next to one. He fantasised about working in the factory's inventing laboratory among the bubbling pots of chocolate and fudge, creating something fantastic that would sell by the millions.

'I have no doubt at all,' Dahl later wrote, 'that thirty-five years later ... I remembered those little cardboard boxes and the newly-invented chocolates inside them [when] I began to write ... Charlie and the Chocolate Factory.'

Dahl enjoyed hearing about an extraordinary lecture we had from one of Oxford's most flamboyant colorectal surgeons. This doctor, like his colleagues, preferred to be described as a *colorectal surgeon* rather than a *bottom chopper*, although Dahl and I agreed the latter is what he really spent his time doing. For an hour the surgeon held us captivated as he talked all about faeces. He made us ponder all sorts of things, such as the ideal consistency of a stool: 'imagine if it hit the pavement: it should not bounce (too hard) or splat (too soft), but should just settle (perfect)'. This was decades before the Bristol Stool Chart addressed the same issue. He spoke of the intricacies of recreating someone's back passage after it had been removed because of cancer. The anatomy was not too tricky, but one of the great unknowns was how well it would work after surgery: particularly when there was the *pressing matter* of someone feeling they need to go, but being unsure of whether it were all *hot air*, or something *more substantial*. The point was, we don't really understand how someone knows if they are about to pass flatus or faeces. This question applies not only to colorectal patients, but to all of us, if you stop to think about it. We don't even have the vocabulary to describe the different sensations. Dahl and I tried out some terms:

'A *perumble* is the feeling that you are about to break wind ...'

'No,' I retorted, 'a *flube* is better!'

'A *storb* is an imminent stool!'

'How about a *plute*?'

Although we barely knew each other, Dahl and I took great delight in this rather frivolous exchange. Thinking about it later, I wondered if he were actually trying to shock me, or test me out in some way.

Daily Deposit

Lavatorial rituals were an important part of boarding-school life for the young Dahl. At St Peters in Weston-Super-Mare the school porter would hand out numbered brass discs every morning to six lucky boys allowed to use one of the lavatories and thus escape the headmaster's morning inspection. An unscheduled visit to the toilet was only allowed if you had diarrhoea, but would result in 'a dose of thick white liquid being forced down your throat by the matron', which would make you constipated for a week.

At Repton one of Dahl's jobs as a 'fag' was to sit on the seat in the winter, warming it up for one of the Boazers, as the prefects were known. 'I must have read the entire works of Dickens sitting on that Boazer's bog during my first winter at Repton,' he later wrote.

When living in Africa, he took great delight in a book called *Culture of the Abdomen – The Cure of Obesity and Constipation* by Professor F. A. Hornibrook. This 1924 bestseller, which ran to eighteen editions and was published until 1960, described a series of abdominal exercises, based on native dances, to deal with middle-aged spread and ensure thorough and regular bowel evacuations. 'We do Horniblow [as Dahl renamed him] every morning,' he wrote to his mother. 'It's the funniest thing you have ever seen, George, Panny and I sprawling over the floor of my bedroom groaning, panting and sweating and cursing the old Professor. But I think it's done me lots of good.' His daily 'deposit in the bank of good health' would be an important concern for the rest of his life.

In the 1980s Dahl's bowel problems were finally diagnosed as diverticulitis, an inflammatory bowel condition, and he had a large section of colon removed. His daughter Ophelia thought that perhaps the tropical bugs from his time in Africa had finally caught up with him. For a few weeks, whilst the bowel healed, he had a colostomy, which he did not enjoy at all. The surgeon Mr Brian Higgs, who lived locally, operated on Dahl. They became good friends afterwards, with Higgs a regular visitor to the Dahl family home. His wife, Rosemary, was already well known to Dahl, who had first met her years earlier at the private Chiltern clinic.

Chapter 2

Prodding and Poking

Sometime during the 1880s Dahl's father, Harald, left Norway on a boat, spending a few years in Paris before settling in Cardiff, South Wales. At the time, Cardiff was a thriving coal metropolis where enterprising Norwegians could make their fortune. Dahl's mother, Sofie Magdalene, also came from Norway, and even after his father had died she stayed in Cardiff for the sake of the children's education. Dahl's first school was Llandaff Cathedral School in Cardiff. However, following *The Great Mouse Plot*, in which he left a dead rodent in a sweetie jar to terrify a local shopkeeper, he was moved to St Peters School in Weston-Super-Mare.

At first the nine-year-old boarder was terribly homesick, but, as recorded in *Boy: Tales of Childhood*, his detailed observation of his sister Ellen's appendicitis would prove useful: with considerable dramatic skill he faked the condition to fool the school matron.

> *I lay on the bed and she began prodding my tummy violently with her fingers. I was watching her carefully, and when she hit what I guessed was the appendix place, I let out a yelp that rattled the windowpanes. 'Ow! Ow! Ow!' I cried out. 'Don't, Matron, don't!' Then I slipped in the clincher. 'I've been sick all morning,' I moaned, 'and now there's nothing left to be sick with, but I still feel sick!'*

She called the school doctor who was also duped by Dahl's antics and so Dahl was sent home. Here he was examined by the family doctor, who was a wiser and more skilful physician.

> *He himself sat down behind his desk and fixed me with a penetrating but not unkindly eye. 'You're faking, aren't you?' he said.*
> *'How do you know?' I blurted out.*
> *'Because your stomach is soft and perfectly normal,' he answered. 'If you had any inflammation down there, the stomach would have been hard and rigid. It's quite easy to tell.'*

I kept silent.
'I expect you're homesick,' he said.
I nodded miserably.
'Everyone is at first,' he said. 'You have to stick it out.'

Dahl was worried about what the general practitioner would tell his school, but they struck a deal: the doctor would say Dahl had a very severe infection of the stomach, which was being treated at home with pills for three days, so long as he promised never to try anything like this again.

The Baron

'You were lucky not to end up under the knife,' I told Dahl, 'like a patient with Munchausen's.'

I had been reading about this extraordinary syndrome, and Dahl was fascinated. In the 1950s, Richard Asher, a great doctor and medical writer, described in *The Lancet* patients who travelled around the country with dramatic and untrue stories of acute illness, which sometimes resulted in unnecessary abdominal operations. They would make up excruciating symptoms, rolling around the bed in agony hoping someone would operate. But often they would be recognised by a member of staff who remembered them: 'Good heavens, you haven't got Luella Priskins in again, surely? Why she's been in here three times before and in Bart's, Mary's and Guy's as well.' *Lancet* publications were rather more lyrical in the 1950s than they are today.

Asher noted these patients were recognisable by their many abdominal scars, extraordinary tales and many falsehoods: 'He's the man who always collapses on buses and tells a story about being an ex-submarine commander who was tortured by the Gestapo.'

Asher named the syndrome after the eighteenth-century Baron von Munchausen who entertained dinner guests with tales of his adventures in the Russo-Turkish war. Munchausen's stories were exaggerated even further in a book about him. I wondered afterwards whether this fantastical storyteller might have appealed to Dahl, but at the time he was more interested in the medical side.

'Why would patients do that?'

'Asher thought there was a range of motives: attention seeking, the pleasure of fooling the medical staff, wanting the drugs, avoiding the police, maybe even free board and lodging.'

We now recognise a whole range of fictitious disorders, including the more sinister Munchausen syndrome by proxy in which a parent or carer fabricates illness in their child. My wife, Rachel Kneen, a paediatric neurologist, comes across this occasionally, and finds it one of the most challenging areas of her work.

'What about the appendicitis?' Dahl asked. 'Are the symptoms so clear cut?'

I told him about a typical case I had seen just a few months earlier, when I was a student on the surgical firm.

The patient is a nineteen-year-old man who works at the Cowley Car Works outside Oxford. He presents with two days of fever, nausea and vomiting, and a pain that started around the umbilicus, and then moved to the right lower quadrant of the abdomen, the iliac fossa. This shifting of the pain is characteristic. Even through the appendix lies down on the right, the aching starts in the central abdomen, reflecting the bowels' embryological origin as a single central tube. However, as the inflammation builds up around the organ, it involves the fatty tissue, the omentum, which overlies it, and then the abdominal wall, so pain is then felt locally at the surface. When I examine him, he looks sweaty and anxious. This is more than the fear of someone who does not like doctors, or being in hospital; it is a raw and vulnerable fear. As I reach to touch his abdomen, he flinches, even though I have not yet made contact. I find he is tender all over, but especially at McBurney's point, the anatomical landmark, named after an American surgeon, which lies one third of the way between the anterior superior iliac spine, the hip bone, and the umbilicus. He is tender when I press here, but even more so when I suddenly let go, almost bouncing off the trolley.

I apologise, but am not really sorry. Eliciting this sign, rebound tenderness, is crucial to clinching the diagnosis. There is no specific blood test or X-ray for appendicitis. It is a clinical diagnosis, and the decision to operate is based almost entirely on the history and examination. The senior house officer, Jim, and the registrar agree he needs to go to theatre, and it is booked for later that afternoon.

An appendectomy is one of the most common emergency operations, and performing it is usually the prerogative of the senior house officer, or the houseman. So as a student I will probably just watch or, at best, get to help. But I get lucky. The houseman, who is training to be a GP, is not interested, and as I am scrubbing up to assist Jim he asks if I would like to do the operation. My heart leaps, and in my head I shout out, 'YES, YES, YES!' but to Jim I offer a nonchalant, 'Sure, why not?'

I have learned it is not the done thing to be too excited or emotional in theatre. I am lucky, but, also, I deserve the privilege. Three nights earlier, I assisted Jim with two appendectomies. 'You've just seen me do one,' he said after the first. 'What's the point of staying up for another?' But at that stage I couldn't get enough of it. I wanted to do surgery; I wanted to do medicine; I wanted to do obstetrics; I wanted to do anaesthetics. I loved being a medical student, and wanted to do everything.

Another World

Dahl's sister Ellen was not the first in the family to have appendicitis. Tragically, his oldest half-sister, Astri, had died from it when she was aged seven. Dahl was only three at the time. Astri had woken in the middle of the night with a terrible stomach ache; her sister Alfhild, with whom she shared a room, went to wake their mother and the doctor was summoned. The clinician diagnosed acute appendicitis, and operated at home on the scrubbed nursery table. However by then the appendix had burst, causing infection and inflammation of the whole abdomen – peritonitis. Astri never came round from the anaesthetic, and died about a week later. As Dahl wrote in *Boy*, his father was heartbroken.

> *Astri was far and away my father's favourite. He adored her beyond measure and her sudden death left him literally speechless for days afterwards. He was so overwhelmed with grief that when he himself went down with pneumonia a month or so afterwards, he did not much care whether he lived or died.*
>
> *If they had had penicillin in those days, neither appendicitis nor pneumonia would have been so much of a threat, but with no penicillin or any other magical antibiotic cures, pneumonia in particular was a very dangerous illness indeed. The pneumonia patient, on about the fourth or fifth day, would invariably reach what was known as 'the crisis'. The temperature soared and the pulse became rapid. The patient had to fight to survive. My father refused to fight. He was thinking, I am quite sure, of his beloved daughter, and he was wanting to join her in heaven. So he died. He was fifty-seven years old.*

We talked about the enormous impact antibiotics have had on medicine. Dahl was familiar with the story of Alexander Fleming's famous discovery of penicillin at St Mary's in London. He even dropped a reference to it into his children's book *Matilda*. Mr Wormwood, her brutish and ignorant father, explains: 'I tell you, I felt exactly like that other brilliant fellow must have felt when he discovered penicillin. "Eureka!" I cried. "I've got it!"'

Dahl hadn't realised that when penicillin was first used, on a policeman in Oxford with an eye infection, it was so scarce that Florey and his team extracted the drug from the man's urine so they could keep treating him. It was a privilege, Dahl felt, to live in the era of antibiotics and so many other important scientific discoveries ...

He turned to me suddenly. 'What about your patient?' He was eager to hear every detail. 'The young man with appendicitis. What happened? Did you do the operation? What was it like?'

I think back to the operating room. I tell Dahl everything, knowing he of all men will relish the sights, sounds, smells and sensations of my very first operation.

The patient has been wheeled in under anaesthetic, the abdomen scrubbed with iodine, and the drapes placed across the top of his torso. I hear the gentle wheeze in and out of the ventilator, and the *blip, blip, blip* of the heart monitor. I look to my left to check with the anaesthetist that we are okay to start. His eyes widen slightly when he realises it will be me, not Jim the senior house officer, operating. I hold my breath. If he objects, the game is over. It is not that medical students are not allowed to operate – there is no rule. It is not as if the anaesthetist could tell the surgeon what to do – he cannot. But if the anaesthetist is not happy with the arrangement it would be foolish of Jim to insist, especially because there might be repercussions if anything went wrong.

'Start, gentlemen, please!' declares the anaesthetist, and then he winks at me. Although I am wearing a face mask, I think he has recognised me by the John Lennon glasses perched on my large nose, and the dark brown curls that escape the edges of my theatre cap. Only a month ago, I was doing anaesthetics and intubating as many patients as he would allow me to.

Jim positions the operating light so that it is directed on to the patch of exposed skin, no more than seven centimetres squared. I focus on that patch. For the next hour it is my whole world. With the scalpel, I draw a line five centimetres across the flesh. I worry I have not pressed hard enough to cut through the skin, but moments later there is a ruby red wax-like bead tracing my move. I tease apart the flesh. More dark round beads appear, and Jim leans forward with the electrified diathermy. There is a crackle, fizz and pop as each bead is burnt and the vessel cauterised. A curl of smoke rises with the faint but unmistakable whiff of burning flesh.

Under Jim's gentle guidance I cut, tease and push my way through the subcutaneous fat, fascia and abdominal musculature. Suddenly there is a spurter – I have cut across a small artery that is now squirting a bright red jet into the air. Jim clamps the artery, and I tie it off. I press on, cutting through the peritoneum, and levering aside the fatty omentum to reveal the raw uncooked sausage of the small bowel glistening in the light. I start feeling my way along it; the caecum and appendix lie at its end, but which way to go? I become aware that the scrub nurse is getting restless. She could object, and Jim may have to take over. I start again and travel in the opposite direction, and suddenly I have it. I can feel it. The appendix is lying tucked behind the caecum.

I prise it gently forward, and lay it out on the abdominal wall, still attached to the bowel. It seems slightly darker than the rest of the bowel, but not as inflamed as I'd expected.

'What do you think?' I ask Jim, worried that it looks too healthy.

'Roll it over,' he instructs, and immediately I see it is much more engorged on the other side.

'Ah ha!' says Jim, with theatrical flourish.

'Nasty!' chimes the anaesthetist, who has lowered his newspaper to peer over the top of his spectacles.

Having found the offending organ, I set about removing it. With a fine curved needle and nylon thread, I sew round the base of the appendix to make a purse string, which I then tighten as Jim cuts through the angry flesh. He places the appendix in a pot, and then swabs the stump with iodine; it dribbles down the drapes, along with blood from the wound. A few seconds later, I feel it trickle round my ankle and into my boot; my plastic apron must have somehow got tucked into it. But I am barely aware of this, or the light banter between Jim and the scrub nurse, relaxing now that the work is almost done. All that exists for me is the gash in the skin before me, the bowel within it, my two hands and the instruments I hold. Beyond me the walls could have disappeared, the whole hospital gone in a great tornado, but it would not have affected my focus. This concentration, which is almost like yoga or meditation in its intensity, is what attracts surgeons to the specialty. They enter another world.

With the appendix removed, I suture the peritoneum back together, and reconnect the various layers of muscle and fascia.

'Would you like me to close up, Mr Solomon?' asks Jim. Suturing together the final layer of skin is often done by the assistant, and this offer, along with the use of the surgical title *Mr*, is the ultimate compliment.

'Yes. Thank you.' I breathe a huge sigh. Rather than heading off to get changed I continue to peer at the wound. I am relieved, exhausted and elated: my first operation is successfully completed. I rest my hands on the abdomen in front of me. Some moments pass.

I look to my left. The eyes peering at me over the spectacles are not those of the anaesthetist, they are those of my patient, Roald Dahl. He stares at me for a long time, saying nothing. Eventually his face softens.

'Do you write?' he asks.

'Sort of, a bit,' I reply evasively. I gather up my files, and leave the room; it seems absurd to admit to this world-famous author that just as he, a writer, has always wanted to be a doctor, so have I, a doctor, always wanted to be a writer.

Flesh and Blood

Medicine was very different in the 1920s when Dahl was a child. Not only were there no antibiotics to fight infection, but the anaesthetics to put you to sleep for an operation were also much more dangerous than they are now, so doctors avoided using them if at all possible. When Dahl was eight and on holiday in Norway, he had his adenoids, the soft glands at the back of the throat, removed without an anaesthetic, as he recalled in *Boy*.

> '*Open your mouth,*' *the doctor said, speaking Norwegian.*
>
> *I refused. I thought he was going to do something to my teeth, and everything anyone had ever done to my teeth had been painful.*
>
> '*It won't take two seconds,*' *the doctor said. He spoke gently, and I was seduced by his voice. Like an ass, I opened my mouth.*
>
> *The tiny blade flashed in the bright light and disappeared into my mouth. It went high up into the roof of my mouth, and the hand that held the blade gave four or five very quick little twists and the next moment, out of my mouth into the basin came tumbling a whole mass of flesh and blood.*
>
> *I was too shocked and outraged to do anything but yelp. I was horrified by the huge red lumps that had fallen out of my mouth into the white basin and my first thought was that the doctor had cut out the whole of the middle of my head.*

After the operation Dahl's grandmother warned him: 'That won't be the last time you'll go to a doctor in your life, and with a bit of luck, they won't do you too much harm.'

'Back then it was fashionable for doctors to remove adenoids and tonsils at the slightest excuse,' I explained to Dahl. 'Nowadays we are much more conservative about it.' Adenoids and tonsils are specialised lymph glands sitting at the back of the nose and mouth to fight infection. The lymph nodes you sometimes feel swelling up in your neck are part of the same lymphoreticular system. As well as tackling infection, they also screen for other abnormalities, like cancer cells. The lymph nodes act like a filter. Lymph fluid drains to the nodes, carrying any pathogens – viruses or bacteria that can cause disease. Here such microbes are recognised as being 'alien' by the lymph glands, and they immediately get to work making lots of white cells, called lymphocytes, to try to kill off the bugs. The lymph tissue swells due to the great number of new cells being produced within.

The adenoids and tonsils function in the same way: they swell up to deal with infections, and go down again afterwards. You can see, then, that there is no sense at all in cutting out these hard-working glands that are doing their best to fight the invaders. Back in Dahl's day, doctors seemed happy to chop out anything they could. These attitudes persisted even into the 1970s. I can remember as a child being threatened by my mother with a tonsillectomy when I was trying to stay off school with a sore throat. I soon jumped out of bed and put on my uniform.

The lymph system extends through the whole body, and is especially important at sites where microbes try to gain entry. As well as the nose and mouth, this includes the lungs, the guts and of course the skin. Occasionally a bacterium manages to cross the tough outer layers, the epidermis, and evade the body's initial immune defences. In that case an army of white cells is sent to isolate the bug, and deal with it. This collection of white cells forms a boil, or abscess, around the site of infection. If you look under a microscope at a place where pus has formed, that is exactly what you will see: thousands of white cells. Because there is no space for this mass of white cells in the skin, they stretch it, causing terrible pain, until the skin ruptures, or someone lances it with a scalpel.

Rule Breaker

When Dahl was at St Peter's School, one of his friends, called Ellis, had just such a boil on his thigh that needed to be lanced. Nowadays you would be put to sleep by an anaesthetist for this, but in the 1920s doctors had to use their ingenuity to get round the problem. The doctor prepared his scalpel at the end of the bed, out of sight of Ellis, before asking the matron for a large towel.

> *Still crouching low and hidden from little Ellis's view by the end of the bed, the doctor unfolded the towel and spread it over the palm of his left hand. In his right hand he held the scalpel. Ellis was frightened and*

suspicious. He started raising himself up on his elbows to get a better look. 'Lie down, Ellis,' the doctor said, and even as he spoke, he bounced up from the end of the bed like a jack-in-the-box and flung the outspread towel straight into Ellis's face. Almost in the same second, he thrust his right arm forward and plunged the point of the scalpel deep into the centre of the enormous boil. He gave the blade a quick twist and then withdrew it again before the wretched boy had had time to disentangle his head from the towel.

Ellis screamed ... I couldn't blame the doctor. I thought he handled things rather cleverly.

Although medical practice had advanced considerably since Dahl's childhood, he felt that the essence of a great doctor remained the same – a combination of clinical skill, empathy and common sense. We were agreed that my boss in Oxford, Professor Sir David Weatherall, had all of these in great abundance.

I remember asking Dahl why, if he was so interested in medicine, he hadn't actually become a doctor himself. He was certainly bright enough, and back then, so long as you had the money you could easily go to university. In fact, his mother begged him to go to Oxford or Cambridge after school, but he had other ideas. He wanted to get out into the big wide world.

Dahl had never been completely happy at school. He'd always felt like a bit of an outsider, perhaps because his family were Norwegian. He didn't agree with his parents' thinking that English schools were 'the best in the world'. At St Peter's school in Weston-Super-Mare, and later at Repton in Derbyshire, he objected to the regular beatings with a cane to which the boys were subjected. Usually this was done by the teachers, but sometimes it was the older pupils, or 'Boazers'.

The indignation Dahl felt is passionately conveyed in his adult short story 'Galloping Foxley'. Decades later, if Dahl had to sit for any length of time on a hard bench or chair, he could feel his bottom, at the site where he had been caned, throbbing at the same rate as his heartbeat. Indeed, as he lay in bed chatting with me he said he could still feel it, if he thought about it, even though there was nothing to see.

This palpable reminder of his clashes with authority, which was carried by Dahl for his whole life, helps explain why he did not go to university. He distrusted people with authority and those who were part of the establishment, especially if their positions were gifted to them rather than being earned. Having hated much of his school life, Dahl had no intention of spending any further time in education. His academic record at Repton was not outstanding, but was good enough: he passed the school exam with credits in English,

History, General Science and other subjects. But he preferred spending time in the dark room producing photographs, or rolling through the countryside on his Ariel motorbike, which he kept hidden off site. So instead of going to university he left school to join the international Asiatic Petroleum Company, which later became part of Royal Dutch Shell. His hope was to be sent somewhere far away and exotic, like Africa.

Chapter 3

Into Africa

Often junior doctors dread their night-time work. They have already done a full day on the wards, and as soon as the evening jobs are finished, they want to get to bed. However, I looked forward to the evenings. Once everything was under control I would head to ward 5E, the haematology ward, and the side-room where Dahl was in bed.

I remember one evening it seemed especially quiet, and so I eased the door open slowly, in case he was asleep. I found him reading, concentrating on a novel by Ed McBain. His solid meaty hands, with well-groomed nails, seemed almost too large for the book. His great bald shiny pate, with a neat rim of hair around the back and sides, was reflecting the reading light, and his brow was furrowed. His face lit up when he saw me.

'How was the day?' he asked, pointing for me to sit on the bedside chair.

'Oh, fine,' I replied. 'Not much excitement.' Even though it was a very busy day, with lots going on, I didn't want to waste precious time talking about that. I wanted to hear more about his adventures.

'An autobiography is a book a person writes about his own life and it is usually full of all sorts of boring details,' Dahl wrote in *Boy: Tales of Childhood*. As one of the world's greatest storytellers, he had little time for biographies; he saw no joy at all in accurately documenting every detail of an individual's life. Why would anyone choose to read a collection of tedious facts when there was so much good fiction around? Invention, he felt, is always more interesting than reality. Indeed when he came to recount details of his own life story the distinction between fact and fiction often became blurred. His second autobiographical book, *Going Solo*, continued his life story where *Boy* left off, with Dahl leaving school and planning the future.

After Repton, Dahl spent a few years working for Shell in England, before being posted to work in Tanganyika, as Tanzania was known back then. He was thrilled to be going. Now he would have the chance to see the 'jungles and lions and elephants and tall coconut palms swaying on silver beaches' of which he had dreamed.

'But also there were snakes,' he told me, with a deadly serious expression one evening. 'Oh, how I hated those snakes.'

In *Going Solo*, Dahl describes a memorable encounter between a green mamba and a snake-man who was advancing slowly towards it, with a pole out in front:

> *What the snake did next was so fast that the whole movement couldn't have taken more than a hundredth of a second, like the flick of a camera shutter. There was a green flash as the snake darted forward at least ten feet and struck at the snake-man's leg. Nobody could have got out of the way of that one. I heard the snake's head strike against the thick cowhide boot with a sharp little* crack, *and then at once the head was back in that same deadly backward-curving position, ready to strike again*

Thankfully, the cowhide boot the man was wearing was thick enough to stop the bite penetrating through to his skin; a thin dark trickle of venom simply ran down the front of it. In *Going Solo*, Dahl also describes an encounter between a black mamba and his servant, Salimu, who is raking the drive as a snake approaches:

> *Wham! Salimu struck first. He brought the metal prongs of the rake down hard right on to the middle of the mamba's back.*

There was never a dull moment in East Africa, and rarely could you forget about the deadly venomous creatures.

Snakes also featured in several of Dahl's short adult tales. In 'The Wish', a boy pretends he must cross the carpet in front of him without stepping on any of the black patterning: '... yes, the black parts are snakes, poisonous snakes, adders mostly, and cobras, thick like tree-trunks round the middle, and if I touch one of them, I'll be bitten and I'll die before tea time.'

As he crosses the carpet, the snakes become more and more real, poised to attack. But it is just his vivid imagination. Or is it?

Dahl's most memorable snake tale is 'Poison', a short story set in India, home of the deadly krait. The narrator comes home to his bungalow late at night, surprised to find his housemate Harry Pope still up, lying in bed motionless and terrified:

> *'I was reading,' Harry said, and he spoke very slowly, taking each word in turn and speaking it carefully so as not to move the muscles of his stomach. 'Lying on my back reading and I felt something on my chest,*

behind the book. Sort of tickling. Then out of the corner of my eye saw
this little krait sliding over my pyjamas. Small, about ten inches. Knew
I mustn't move ...

One false move and it will be curtains for poor Harry. The doctor is called, and over nine tense sweat-drenched pages, he gives Harry anti-venom then pumps chloroform under the sheets to try and anaesthetise the krait. I won't tell you what happens in the end, but don't be surprised if there is a twist in the tail. The story was made into a television programme, one of the *Tales of the Unexpected* series shown in the early 1980s. I can remember as a youngster watching the programmes on Saturday nights, sitting with my brothers Guy and Bruce huddled on our big sofa. We would peep out from behind our cushions, hardly daring to see what would come next.

Medicine in the Real World

In Dahl's world, as in much of the popular imagination, a snake bite was almost always fatal. 'If a black mamba bit you, you died within the hour writhing in agony and foaming at the mouth.' Certainly snake venom causes a lot of deaths, one hundred thousand a year globally, according to David Warrell, a world leader in this area, and Professor of Tropical Medicine at Oxford. But many snakebites don't result in envenomation, and even if they do they are more likely to result in severe injuries rather than death. Dahl was fascinated, and horrified, to hear about some of the cases I had encountered as a medical student, sent to Thailand by Warrell to 'see something of medicine in the real world'.

You can smell the ward even before you step onto it: the stench of rotting flesh drifts down the corridor. I am greeted by one of the elderly Thai professors who has offered to show me around. He is polite and gentle, encouraging me to ask questions as we move from bed to bed.

The third patient is a young farmer, just twenty years old, who stepped on a Malayan pit viper whilst clearing a rice paddy. The venom has destroyed the skin and subcutaneous tissue, and his leg is peeled back to the muscles and tendons, like an anatomy dissection from my first year. While a nurse is preparing to dress the limb, fluid oozes from the flesh on to the green drapes. The toes are turning black and gangrenous.

The professor catches my eye then nods discreetly at the toes before giving a barely perceptible shake of his head. He says a few encouraging words in Thai to the young man, who is heavily sedated, and then explains to me, 'If he come straight to hospital we have chance to save leg. Now he lose toes, probably whole foot'.

I do not understand. 'Why would anyone wait?'

'Most people,' he explains, 'go to traditional healer first. Healer apply herb, and harmful treatment. Only when limb rotting patient comes to hospital. Then is too late for anti-venom.'

As long as the leg is looking like an anatomical dissection, I can cope with it. But as the nurse cleans his wounds, the young man extends his toes, and the dissection comes to life: the muscles contract and the tendons slither across the bones. Suddenly the ward is too hot for me. I can feel sweat trickling down my chest. The professor's voice becomes a distant echo. My vision closes in. All I can see are the sinews, sliding like snakes up and down the leg. I feel a wave of nausea and my head is spinning. Just as I am about to teeter over, a firm hand grips my arm and guides me into a chair.

'Here,' says the professor with a smile. 'Why don't you look at drug chart? I get water. It very warm today.'

I sometimes wonder whether my career would have taken a totally different direction had that wise old professor not been so shrewd and sympathetic. Medical students are easy prey for humiliation. I remember a friend who fainted during his first time in theatre. He had been all set on a surgical career, but he was so demeaned by the surgeons that day that he changed course to become a GP.

David Warrell, who is still working despite being nearly eighty, was quite an inspiration for me, and a whole generation of medical students. His expertise extends beyond snakes to all manner of venomous creatures, including poisonous fish, scorpions and spiders. For snakes, he was not just knowledgeable about envenomation and its treatment, he was the complete herpetologist, seeming to know everything there was to know about them.

'There are up to three hundred thousand people every year left with devastating disabilities from snakebite injuries,' Warrell had told us.

And it is the poorest people in the world, the farmers in remote areas, nomads and cattle herders, that are affected, those with the lowest influence on politicians and decision makers. A lot of this is preventable with education and simple protective measures. In South Asia, for example, almost all bites from kraits occur at night whilst people sleep on the ground; a study in Nepal showed that sleeping under a mosquito net reduced the risk by about fifty times. In Burma, where Russell's vipers are extremely common in the rice paddies, some farmers have started wearing simple protective boots made from leather, plaited palm leaves, or even woven grass; others refuse in the unfounded fear that it may provoke the snakes. With a concerted effort, much could be done.

Clever Cocktails

Warrell talked to us about anti-venom. There is simply not enough, and there is too little research into new ways of producing it. Most anti-venom around the world is still made in the traditional way. A snake is milked for venom, much to the delight of travellers to places like Thailand where this has become a tourist spectacle. Tiny amounts of the toxin are then injected into horses, sheep or other animals, which produce antibodies against it. This is then extracted, in the form of immunoglobulin or gamma globulin as it is sometimes known, and prepared for injection into the unlucky recipient of the bite.

However, one of the problems is that anti-venom is specific for each particular type of snake, and the victim usually does not know exactly what bit them. People used to try to capture or kill the snake to guide the treatment, but this is dangerous and is now discouraged. A more recent approach to identifying the snake is to swab the bite site and test for the snake's DNA, which, like a molecular calling card, can help identify the creature responsible.

Anti-venom is a pretty crude treatment, and often produces problems of its own, such as 'serum sickness' reactions where the body fights against this foreign blood product. Newer molecular approaches to designing anti-venom are being developed by analysing the exact proteins in different poisons and trying to look for commonalities.

'The interesting thing,' I said to Dahl, 'is there's a lot we can learn from these snake venoms.' Each one contains hundreds of proteins, carbohydrates, lipids and other small toxic molecules, evolved over millennia to incapacitate the snake's prey. 'It's important to remember humans are not the intended targets – we usually only get bitten because we have encroached on the snake's territory.' The toxins are clever cocktails of molecules that can specifically target the nervous system, or the cardiovascular system, or the blood-clotting system. According to Warrell, snake venoms are like drugs in many ways, small chemicals delivered via injection that must remain inert, and avoid the body's defences, until they arrive at the target tissue, where they cause major physiological changes.

Dahl's face lit up; he could see what I was getting at.

'Half the patients on the ward with high blood pressure are on captopril,' I went on. 'This drug was actually based on a snake toxin.' Blood pressure is maintained by increased muscle tone in all the arteries. One key step in the enzymatic pathway that controls this is the conversion of a protein called angiotensin I into angiotensin II. The venom of the Jararaca, the Brazilian pit viper, contains a small protein that interferes with this conversion, and led to the development of a whole new class of drugs: angiotensin-converting-enzyme inhibitors. A molecule that causes a lethal drop in the blood pressure of a small rodent can, at just the right amount, cause a modest reduction in the blood pressure of a human, thus providing a useful antidote to the salt we all sprinkle on our chips.

Warrell was right. This is a rapidly growing area, and one that shows great promise for the future. This blood-pressure treatment was just the first of many venom-derived drugs which are now in development: a cancer-targeting drug based on chlorotoxin from the deathstalker scorpion, a cobratoxin to dampen the immune system in multiple sclerosis, a toxin from the Cuban sea anemone to treat other immune diseases like rheumatoid arthritis.

Man from the South

Warrell joined me and my wife for dinner one evening, when we were living and working in Saigon, Vietnam, in the mid-1990s. We had moved to Oxford University Clinical Research Unit in Vietnam in 1994 when I was awarded a Wellcome Trust Fellowship to work on brain infections, and Rachel had joined as one of the Unit's paediatricians.

Showing Warrell the progress of our work in the hospital was nerve-racking enough, but to entertain this very senior academic to dinner, who seemed only yesterday to have been examining me as a medical student, felt even more daunting. However, Rachel and I need not have worried. He was the perfect guest.

As the ceiling fan whirred, and the cicadas chirped, he entertained us with his many years of tropical exploits. He was passionate about snakes, which he considered poorly understood and much-maligned creatures. Moved almost to tears, he described some of the terrible things that humans do to these most elegant of animals. Snake wine, a favourite tipple in southern Vietnam, was a disgusting concept. He had brought us a bottle of Australian, and as we polished it off he described how to milk a snake for venom.

'You must hold it just behind the neck ...' His voice became quieter as he concentrated on the detail. 'Grip it carefully ... tight, but not too tight ...'

Rachel and I leaned in to catch every word. 'You need a calm space ... no distractions ... because if you slip ... *SHISH*.' He suddenly whipped his hand round in a dramatic flourish. Rachel shrieked and I jumped back, knocking over my wine, in surprise at the sudden movement and the sight of Warrell's thumb and forefinger, which were badly deformed, scarred by the bites of the venomous creatures he so loved.

I was reminded, instantly, of Dahl's 'Man from the South': the heat of the tropics, the suspense, the allure of an encounter with danger, the deformed hand. I do not think Dahl and Warrell ever met, but I am sure if they had there would have been some interesting discussion, especially given Dahl's fascination with spiders and other arachnids, as conveyed in *My Uncle Oswald*.

Fighting the Battle

I have often found that when someone is ill in hospital, especially towards the end of their life, you see what they are really like as a person. All the airs and graces are peeled away. Sometimes the most charming person can turn out to be quite the opposite. But other patients who you might expect to be a little bit troublesome can surprise you.

I did not know it at the time, but over the years, Dahl had developed a reputation as an occasionally cantankerous, quarrelsome and sometimes downright rude man. If he didn't agree with someone, he did not mind letting them know, and he quite often fell out with his friends and acquaintances.

Dr Michael Streule, Dahl's GP, described the first time he met Dahl as 'petrifying': a couple of Dahl's children were having treatment at the local dentist, and Streule had to give the gas and air anaesthetic, with Dahl watching his every move 'like a hawk'. He found Dahl 'dominating, powerful, strong-willed and independent; a terrifying patient who was sometimes critical of the medical profession'. Dahl wanted to know everything, and liked to take charge; 'there was no fobbing him off'.

This was nothing new. In 1961, when he was a young man in New York, Dahl had broken his ankle after slipping in the snow.

'They wanted to take me to hospital and put the bloody thing in plaster, but I refused.'

However, in the John Radcliffe hospital in 1990 we found Dahl was a delight, even when he was very ill. He really cared about all those around him. Not just the doctors and nurses who were looking after him, but the other patients too.

Throughout the day, he kept himself to himself, especially during visiting time; he didn't want everyone's relatives gawping at him. But when all was calm, and we were chatting in the night, he was very concerned to know how the others on the ward were getting on in what seemed like a battle they were all fighting against their illnesses. He was especially bothered about a teenage boy called Mohammed, who had leukaemia. There had been quite a kerfuffle when he was first diagnosed.

Mohammed is a normal, healthy young man who has never been ill. He has been suffering from bleeding gums after brushing his teeth, and so his rather diligent GP sent in a blood sample for a full blood count. The counts are off: his haemoglobin is too low, and there are too many white cells, many of which are abnormal. He simply cannot believe it when he is called in to hospital to be told he has leukaemia. He feels so well – out partying at night, working on his various business interests in the daytime.

'There's nothing wrong with me,' he cries out angrily, and before we have the chance to explain properly he runs off the ward. Hours later there is growing concern when we still have not located him. He is not with his family, nor with his friends or fiancée. In the end, he is tracked down with a secret girlfriend nobody knew about. She brings him back to the ward. It is not an easy situation for anyone.

Now that he has calmed down, I try to explain the problem. I sketch out for him a normal blood film: the regular disc-shaped red blood cells, pale pink Smartie shapes separated by the occasional larger white blood cells, each of which has a central nucleus of three or four purple blobs. Then I show Mohammed what *his* blood film looks like. The red cells are paler, and some contain fragments of nucleus – Howell-Jolly bodies, that should not be there. But the striking thing is the white cells: there are far too many with dominant, ugly purple blotches – undifferentiated immature blasts. His bone marrow, the factory producing the cells, has gone into overdrive, pouring millions of these immature white cells into the blood.

If we do nothing he will become more and more tired, and develop severe infections because the white cells, meant to fight bacteria and viruses, do not work properly. Somehow it would all be a lot easier if the GP had not been so diligent, and Mohammed had actually started feeling unwell before the diagnosis was made.

He understands eventually.

He just needs a couple of days away, to sort out his business interests, and other family concerns. Then he will come in for treatment. Two days is too risky, I say. We settle on twenty-four hours.

Ahead of him lie months of nausea, vomiting, pain, exhaustion, tears, and frustration. He will lose his hair and his dignity. He will have countless needles in his arm for blood, and in his spine to check his nervous system is unaffected. He will have course trocars forced into his hip bone. He will face the ignominy of producing semen to be preserved in case of infertility from the chemotherapy.

Mohammed is young and tough, the cool dude among his friends. In the months ahead he will be jabbering and sobbing like a baby. Although he will come out of it a different person, he will survive the ordeal; his engagement will not.

In a side room at the far end of the ward is a middle-aged man called Toby who is also having a really tough time of it. He has a rare cutaneous form of leukaemia, mycosis fungoides, in which the abnormal white cells infiltrate the skin, looking vaguely like a fungal infection. His problem is that he is simply terrified that he is going to die.

Like everyone with cancer, Mohammed is frightened of course. But for the most part he can ignore it, grit his teeth and get through it. On good days, he will get out of the hospital; between treatments he can spend weeks away. Toby is too terrified. He can barely leave the ward, let alone the hospital. Even when his cell counts are okay, and we try to convince him that everything is under control, that he could have a few days at home, he is just too anxious. Every minor setback – a cough, a flicker of fever, a pain in his foot – convinces him that he is dying. He does not do well in the end.

Dahl knew he was very ill himself, and might die soon. But he said he was not frightened. 'Make things a laugh and a joke,' he told me, 'and life will be fun!'

A Bad Go of Malaria

Dahl certainly had fun in his few years in Africa, enjoying the colonial lifestyle, and playing tennis and football, sailing, and getting his golf handicap down to scratch. The work for Shell involved touring the country, supplying fuel and lubricants for farm equipment, as well as for the flying boats that visited the harbour every few days. There was also a fair amount of drinking. Dahl proudly wrote home to his mother about one party at which he had drunk 'Beer, Gin, Whiskey, Rum, Champagne, Sherry, Crème de Menthe, Brandy'. Like many of his generation, he continued throughout his life to enjoy a drink at lunchtime and in the evening. Years later when a biopsy revealed there was no damage to his liver at all he was 'delighted and felt vindicated'.

In Africa, Dahl managed to keep away from the dreaded snakes, but he was not so lucky with other tropical diseases.

'Last week I finally succumbed to Malaria and went to bed on Wednesday night with the most terrific head and a temp of 103°,' he wrote to his mother in 1939. 'Next day it was 104° and on Friday 105°.'

He was impressed with the treatment he received. 'They've got some marvellous new stuff called Artebrin which they straightaway inject into your bottom in vast quantities which suddenly brings the temperature down; then they give you an injection of 15 or 20 grams of quinine and by that time you haven't got any bottom left at all – one side's just Artebrin and the other's quinine.'

Artebrin was the trade name for mepacrine, a new antimalarial drug developed in the 1930s. Previously quinine was really the only effective malaria treatment, and had been in use for more than three hundred years. It was the Peruvians who initially worked out that the bark of the cinchona tree, which contains quinine, could be effective against fevers. This was long before the Frenchman Laveran first described, in 1907, the parasite that causes malaria. The Jesuits brought cinchona back to Europe in the sixteenth century, and it has been used ever since. The bark was dried, ground and mixed with sweet liquid to offset the bitter taste. In India and across the Empire the British would drink this 'tonic water' as a prophylactic to keep malarial fevers away; it seemed to go down especially well with a splash of gin. Nowadays the amount of quinine in Indian tonic water is too tiny to have any therapeutic effect.

From the 1930s onwards, newer antimalarials were developed. Mepacrine, as Dahl found, was very effective at killing parasites, but it went out of favour because of side-effects including psychosis. Choloroquine, developed around the same time, has been employed more widely although the parasites have now developed resistance to it. Thankfully quinine still proves effective, especially in severe disease.

'You mean after all these years doctors are still using quinine?' Dahl was amazed that things had not moved on.

'Yes, and we still don't even know the best way to give it.' I told Dahl all about a study I had been running in Mozambique. 'We know quinine is very effective in children with severe malaria if you give it straight into a vein. But what do you do in a rural health clinic, if you don't have facilities to set up a drip? Does it work if you give quinine into a muscle, and is it safe?' My study was a comparison of intravenous versus intramuscular quinine. 'Half the children got the drug into a vein, and the other half into a muscle.'

Dahl pulled a face and rubbed his buttocks. 'I know which I would prefer.'

I showed him the graph of parasite clearance times. 'You can see, i.m. quinine is just as effective as i.v., and it is a lot easier to administer.'

'Yes, very useful, I suppose.'

Antimalarial research has come on apace in the last twenty-five years. In Vietnam I was studying encephalitis and other brain infections, but much of the work of the Unit, where I was based, was in testing a new antimalarial drug, artemether. This is derived from *qinghaosu*, a herb the Chinese have been using to treat fevers for more than two thousand years. The programme was led by Professor Nick White, who supervised my PhD, and whom I found to be another inspirational academic.

Tropical Exploits

'If you are going to Thailand, you must go and see Nick White,' David Warrell had told me before my first trip to Southeast Asia as a student. Like the Taj Mahal in India, or Angkor Wat in Cambodia, Nick White sounded like a spectacle not to be missed. I first met him in Bangkok as he was cramming the last few pieces of equipment into a battered Toyota Corolla, ready for the eight-hour drive up to Ubon Ratchathani, near the Thai-Cambodian border. Oy, his laboratory technician, was navigating, and I was squeezed in the back between a freezer and a centrifuge.

After two hours of frosty silence – was it me, the humidity, the terrible Bangkok traffic or something else? – there was a gradual thawing. The rickshaws, scooters and buses gave way to breathtaking scenery: a patchwork quilt of green paddy fields dotted with occasional bamboo huts, naked children dipping in and out of the water, and buffaloes wallowing in the mud. Nick captivated me with descriptions of the tropical ailments we would see in Ubon, and the research taking place there. I entertained him and Oy with gossip from Oxford, the shenanigans on the wards and medical-student politics. I was teased for my inability to recall famous cricket scores from the last decade, and my failure to make diagnoses based on Nick's classical descriptions of the diseases: even Oy could diagnose anthrax.

After a few hours we were stopped by police at a roadblock. The fact that Nick's international driving licence was out of date by two years looked problematic until he simply changed the date with his biro. We drove on. My unwitting renaming of the antibiotic Fortum as *Fortnum* caused such hilarity that we nearly came off the road. Nick has called me Fortnum ever since. As the sun dipped behind the mountains, he screeched the brakes full on, and leapt out of the car. I wondered at his sanity, until I saw him dig out his camera and capture the orange rays glistening on the rice paddy, silhouetting palm trees and egrets. I still have the picture.

After eight hours on the road, I was stiff, aching and tired, but exhilarated. The work at the hospital in Ubon proved hard. We started before sunrise with a breakfast of noodles and chilli that I could barely stomach, and ended after midnight. A twenty-two-year-old Buddhist monk was admitted with cerebral malaria. His parasite count fell as the treatment took effect, but we watched helplessly as his coma deepened, his urine dried up and his skin yellowed. There must be some explanation, something we could do. In the next bed a child who had been bitten by a snake stopped breathing. Her face and larynx were swollen, and the staff were unable to intubate. When Nick effortlessly placed the tube into her larynx, I could not hide my admiration: most consultants in Oxford would not even know which way up to hold the laryngoscope.

Sadly, the monk died a few hours later. Nick found me at the end of his bed, tears in my eyes, pouring over his charts. Later two delightful nurses squeezed me on to their Honda Dream and took me to a remote pagoda on the hill to drink cooling tea. That evening, as Nick and I smoked cheroots on the roof of the hospital and admired another breathtaking sunset, I had a strong feeling about where my future lay.

Urgencia

'My friend died of malaria,' said Dahl. 'Charles Marsh – a terrific fellow. He didn't die straight away, but it killed him all the same.' Marsh was more than just a friend: he was a mentor, advisor and in many ways the father Dahl never had. Older than Dahl by nearly thirty years, he was a well-connected Texan newspaper tycoon who shared Dahl's sense of fun. In the 1950s, Marsh was entertaining Dahl and his first wife, the actress Patricia Neal, at Jamaica Inn, the hotel he built on Jamaica Island. It was here that he caught malaria and slipped into a coma.

'Cerebral malaria,' I said to Dahl. 'It's the worst form.' Back then nearly two million children were dying of malaria in Africa every year. The big unknown was why some of those infected with *Plasmodium falciparum*, the malaria parasite, developed severe disease, whilst others were fine. 'And by fine I mean really fine,' I told Dahl. 'We did a study in Mozambique where we bled every child in a village, and one third of them had malaria parasites in the blood. They were not lying at home in bed – they were playing football in the scrubland.'

'So they weren't feeling sick at all?'

'No, they were absolutely fine.' One theory was that the children who became comatose had a low blood sugar, hypoglycaemia. So for my student elective project I took hundreds of Glucostix for assessing blood sugar. The plan was to study every child admitted with malaria.'

'And?'

'Well, just as I was leaving the UK, there was a paper in the *Lancet* showing just that – hypoglycaemia is common in African children with severe malaria.'

'Ah, beaten to it.'

'Exactly. So we had to change the study.' I spent a fortune on a phone call from Mozambique to my supervisor, Rodney Phillips, back in Oxford, as we redesigned the protocol. 'We decided to measure the sugar level of every child admitted: maybe it wasn't just a problem in malaria.'

'You tested every child?' Dahl asked, 'Was it busy?'

'It was a bit of a mad plan. For five days and five nights I studied every child admitted to the Pediatria Urgencia, the emergency paediatrics department. I was OK for the first two days. But by the second night I was pretty tired.'

'You didn't sleep.'

'Well, the patients kept coming in, and I didn't want to miss any. There was no one really to help because the hospital was so busy. By the third night I was exhausted, and by the fourth I was hallucinating, but I was determined to go on.'

'So what happened?'

'The nurses took pity on me. They sent me to rest in their coffee room, but I wouldn't go unless they promised to call me for any children that came in. About four hours later I woke with a start, thinking I had messed up the whole study. But the nurses had kept recruiting whilst I slept. There was only one form to fill in for each child, and a single blood sugar measurement, so it wasn't too onerous. But it meant I didn't miss any children. The nurses did the same every night after that. I'd stay in the department until everything quietened down, then they would take over.'

'So it worked.' Dahl popped a wine gum in his mouth, and then passed the jar across to me. I took a red one.

'It just about worked, yes.'

'And what did you find?'

'Well, that was the interesting thing. It wasn't just malaria. We saw hypoglycaemia in malnutrition, and other diagnoses in which you wouldn't expect it.' This was in the middle of Mozambique's civil war; kwashiorkor and other forms of malnutrition were very common. Overall, nearly ten per cent of the children were hypoglycaemic, and those with low sugar were much more likely to die. The overall mortality for children under five in Mozambique was thirty per cent at the time. 'A staggering one in three children never reached their fifth birthday.'

'That's truly horrific,' said Dahl, and I could see him starting to brood. Luckily one of his favourite nurses, 'Bluebird' he called her, came in with the night-time drugs, and lightened the mood.

Since my late-night discussions with Dahl, the number of children dying of malaria has come down considerably. This is largely due to the use of bed-nets impregnated with insecticide, and better treatment for those that get sick. Every child now gets a blood sugar level checked on arrival at hospital, and we are much smarter at using the drugs we have. However, there are still half a million deaths every year, which is far too many. We also now have a much better understanding of the disease mechanisms in cerebral malaria – low blood sugar only accounts for a small proportion of the children in coma and fitting. In most, the cause of coma is more complicated.

Malaria is caused by an anopheles mosquito taking a blood meal, and injecting *Plasmodium falciparum* into the blood. The parasite enters the red blood cells, and replicates within them. This seems to make the cells less flexible than normal; they also develop surface 'knobs' containing parasite proteins, which interact with sticky cellular adhesion molecules that line the surface of the blood vessels. Together this means that instead of red blood cells squeezing through the small blood vessels in the brain, as they normally do, they get stuck or sequestered. This sequestration is the cardinal feature of cerebral malaria, disturbing the brain's normal function to cause coma and fitting.

But other processes may also contribute.

Dr Mac Mallewa was a Malawian Wellcome Trust-funded Research Fellow with the Liverpool Brain Infections Group for many years. Together we studied hundreds of children in coma and showed many of them had a viral brain infection as well as malaria parasites in their blood. Those with both infections have an especially bad outcome. It may be that the viral infection makes sequestration more likely by causing increased expression of the cellular adhesion molecules. He and others are now doing studies to see if he can improve the outcomes in such children.

Ultimately malaria vaccines may offer the best hope for control, but, until we have good vaccines widely available, a better understanding of the disease processes, leading to newer treatments, will remain a key way to save lives.

'"An aesthetic disease but a deuced nuisance,"' I declared, challenging Dahl to name the author of this quote on malaria. He looked around the room thoughtfully.

'Keats, maybe ... ?' He leaned his head to the side. 'But I don't recognise it.'

'It's Oscar Wilde.'

'Ah, of course … Though *I* would say malaria is *more* than a nuisance; and I'm not sure it is very aesthetic either.' He laughed sardonically, rubbing his buttock again.

Chapter 4

Crash

Dahl and I chatted every few nights, whenever I was on call, and I found I liked him more and more. He was one of many patients to whom I have become close over the years. I used to keep notes of what I learned along the way in a green notebook, important things patients taught me about medicine and about life. In five or six packed years as a medical student, you discover so much about what is important. By seeing people at their most difficult times, their most vulnerable, you understand how some cope, and even grow, whilst others really struggle and wither.

I still have my green notebook from all those years ago. 'GP Roger X,' it begins. 'Shouts at old people or anyone Asian etc. and thus distances them.' There follow two pages of my critical observations of this hapless general practitioner, who I, a twenty-one-year-old medical student, clearly felt was getting it all wrong. 'He ought to read the notes of their last visit before they come in, so he knows what it may be about ... Best to talk to them *before* starting to write anything down; not make notes as they talk – it's RUDE.'

Like generations of medical students before me and since, I must have sat there wincing with embarrassment at what seemed like the clumsy behaviour of an ignorant doctor. Do my own students similarly sit in silent horror and observe my cumbersome performances today? Probably. I catch myself occasionally shouting at an old person, and then will ask apologetically, 'Are you actually hard of hearing? No? Then there's no need for me to shout, is there?'

I do try to listen to patients before I start scribbling notes. Time is very pressured, but I have found if you look people dead in the eye, listen carefully to what they are saying, and try not to cut them short, it actually takes less time overall. I'm not sure why. Maybe because they know the messages are getting across first time, and they don't need to repeat things.

'It would be good to have BUZZWORDS on the front of their records,' my notebook continues, 'which remind you at a glance of past medical history and important things, e.g. *Diabetic 1960, 1972 MI, 1980 broke leg; 2 sisters* ... Gives the impression you know them really well and remember all about them.'

Below this entry I added a further comment three years later, when I had spent a few weeks with a wonderful GP, Dr Andrew Markus, in Thame, who did exactly this. In fact, I learned a great deal from Dr Markus, including the recipe for Dr Markus's Spicy Apple Chutney, which we still make every autumn.

My green notebook is full of other pearls of wisdom, and patient memories, such as 'Lesson of the Take', 'Surviving as a Houseman', 'My First Patient', 'Bringing up Children', 'Bad Surgery', 'How to Run a Committee', 'The Simple Solution' and 'Hell of a Night'. But far and away the largest section of the book is devoted to one patient, 'Roald Dahl'.

I did not know it at the time, but Dahl, too, always kept a notebook to hand for jotting down ideas, and anything he came across that was interesting. Some of these were just observations of people he met, like Max Aitken (Lord Beaverbrook). Dahl's sloping handwriting indicates he was obviously impressed:

> *Most dynamic man in world comes into room shouting well, well, well ... His knowledge of facts and his memory superhuman ... the hours he talked about hotel keeping in Bermuda ...*

Many of Dahl's notes were eventually developed into short stories. 'The man with the picture tattooed on his back' became 'Skin', whilst 'Story – sound apparatus that could hear trees scream' led to 'The Sound Machine'. One of the most significant notes was:

> *What about a chocolate factory that makes fantastic and marvellous things – with a crazy man running it?*

Bust Up

Dahl was still a young man working for Shell in Dar es Salaam when World War II broke out. As soon as he could, he drove the hundreds of miles north to join the RAF in Nairobi. On the journey, as he recalls in *Going Solo*, he encountered groups of giraffes, 'Hello! Hello!' he would call to them. 'How are you today?' There were also elephants moving with 'a great sense of peace and serenity ... Their skin hung loose over their bodies like suits they had inherited from larger ancestors, with the trousers ridiculously baggy.' This was the continent of which he had dreamed, as promised by Isak Dinesen's *Out of Africa*.

'Did you see much game in Mozambique?' Dahl asked me.

'Unfortunately not. I couldn't travel through the countryside because of the war.' The Front for the Liberation of Mozambique (FRELIMO) and the National Resistance Movement (RENAMO) were still locked in battle in 1990. In fact, that was one of the reasons I chose the country for my elective; I wanted somewhere you could not otherwise visit, and I was also interested in refugee health, having spent time in camps on the Thai–Cambodian border.

In Mozambique, I was mostly confined to the capital, Maputo, because of the fighting. Just before I arrived, a European doctor had been found in his car a few hours away from the city with a bullet in the head. He had worked in Mozambique for years, and was supposed to have been guaranteed safe passage by both sides. If he was not safe, then no one was.

When the desperate plight of the children in the *Urgencia* became too much for me, my only chance to escape Maputo was to hitch a ride in a tiny Save the Children plane that was shuttling up the coast to Quelimane. Even that was not entirely risk-free. I was told to sit on the sacks of rice in the back of the plane because occasionally the bored RENAMO fighters would take a pot shot at passing planes from below, and the sacks would buffer the bullets.

'The views from the plane were amazing,' I was telling Dahl, 'lush green jungle giving way to brilliant white beaches, fringed with palm trees and washed with breaking surf.'

'Ah, yes,' he agreed. 'I loved flying in Africa, soaring through the sky, gazing at the buffalo and the wildebeest and impala.'

'Impala?'

'Like eland, but smaller and faster.' I frowned, none the wiser. 'Types of antelope. Tom, you really must go back to Africa and see it properly.'

I have been many times since then, visiting Blantyre in Malawi, where Liverpool has a long-standing research collaboration with the local college of medicine, and have seen some amazing wildlife.

After a few weeks of training with an RAF instructor in a two-seater Tiger Moth, Dahl was allowed to go solo, learning how to loop-the-loop, navigate and make forced landings with the engine cut. He and his peers were flown to Iraq for six months of further fighter training on a range of planes. Here there were 'sand vipers ... the old scorpions and tarantulas to add to the excitement'.

Dahl was commended with a Special Distinction as one of the top trainees, and was made a Pilot Officer. He came third out of forty in his final exams, being beaten only by two men who had flown as civilian pilots before the war.

With training completed, he was sent to Northern Egypt from where he was to fly west and join 80 Squadron.

'Proceeding to fighter squadron in Western Desert immediately,' Dahl wrote in a telegram home in September 1940. 'Address RAF Cairo. You won't hear much from me, so don't worry.' Dahl was right – they would not hear much from him – but wrong that they should not worry. Just days after sending the telegram, Dahl's plane came down in the Libyan desert, and he was lucky to survive.

'My injuries in that bust-up came from my head being thrown violently against the reflector-sight when my plane hit the ground,' he wrote in *Going Solo*, decades after the event, 'and apart from the skull fracture, the blow pushed my nose in and knocked out a few teeth and blinded me completely for days to come.'

The plane had burst into flames, and Dahl lost consciousness, but he was soon brought round by a *whoosh* as the petrol tanks in the wings exploded. He sat there comfortably drowsy in no pain, but unable to open his eyes and just wanting to go off gently to sleep. The heat was increasing around his legs, but he was slow to do anything about it.

> *I think there was something wrong with the telegraph system between the body and the brain ... But I believe a message eventually got through, saying, 'Down here there is a great hotness. What shall we do? (Signed) Left Leg and Right Leg.' For a long time there was no reply. The brain was figuring the matter out.*
>
> *Then slowly, word by word, the answer was tapped over the wires. 'The–plane–is–burning. Get out–repeat–get–out get–out.'*

In his dazed state, it took Dahl a while to figure out how to undo his shoulder straps and buckle to get free. But he managed to hoist himself up, tumble out of the cockpit and crawl on all fours away from the heat before collapsing.

> *'I'm a wreck!' groaned the Centipede. 'I am wounded all over ... My legs!' he cried. 'They are all sticking together! I can't walk! And my eyelids won't open! I can't see!'*
>
> – James and the Giant Peach

As Dahl lay there, the machine gun ammunition exploded in the flames, with bullets pinging off in all directions, and he began to feel pain.

'My face hurt the most. I slowly put a hand up to feel it. It was very sticky. My nose didn't seem to be there.'

Suddenly he was joined by a fellow fighter pilot, who'd been flying alongside and who had managed to put his plane down safely.

> *'Where's your blasted nose? What a mess! Does it hurt?'*
> *'Don't be a damn fool. Of course it hurts.'*
> *'You'll look funny without a nose. I've never seen a man without a nose before. They'll laugh like hell.'*

Dahl's fellow pilot stayed with him throughout the night, lying alongside him for hours to keep him warm. Eventually a British infantry patrol came to find them, astonished that he had survived the crash. He was taken to an army first-aid station where one of the doctors initially mistook him for an enemy Italian. Here he was patched up, and then sent by train to the Anglo–Swiss hospital in Alexandria. Because of the swelling to his face, Dahl could not open his eyes for many days, and initially he thought he might be permanently blinded: '... blindness, not to mention life itself, was no longer too important ... the only way to conduct oneself in a situation where bombs rained down and bullets whizzed past was to accept all the dangers and the consequences as calmly as possible'.

Rudolph Valentino's Nose

The medical staff sheathed Dahl's whole head in bandages, with only small holes left for breathing. He had many X-rays and operations. Before one procedure, the anaesthetist told him they planned to use a brand-new anaesthetic, just come from England, that was given by injection, rather than the usual chloroform gas. Dahl described the conversation in *Going Solo*.

> *'What is it called?' I asked him.*
> *'Sodium pentathol,' he answered.*
> *'And you have never used it before?'*
> *'I have never used it myself,' he said, 'but it has been a great success back home as a pre-anaesthetic. It is very quick and comfortable.'*
> *'You mean this is the very first time you've ever used this anaesthetic?' I said to the anaesthetist.*
> *'You'll love it,' was the response. 'You go out like a light ...'*
> *I was quite unafraid. I have never been frightened by surgeons or of being given an anaesthetic, and to this day, after some sixteen major*

operations on numerous parts of my body, I still have complete faith in all, or let me say nearly all, those men of medicine.

Unfortunately, Dahl's confidence was misplaced on this occasion, and the anaesthetic did not appear to be working. He described what happened next as he lay on the operating table.

> *'I'm still awake,' I said.*
> *'I know you are,' he said*
> *'What's going on?' I heard another man's voice asking. 'Isn't it working?' This, I knew, was the surgeon, the great man from Harley Street.*
> *'It doesn't seem to be having any effect at all,' the anaesthetist said.*
> *'Give him some more.'*
> *'I have, I have,' the anaesthetist answered, and I thought I detected a slightly ruffled edge to the man's voice.*
> *'London said it was the greatest discovery since chloroform,' the surgeon was saying. 'I saw the report myself. Matthews wrote it. Ten seconds, it said, and the patient's out. Simply tell him to count to ten and he's out before he gets to eight, that's what the report said.'*
> *'This patient could have counted to a hundred,' the anaesthetist was saying.*
> *It occurred to me that they were talking as though I wasn't there. I would have been happier if they had kept quiet.*
> *'Well, we can't wait all day,' the surgeon was saying ... 'I'd forget that pentathol stuff if I were you. We really can't wait any longer. I've got four more on my list this morning.'*

Whether it quite happened like this is anyone's guess. A letter home to his mother confirms that Dahl's surgeon was indeed a plastic surgeon from Harley Street, seconded to the navy as a surgeon-commander. Pentothal (as it is correctly spelled) was certainly being introduced at that time, and there are relevant publications in the medical literature, but none by anyone called Matthews. However, the tension and banter between surgeon and anaesthetist rings true, and is heard in operating theatres up and down the country to this day.

The typical surgeon just loves operating, and wants to get through as many procedures as possible. They are characteristically full of bravado and self-confidence, which I suppose is what you need if you spend all day cutting people open and trying to fix them. Anaesthetists, on the other hand, are typically more cautious and careful and conservative. They have the tricky job of putting you to sleep, so the operation can be done, without putting you so deeply asleep that you never wake up again. According to *Going Solo*, the day before the operation, the surgeon had visited Dahl and examined his face carefully.

> *'We can't have you going about like that for the rest of your life, can we?'*
>
> *That worried me. It would have worried anyone. 'Like what?' I had asked him.*
>
> *'I am going to give you a lovely new nose,' he had said, patting me on the shoulder. 'You want to have something nice to look at when you open your eyes again, don't you. Did you ever see Rudolph Valentino in the cinema?'*
>
> *'Yes,' I said.*
>
> *'I shall model your nose on his,' the surgeon said. 'What do you think of Rudolph Valentino, Sister?'*
>
> *'He's smashing,' the Sister said.*

The Number One Attribute

Roald's nose recovered from the operation, but as he recuperated in hospital he still couldn't see.

> *It seemed to me that I had been permanently blinded, and as I lay there in my quiet black room where all sounds, however tiny, had suddenly become twice as loud, I had plenty of time to think about what total blindness would mean in the future. Curiously enough, it did not frighten me. It did not even depress me.*

Every morning a nurse would sit on Dahl's bed for an hour, bathe his swollen, sealed-up eyes, and talk with him.

'She had a lovely soft voice ... and sometimes as she worked very close to my eyes, I would feel her warm and faintly marmalade breath on my cheek and in no time at all I began to fall very quickly and quite dizzily in love with Mary Welland's invisible image.'

One day, as she was working away on his eyes, an eyelid began to open and he started to see things. The first objects he could make out were beautiful shining images of red and gold; he wondered whether he was perhaps catching a glimpse of paradise. In fact, it was the golden crown, the scarlet-rope-entwined anchor and the bright red cross that constitute the emblem of the Royal Naval Nursing Service. It was pinned to the nurse's white uniform.

'Hello,' she said. 'Welcome back to the world.' Although she was a lovely-looking girl, Dahl found that his passion soon evaporated. However, he retained a soft spot for nurses for the rest of his life. He realised that, while the skill and knowledge of doctors are essential for people to recover, the care and kindness of nurses are often equally important.

'Kindness is the number-one attribute in a human being,' he would often say afterwards.

Fashion

At the John Radcliffe Hospital in Oxford many years later, I could see that Dahl still had a fondness for the nurses, giving them each a nickname. He appreciated all their efforts, and was glad when he had the opportunity to do something for them in return. At the time, in 1990, the NHS was going through one of its strange experimental phases, which more recently seem to have become a persistent feature of hospital life. Someone had hit upon the idea that nurses on the ward should wear their own clothes, rather than nursing uniforms: you can imagine somebody 'upstairs' in hospital management thinking what a splendid idea this would be. We were told it would help the patients feel more at home, and create a friendlier atmosphere.

Dahl, like many of the patients, nurses and doctors, thought the ideas was ridiculous. Firstly, it meant no one knew who the nurses were, so there were all sorts of embarrassing misunderstandings. Secondly, Dahl was outraged that the nurses' own lovely clothes might be ruined at work by spills of blood and other even more unsavoury bodily fluids. Despite being terribly unwell, he decided to do something about it. He couldn't change the hospital rules, but he could stop the nurses spoiling their own clothes. How? He asked Liccy, his second wife, to go down to Marks and Spencer's and buy all sorts of different outfits. She came back to the ward with huge bags of cardigans and blouses and shirts and trousers. Then Dahl laid them all out on his hospital bed, and invited the nurses in to choose what they wanted. His face beamed with pleasure, as he stood back and watched the excitement and hilarity caused by this impromptu clothing sale. It showed the nurses just how much he cared about them. It was typical of Dahl – he always sought a practical solution to any problems that came up.

That evening I found Dahl standing at his open window looking contemplative. 'Just enjoying the evening air,' he explained with a sheepish smile as he hastily stubbed out a cigarette. 'Now, how is your work coming on?' he asked before I could say anything.

I told him about a review on malaria we had just finished that would be published soon in the *Lancet*. I showed him the figures, and tables, but he did not want to read the whole thing.

However, something else in my bundle of papers caught his eye, the spoof column I was writing for the *Oxford Medical School Gazette*. 'Hepatticus' described the musings of Professor Sir Hepatticus Oath TS FRS, an 'ancient Oxford academic' who was clinically and academically brilliant, but often baffled and bewildered by the mores of modern medical life.

I watched intently as Dahl sat down on his bed and began to read the piece. He paused and looked up. 'Humph! Are all the professors like that?' I thought about Hepatticus, about Weatherall, Warrell and others.

'They are all characters in their own ways.'

Dahl continued reading. He smiled, *humphed*, smiled again. I waited eagerly, pretending to be busy with his charts.

'Ha!' he snorted, and carried on.

Before I could get any feedback on the piece I was bleeped to go and see another patient. We never got round to discussing it properly. Did he think it was rubbish? Did he like it? I won't ever know. As I was closing the door behind me, however, I heard him mutter 'Dippy Dud!' At the time I thought I had misheard him; or maybe he was being rude. It was only years later, when I read about a spoof character Dahl had created for Shell's internal magazine, that I made the connection. For Dahl, 'Dippy Dud' had been a bit of light relief, an escape from the confines of corporate life. For me 'Hepatticus' was a chance to deliberate on some of the crazy antics of hospital and academic life, and take an occasional potshot at those who I felt deserved it. The column was written behind the cloak of anonymity, the author's identity closely guarded by all involved in the *Gazette*. It was later moved to the British Medical Association's monthly *News Review* magazine. On more than one occasion the recipients of the teasing failed to see the funny side. The Oxford radiologists in particular took great offence at some mild criticism of the way the department was run; they were on the warpath for a while, determined to discover the author, until Professor John Ledingham, who was Weatherall's closest colleague, intervened.

A little nonsense now and then, is relished by the wisest men.

– Willy Wonka in
Charlie and the Chocolate Factory

PART TWO

THE GREAT INVENTOR

Chapter 5

A Lucky Piece of Cake

'A man with congestive cardiac failure, two patients with myocardial infarctions and an old boy who had fallen out of bed and hit his head ...' I was telling Dahl a bit of what I had been up to earlier in the evening.

'My writing career was started by a bang on the head, you know.' Dahl had a mischievous twinkle in his eye. 'Yes, it was the great bash on the head.' I suspected he was ribbing me, but I let him go on. '... The plane coming down in the desert. Mind you, there was quite a bit of good fortune involved too ...'

After five months in hospital in Alexandria, Dahl was sufficiently recovered to rejoin his flying squadron, who by this stage were in Greece. Their equipment had been upgraded to the Hawker Hurricane.

This was a magnificent plane, not like the ancient Gladiator; four Browning machine guns on each wing, all firing at the push of a button.

Downing his first enemy plane, a Junkers 88 was a big moment:

Good heavens, I thought, *I've hit him! I've actually hit him!*

But the RAF squadron protecting Greece was vastly outnumbered by the Luftwaffe. Day after day their numbers were reduced as planes came down, especially during the Battle of Athens: 'an endless blur of enemy fighters whizzing towards me from every side'. As the Germans pressed on Athens, the squadron was evacuated to Palestine, as Israel was then known. Landing at a remote strip near Haifa, Dahl was astonished to find 'a welcoming committee of fifty screaming children and a huge man with a black beard, who looked like the prophet Isaiah and spoke like a parody of Hitler'. The man was a German Jewish settler, and the children were orphans. Dahl downed further enemy planes above Haifa, and having five aerial victories met the criteria to be classified as a flying ace. However, he suddenly started to get blinding headaches.

I got them only when I was flying and then only when dog-fighting with the enemy. The pain would hit me when I was doing very steep turns and making sudden changes of direction, when the body was subjected to high gravitational stresses, and the agony when it came, was like a knife in the forehead. Several times it caused me to black out for seconds on end.

The squadron doctor attributed the headaches to the severe head injuries Dahl had received in the earlier plane crash. He was worried that Dahl might lose consciousness altogether while up in the air – that would be the end of both plane and pilot. So Dahl was ordered to stop flying, and sent back to England. After a brief period, he was transferred to work as assistant air attaché at the British Embassy in the United States. The Americans had recently joined the war, but many of them still felt this was a European fight they should keep out of. Dahl, a dashing RAF war hero who had won countless dogfights, and even survived when his own plane went down, was sent to win the Americans over. He was also told to report back to the British government anything he heard that might be useful. He ingratiated himself among the American political elite, and counted Vice-president Henry Wallace, and Eleanor Roosevelt, the president's wife, among his friends – making him a very well-placed spy. After a year and a half at the embassy he took on a more secretive role with Canadian spymaster William Stephenson, working for British Security Co-ordination in New York.

Shot Down

It was in Washington that Dahl wrote his first paid piece of work, but even that was only by chance. Dahl met the famous author C. S. Forester, who had heard about his wartime adventures and was planning a newspaper article. Forester was one of Dahl's heroes, and at first he could not believe the little bespectacled man popping his head round the door was really the famous author.

They agreed to go to lunch at a French restaurant nearby as Dahl recalled in his short autobiographical story 'Lucky Break', which describes how he became a writer. Forester was struggling to enjoy the sumptuous smoked salmon and roast duck, whilst also making notes of the adventures.

So Dahl offered to write some notes himself, and send them to Forester the next day.

'Wouldn't that be easier? I could do it tonight.'
That, though I didn't know it at the time, was the moment that changed my life.

'A splendid idea,' Forester said ... 'Let me have plenty of detail. That's what counts in our business, tiny little details ... Try to think back and remember everything.'

Dahl set to it that evening with a glass of brandy. 'For the first time in my life, I became totally absorbed in what I was doing ... The story seemed to be telling itself, and the hand that held the pencil moved rapidly back and forth across each page.' He had finished by midnight, and sent it to the great author the next day. Forester was so impressed with what Dahl had written that he submitted it, unchanged, to the newspaper. 'Your piece is marvellous,' he wrote to Dahl. 'Did you know you were a writer?'

'Shot Down Over Libya' was published in the *Saturday Evening Post* in August 1942. This was more than forty years before Dahl wrote *Going Solo*. The article is prefaced with a note from the editors: 'The author of this factual report on Libyan Air fighting is an RAF pilot at present in this country for medical reasons.'

In the piece the anonymous author describes his mission, along with five other Hurricane pilots, to attack a large number of Italian vehicles in the Libyan desert. They destroy lorries and tankers, despite coming under attack from enemy ground fire. They are preparing to head home, when:

> *'Hell's bells, what was that? Felt like she was hit somewhere. Blast this stick; it won't come back. They must have got my tail plane and jammed my elevators ...'*
>
> *The Hurricane dipped its nose and dived towards the ground, and there wasn't a thing I could do ... I was doing about 250 miles an hour, so I suppose it took, roughly, two seconds to hit the deck, but it seemed a long two seconds. I remember the dipping nose of the aircraft and I remember looking down the nose of the machine at the ground and seeing a little clump of camel thorn growing there all by itself, and my stomach felt as though someone were using it as a pincushion for rusty hatpins.*

Dahl then described the plane bursting into flames as it hit the earth, and his struggle to escape. He was paid US$900 for the piece.

'But surely it can't be as easy as all that,' Dahl wrote in 'Lucky Break'. 'Oddly enough, it was.'

The newspaper article was reworked as 'A Piece of Cake' and published in Dahl's first collection of short stories, *Over To You*, in 1945. Whereas 'Shot Down Over Libya' included a vivid description of Dahl attacking the Italians, and his plane being shot at, in 'A Piece of Cake' it is all less clear.

'I don't remember much of it,' the story begins, 'not beforehand anyway, not until it happened.' Dahl then describes an older RAF man strapping him into his plane before take-off:

> *'Be Careful. There isn't any sense not being careful.'*
> *'Piece of cake,' I said.*
> *'Like hell.'*
> *'Really. It isn't anything at all. It's a piece of cake.'*
> *I don't remember much about the next bit ... I only know that there was trouble, lots and lots of trouble ...*

The next thing Dahl's plane was hurtling out of the sky towards the dessert below. Once the plane hit the ground, the events are largely unchanged from 'Shot Down Over Libya', save for some hallucinations that Dahl experienced as he lay semi-comatose. But how the plane ended up on the ground is much less clear in 'A Piece of Cake' than it was in 'Shot Down Over Libya'. It was published only three years later, so at face value it is hard to understand why the story had become so vague. Even more puzzling, somehow the plane had also changed from a Hurricane to a Gloster Gladiator.

A Web of Mythical Stories

Forty years later, in *Going Solo*, Dahl gave yet another account of what had happened over the Libyan desert that September evening in 1940. He begins by referring to 'A Piece of Cake', 'but,' he confesses:

> *... there is an aspect of that story that I feel ought to be clarified by me and it is this: There seems, on rereading it to be an implication that I was shot down by enemy action, and if I remember rightly, this was inserted by the Editors of an American magazine called the Saturday Evening Post who originally bought and published it ... The fact is that my crash had nothing whatsoever to do with enemy action. I was not shot down either by another plane or from the ground. Here is what happened.*

In *Going Solo*, Dahl then explains what really happened, or he almost does. He had left Fouka in Egypt in the Gloster Gladiator, heading West for Mersah Matruh near the Italian front line. But, as a subsequent enquiry confirmed, the commanding officer had given him the wrong directions for the airfield where he was meant to land. He was ordered to set off as dusk was approaching, and had received little training for the Gladiator, an out-of-date plane from World War I. Unable to find the landing strip, as the sun disappeared and it started to go dark, Dahl had no option but to make a forced landing. He searched frantically for suitable ground, but in the end had to put down where he was. The plane's undercarriage hit a boulder, and nosedived into the ground.

Although Dahl later proved his worth in the dogfights over Greece, it would seem that the ignominy of crashing his plane, before he had even been involved in hostile action of any kind, was too much for Dahl. All his life he talked about being 'shot down', even after he had written *Going Solo*, which clarified what had happened. In many ways, one can understand how Dahl ended up in this situation. 'Shot Down Over Libya' was written to help garner American support for the war effort. Dahl clearly based it on the very real experiences of his crash landing, plus all the subsequent action that he saw. But as a propaganda piece for an American newspaper it would not have worked had Dahl explained he'd crashlanded an out-of-date plane, for which he was poorly trained, because an incompetent officer sent him to the wrong location. When Dahl rewrote the story as 'A Piece of Cake', he did not want to lie, but nor did he want to completely contradict the earlier version, and so he cleverly implied he had been shot down, without actually saying it.

In *Going Solo* he tried to set the record straight, but still did not come clean on everything: in the book, and whenever he recounted the story he claimed he was flying alone, but, as the two earlier versions made clear, there was another pilot flying alongside in his own Gladiator. Douglas Macdonald, who had grown up in Kenya and learned to fly before the war, managed to put his plane down safely, and came to assist the injured Dahl. Did Dahl feel Macdonald's successful landing somehow put Dahl's own abilities into doubt? Maybe. It seems extraordinary that Dahl, the flying ace who had undoubtedly proven his bravery in subsequent battles as recorded in the official squadron records, and who was among only three survivors of the eighteen with whom he'd trained, should still have been sensitive about this. Perhaps he had just told the tale so many times that fact and fiction had become blurred.

Maybe we shouldn't be too harsh on Dahl. As most people get older and tell their favourite stories again and again, they tend to get modified over the years: the ladder gets taller; the tiger becomes closer; the adoring crowd grows bigger. The problem for Dahl, though, and for those writing about him, is that so much was documented. He might have first mentioned something in one of the nine hundred letters he wrote to his mother; the tale may then have resurfaced in a short autobiographical story, and been reworked for younger readers many years later. He probably recounted the story dozens of times on radio and television programmes, and in speeches and talks. And each time the tale might have been slightly different. His biographers may then have found some corroborating evidence in the archive, or from eyewitness accounts. And then one night in Oxford Dahl told the tale one last time to a fresh-faced gullible young doctor. How does one decide what was actually true? And does it matter anyway? For me, the episode serves as a lesson that not everything Dahl claims should necessarily be taken at face value.

Dahl's first biographer, *Life* magazine journalist Barry Farrell, took pretty much everything he was told as gospel truth when he wrote in 1970 *Pat and Roald*, about Dahl's marriage to Patricia Neal. Jeremy Treglown, who wrote an unauthorised biography a few years after Dahl's death, took more trouble to dissect the inconsistencies: Dahl claimed to have been shot down over Libya, when in fact he crashlanded; Dahl took credit for coining the term 'the Gremlins', when it was actually already in RAF parlance; Dahl attributed severe school beatings to the future Archbishop of Canterbury, when in fact it was a different headmaster. Treglown's thorough assessment of Dahl's life comes across as perhaps over-judicial and admonitory.

With access to Dahl's letters and other material in the archive, plus the support of all the family, Donald Sturrock's excellent account, *Storyteller*, provides a more sympathetic picture. Unlike Treglown, Sturrock had actually met his subject. In *Storyteller* the reader can usually see how the exaggeration happened, and forgive Dahl for taking a shortcut to convey the right impression, without being bogged down in too much detail.

'I don't lie,' Dahl wrote on the inside cover of one of his small notebooks. 'I merely make the truth a little more interesting.'

As a young researcher living in Asia in the 1990s, I became intrigued by the story of Alexandre Yersin, a doctor working in French Indochine one hundred years before me. He was at the centre of a major controversy about who had discovered the cause of plague; this was during a large outbreak of the disease in Hong Kong in 1894. I set about investigating the question. This project was my only prior foray into historical research before getting embroiled with Mr Dahl. I had access to the few scientific publications from the era, the colonial records, Yersin's diary, and that of the colonial medical officer, Dr James Lowson, which I had also stumbled across. It felt challenging at the time, but compared to studying the elusive Mr Dahl, who 'had woven around himself' a 'complex web of fictions' which made him more fantastic than he really was, reading Yersin was like a walk in the park.

'The thing about Forester,' Dahl told me when we chatted about writers, 'is that he was nothing like I imagined. I loved his work, Hornblower and all the rest, but he was such an ordinary-looking man ... Have you met many writers?'

I shrugged. I couldn't think of any before Dahl.

'I have met many. They're mostly a dull bunch ... Norman Mailer, a fine writer but a terrible bore to meet, Thomas Mann – no spark at all, John Steinbeck was usually drunk, Evelyn Waugh ... insufferable.'

I couldn't help laughing; did he not have a good word for any of them?

'Hemingway; I knew him well. He was not much fun to be with, but I had such respect and love of his work that I did not mind.' His influence was massive, Dahl continued. He taught a generation of writers to be clean and crisp. Short punchy sentences with lots of full stops. Very few adjectives. 'Did you know he read *War and Peace* and *Madame Bovary* every year to reabsorb their greatness? Have you read them?'

I had read *War and Peace* but had to confess I had never read *Bovary*. Dahl was thoughtful for a moment.

'Let me share something with you that Hemingway told me, a marvellous tip. He said "When you are writing good, stop writing." I must have looked puzzled. 'What he meant was don't write yourself out in one session. If you do, it's hard to get started again. Stop when things are going well, so it's easy to pick up.'

I could see what he meant, and indeed have used this approach ever since. Dahl was horrified to learn I had not read anything by Hemingway, 'You must read some when you are next on holiday.' I promised I would. *A Farewell to Arms* still sits menacingly on my bedside table, but somehow I have never got into it. 'Ian Fleming was the opposite of Hemingway,' Dahl continued, his eyes sparkling and his face animated, 'very witty, extroverted, a sybarite ...'

'A what?'

'A sybarite, a lover of the fine things ... luxuries ... pleasures ... People forget how well he wrote ... a natural. But for me it all started with the bash on the head ...'

A Persistent Muddler

Dahl liked to say his writing career was started by the monumental bash on the head when his plane came down. He had heard that brain injuries can sometimes unleash people's creative abilities, and fancied the idea that his head trauma had turned 'a promising oil executive with no literary talents' into a best-selling author. But was he right? Certainly there are well-described cases of people with no artistic inclinations at all whose brain injuries released incredible unknown creative potential.

We had one such patient at my own hospital, the Walton Centre in Liverpool, who became quite celebrated locally. Tommy McHugh was a fifty-six-year-old builder who had a stroke caused by a haemorrhage into his brain. After ten hours of surgery to stop the bleeding, he woke up a very different person. Previously he had been a bit of a bruiser who was sometimes in trouble with the police, and had shown no interest in art at all. After the operation, he found he was an artist, compelled to draw, paint, make sculptures and write poems. He could not stop himself. All the walls and even the carpet in his house were covered with magical pictures.

The condition has been called 'sudden artistic output' syndrome, or the 'acquired savant' syndrome. Savants are people with a developmental disorder, usually autism, who have an extraordinary ability in one particular area. You may remember Dustin Hoffman in the film *Rainman* brilliantly portraying the autistic savant Raymond, who can remember whole series of playing cards to help his brother cheat at blackjack. Whereas savants have their unusual ability from an early age, *acquired* savants have no such talents until they suddenly arise, typically after some kind of brain injury. There are many examples of acquired savant syndrome in medical literature: a three-year-old child who becomes a musical genius following meningitis; a college dropout who developed mathematical abilities after a blow to the skull; a ten-year-old who was hit on the head by a baseball, after which he could recall the day of the week, for any given date in the calendar.

I do not think the syndrome applies to Dahl, though, because he showed lots of literary potential even before the accident. The weekly letters he wrote home to his mother from boarding school are packed full of entertaining stories, and vivid descriptions, such as the new school matron who had 'hair like a fuzzie-wuzzie, and two warts on her face' and the maths teacher with a 'face like a field elderberry, and a moustache which closely resembles the African jungle'. Dahl's official biographer Donald Sturrock thinks to some extent the purpose of these entertaining descriptions was to divert his mother from the true misery of Dahl's boarding school.

Intriguingly, in one of his school essays Dahl described a little girl who climbed out of bed in the middle of the night, tiptoed to the window and peeped through a chink in the curtains to see what lay outside. This was more than forty years before he wrote about another little girl, Sophie, who 'slipped out of bed and tiptoed over to the window', ducked under the curtains and leaned out to see … 'something very tall and very black and very thin' – the BFG.

Although he clearly enjoyed writing whilst at school, the outputs were not particularly brilliant according to his school reports. As Dahl describes in 'Lucky Break', in 1928 he was taken for Boxing and English Composition by the same teacher – Mr Corrado.

In this particular report it said under English: See his report on boxing. Precisely the same remarks apply. *So we look under boxing and there it says:* Too slow and ponderous. His punches are not well-timed and easily seen coming.

By the time he left school, Dahl's boxing had improved considerably and he had become the champion. His English appears not to have developed alongside. 'I have never met a boy who so persistently writes the exact opposite of what he means,' says the 1930 English composition report. 'He seems incapable of marshalling his thoughts on paper.' In 1931 Dahl is noted to be 'A persistent muddler. Vocabulary negligible, sentences mal-constructed. He reminds me of a camel!'

Despite, or maybe even because of these reports, Dahl continued to dabble in writing as a young man. After leaving school he wrote a short humorous play, *Double Exposure*, which combined his passion for photography with a plot reminiscent of *My Uncle Oswald*. Whilst he was working for Shell, he wrote the small spoof piece for their in-house magazine in which he described 'Mr Dippy Dud' who, if employees came across him, should be 'tackled' to the ground for a prize; and what did he look like? He could be mistaken for town councillors, arch-deacons or retired colonels.

'The thing about writing,' Dahl explained to me, 'is that it is very different to music or art, where special talents are nearly always evident at a young age – think of Beethoven or Mozart.' I knew that both of them had been child prodigies. 'I have asked all the successful fiction writers I know, and not one of them showed any marked ability at school. As far as I can see, fiction writing is something that you slide into gradually, cautiously. Only a madman would set out to write fiction as a sole occupation until he had proven himself.'

Like most writers, Dahl loved books, and was an avid reader from a young age.

As well as Forester he enjoyed W. Somerset Maugham. Indeed Somerset Maugham was a favourite we shared; he trained as a doctor initially before writing fabulous stories about the eccentric characters running the British Empire. 'He once gave me champagne in his New York flat at noon,' Dahl commented, 'a courteous old homosexual who said very little.' Somerset

Maugham's tales had given us both a sense of adventure, a desire to go and see the world. Dahl went off to Africa. I had travelled in both Africa and Asia, and still have ongoing research projects on both continents.

So long before the plane crash I believe Dahl had many of the ingredients that would make him the great writer he was to become. He loved literature, had a keen eye for detail and enjoyed writing mischievous tales. Although I do not think Dahl had acquired savant syndrome, could the plane crash have contributed to his writing in some other way? I'd say the answer is yes, because, for example, it may well be that the head trauma caused mild damage to the frontal lobes of Dahl's brain, affecting his character and personality, and releasing him from some of the inbuilt inhibitions that normally hold people back.

A Bit Frontal

The frontal lobes, as their name suggests, lie at the front of the brain just behind the forehead. One of their functions is to stop us from doing things that we might otherwise want to. They are the natural inbuilt braking mechanism. When you are in a restaurant and someone at the next table has a rather tasty-looking dish, it is your frontal lobes that stop you reaching across to dip your finger in. If you are out on the street and feel a sudden need to relieve yourself, it is the frontal lobes that make you search for a bathroom rather than dropping your underwear there and then. It is well recognised that the frontal lobes are vulnerable in head injuries, and damage here can change somebody's personality and behaviour. Someone with frontal lobe damage might say embarrassing things, be more outspoken and ready to criticise, and maybe even have wild thoughts that wouldn't occur to others.

As doctors, we describe someone as being 'a bit frontal' if they display these behaviours. In Dahl, frontal lobe damage may have just tipped the balance, and allowed someone who was slightly mischievous to go that little bit further, to shock, outrage and horrify. Injury here might explain why in his *Tales of the Unexpected*, Dahl would come up with bizarre, startling and sometimes truly horrible twists that no one could predict. Who else but Roald Dahl would have the investigating police unwittingly eat the murder weapon in 'Lamb to the Slaughter'? Or a sexually repressed vicar, in 'Georgy Porgy', swallowed whole by the spinster who is trying to seduce him like a rabbit eating its offspring? Dahl's stories for children are so popular because of the cruel and outrageous things that happen: the squashing to death of James's two horrible aunties by the giant peach, the terrible fates of the miscreant children in *Charlie and the Chocolate Factory*, the outrageous things Mr and

Mrs Twit do to each other. As long as the stories were funny and made people laugh, he did not care.

I suspect damage to this part of Dahl's brain may have affected not only his writing, but his personal life too. At times he could be troublesome, argumentative and opinionated, and he didn't mind winding people up. He hated small talk at dinner parties, and would come out with outrageous and mischievous comments just to see how people responded. As a patient in the John Radcliffe, he didn't feel the rules were necessarily for him. He would lean out of the window to have a cigarette, even if the smoke wafted into the adjacent room, causing his neighbour to complain. Indeed on one occasion Dahl became stuck and the nurses had to carefully haul him back in. He would have a drink of whisky in the evening and try to tempt the medical staff to join him. I declined saying I was on call and could get sacked. But one of the other housemen, my friend Anwar Hussein, said he would not drink because he was a 'good Muslim boy'. For Dahl, this was an invitation to launch into some lewd limericks, to try and wind Anwar up:

> A plumber who lived in Dundee
> Was plumbing a girl by the sea.
> Cried the girl, 'Stop your plumbing!
> There is somebody coming!'
> Said the plumber, still plumbing, 'It's me!'

Later, in one of Dahl's notebooks, I found he had quite a collection of limericks – always dirty, and often very witty:

> There was a young man of Kildare
> Who was having a girl in a chair.
> At the sixty-third stroke
> The furniture broke
> And his rifle went off in the air.

People with frontal lobe damage, as well as disinhibited behaviours, also have mood lability, being more likely to laugh and cry at the slightest thing:

'The filthy old fizzwiggler!' shouted the BFG. 'That is the horridest thing I is hearing for years! You is making me sadder than ever!' All at once, a huge tear that would have filled a bucket rolled down one of the BFG's cheeks and fell with a splash on the floor. It made quite a puddle.

Sophie watched with astonishment. What a strange and moody creature this is, she thought. One moment he is telling me my head is full of squashed flies and the next moment his heart is melting for me because Mrs Clonkers locks us in the cellar.

– The BFG

What a strange and moody creature Dahl is, I thought as I watched him dozing at last. What squished flies have filled his head all these years? And how extraordinarily privileged I am that he is willing to share them with me.

Chapter 6

Tales

Over the last twenty-five years, evidence has accumulated to support this idea that mild frontal lobe damage could subtly increase artistic abilities. There are cases of acquired savant syndrome caused by fronto-temporal dementia, due to the gradual loss of neurones from the frontal lobes, rather than the sudden trauma or bleeding with which it was first associated. Functional brain imaging techniques such as SPECT (single photon emission computed tomography) show remarkable similarities between savants with fronto-temporal dementia and those with autism: in both situations there is loss of function in the frontal and temporal lobe of the brain and enhanced function in the posterior part involved in visual perception. In other words, in people with savant syndrome the front 'inhibiting' part of the brain appears to have less activity, allowing creative parts of the brain involved in vision unfettered activity.

Functional imaging is giving all sorts of new insights into these creative processes that would have fascinated Dahl. For example, work by Charles Lamb and colleagues at Johns Hopkins in Baltimore shows that during jazz improvisation musicians have extensive deactivation of the frontal cortex: as if this inhibiting part of the brain is switched off to allow the creative juices to flow elsewhere.

In Germany, Martin Lotza examined functional brain changes during writing. He and his co-workers showed very different patterns of activity for those who were creating a story compared with those who were just copying one down. And again the frontal lobes were intimately involved. Intriguingly, for the novice writers the visual cortex at the back of the brain was active; in contrast, for full-time creative writers it was the language centres that were more active. It is as if novices watch their stories like a film inside their heads, while full-time writers narrate it with an inner voice.

I know Dahl would have been intrigued by these imaging studies. The idea that the visual and verbal centres of the brain need to be free from inhibitions and distractions for creativity to occur resonates very much with his own experience. For Dahl to write he would sit in his little work hut every day, cosy and enclosed, 'like being in the womb'. Here, eschewing all interruptions, he would enter a trance-like state. Even the curtain was drawn to exclude the enchanting views of the orchard beyond. 'Sometimes, when I'm trying to think of new twists and turns to a story, it actually feels as though long tentacles are reaching out from my head and groping around in the air, trying to pluck ideas out of nowhere.' In this environment he would work for two hours every morning, and two to three every afternoon. But new story would be considered for months or even years, looked at from all angles, before he would finally take the plunge.

Much of his children's literature began life as bedtime tales for his own children. Other ideas were tried out over dinner or in a speech to see how people responded. At public events Dahl rarely recited from work already published. Partly because he seldom liked reading what he had finished writing, but also because he viewed that as a wasted opportunity. He would far rather try out something in development to see how it was received. This comes across in his literature; it often reads as if he is chatting to you personally. His children's stories, especially, were written to be read aloud. He knew it would often be an adult doing the reading, and so included little witticisms to keep them, as well as their children, entertained: for example Mr Willy Wonka manufactures *buttergin* as well as *butterscotch*; the BFG describes *Nicholas Nickleby* as a book by *Dahl's Chickens*; in *Charlie and the Chocolate Factory* there is a door labelled ALL THE BEANS, CACAO BEANS, COFFEE BEANS, JELLY BEANS, AND HAS BEANS.

Once Dahl started writing, the words would flow from his pencil, and a couple of hours could pass without him even noticing. He followed the same ritual every day: writing from ten till twelve in the morning, having a nap after lunch, then three till five or six in the afternoon. He would walk from Gipsy House, across the orchard with a flask of coffee, to the hut that he built in the 1950s after visiting Dylan Thomas's writing shed in Wales. Dahl was a great admirer of Thomas, including one of his poems, 'In Country Sleep', in *Matilda*, and another, 'Fern Hill', in his list for Desert Island Discs.

Dahl's writing hut was constructed by his friend Wally Saunders, who partly inspired the BFG. Dahl had a set routine: settle into his chair; tuck the legs into an old sleeping bag to keep them warm; place the writing board across the arms of the chair – it was shaped to fit around the body, and covered in snooker-table green baize which was 'soft on the eyes'; clean the glasses; brush away any dust or eraser fragments from the board using the clothes brush owned since Repton; sharpen six pencils – always the same yellow Dixon Ticonderoga HB2 with a rubber on the end; pour some coffee from the flask. Now there could be 'no more delaying tactics'. The yellow legal notepaper, on which he always wrote, would be there 'watching me', waiting patiently for Dahl to begin. If he had followed Hemingway's advice, he would have stopped halfway down a page, in mid flow, and it would not be too difficult to get going again.

Gremlins

Soon after he published 'Shot Down Over Libya', Dahl wrote his first book, *The Gremlins*, in 1943. In the RAF, the legendary gremlins were blamed for anything that went technically wrong on a mission – it was an innocent way of reducing tensions between airmen and ground crews which seems to have gone back as far as the 1920s. In the book, Gus, an RAF pilot loosely based on Dahl himself, is shot down and injured, but is determined to get back into action. He convinces the gremlins to help the RAF, rather than hinder them.

One of Dahl's superiors sent a draft of the book to Walt Disney who bought the rights and planned to make a film. The twenty-five-year-old Dahl enjoyed being fêted by Disney, staying at a palatial suite at the Beverley Hills Hotel in Hollywood. At the party to welcome him, Dahl met Charlie Chaplin, Spencer Tracy, Basil Rathbone and a host of other stars who all pretended to be 'some sort of Gremlin or other'. He later took Ginger Rogers to dinner and spent an evening with Marlene Dietrich.

Dahl was enthralled by his first Hollywood encounter, but after much to-ing and fro-ing the *Gremlins* film was never made. There was a variety of concerns, including anxiety about trivialising what was a very real issue for the British and American pilots. There was also the question of whether the term 'gremlin' could be copyrighted, given that it was used by the entire RAF. Eventually the story appeared as a Walt Disney Picture Book, by Flight Lieutenant Roald Dahl, with his proceeds going to the RAF benevolent fund. Although Dahl did not invent the word 'gremlin', his book brought the term into popular parlance. Although initially he made clear to Disney that he had not created the term, more and more people began to give him credit for it and he became unable to resist the claim.

'I also had a go at a story for children,' he writes in 'Lucky Break'. 'It was called *The Gremlins* and this I believe was the first time the word had been used … news of the gremlins spread rapidly through the whole of the RAF and the United States Air Force, and they became something of a legend.'

The Gremlins certainly helped Dahl become something of a legend, increasing his fame considerably. Indeed it was because Eleanor Roosevelt loved reading the book to her children that she wanted to meet the author.

Losing It

After the success of 'Shot Down Over Libya' and *The Gremlins*, Dahl produced further short stories for magazines and newspapers based on his wartime experiences. He was still employed in Washington by the British government, and struggled to find time for his writing.

'I'm so busy these days ...' he complained to his mother. 'I turn down nearly all my evening dinner invitations, and try to stay at home and write.' Seventy years later, writing about Dahl, I know how he felt.

Dahl's first pieces were collected together in the book *Over to You: Ten Stories of Flyers and Flying*, published in 1946. One of the most compelling, 'Beware of the Dog', includes a gripping account, based loosely on Dahl's own experience, of an injured pilot calmly cataloguing his injuries while slipping in and out of consciousness. It was twice made into a film.

> *He glanced down again at his right leg. There was not much of it left. The cannon shell had taken him on the thigh, just above the knee, and now there was nothing but a great mess and a lot of blood. But there was no pain. When he looked down, he felt as though he were seeing something that did not belong to him ... something strange and unusual and rather interesting. It was like finding a dead cat on the sofa ...*
>
> *He realised that he was no longer feeling good; that he was sick and giddy. His head kept falling forward onto his chest because his neck seemed no longer to have any strength ...*

The collected stories catalogued Dahl's early feelings about fate, life and death. 'Katina' describes a young Greek girl who is orphaned by a Luftwaffe attack on her village. In 'Someone Like You' a pilot considers how a little jink or swerve as he drops his bombs can make the difference between life or death for those in the houses below. 'They Shall Not Grow Old' explores a near-death experience for a fighter pilot, whilst the feelings of relief at finally giving up the fight are conveyed in 'Death of an Old Old Man'.

When the war ended in 1945, Dahl returned to Buckinghamshire for a few years to pursue his writing career, but by 1950 he was back in the States – the Americans seemed to appreciate his short stories more than the British. He stayed in New York with his wealthy friend the oil tycoon Charles Marsh. Moving among elite American circles again, Dahl met the Hollywood actress Patricia Neal. They were first introduced at a dinner party and, although Neal was attracted to the 'lean, handsome, very tall man who towered over the others', he completely ignored the very beautiful famous young actress sitting next to him at dinner. He preferred to chat to the composer Leonard Bernstein who was seated across the table.

'I behaved badly, I suppose. I was getting into one of those arguments with Lennie Bernstein, and there was no backing off from it.'

Pat therefore refused to see Dahl when he contacted her the next day for a date, but she eventually relented and things progressed rapidly from there. She was impressed with this man who was 'acquainted with just about everybody', and seemed interested and knowledgeable on everything: paintings, antique furniture, the English countryside, theatre, gardening, chess and medicine. To Pat 'there seemed to be nothing that he didn't know something about'. Dahl regarded expertise itself as a form of possession, according to the biographer Treglown, perhaps acquiring knowledge to make up for the university education he never had. Pat was also very taken with a photo of Dahl's beautiful nephew and nieces.

'My God, you make beautiful babies,' she blurted out when she saw it in his flat. 'I mean your family does!'

They were married in New York in July 1953. Dahl's second collection of short stories, *Someone Like You*, was published soon after to great critical acclaim. It rapidly became a bestseller, and provided the crucial breakthrough for his career.

Sound and Vision

The collection of macabre tales in *Someone Like You*, many of which had a cruel or unexpected twist at the end, underscored Dahl's fascination with the full range of unpleasant incidents, accidents and injuries that people could suffer. The book includes 'The Man from the South', who likes to chop off people's fingers; 'Neck', in which a woman is nearly decapitated; 'The Soldier', who is suffering from some kind of shell shock; 'Poison' and 'The Wish', which both feature venomous snakes; 'Nunc Dimittis', which ends in a poisoning; 'Skin', which ends in a skinning; and 'The Sound Machine'. In this tale, Dahl began to explore human physiology – the science of how the body works. Klausner, an elderly man, has been trying to create a machine to capture sounds beyond the normal range of human hearing.

> *'Up the scale ... there is another note – a vibration if you like, but I prefer to think of it as a note. You can't hear that one either. And above that there is another and another rising right up the scale for ever and ever and ever, an endless succession of notes ...'*

'I believe,' he said, speaking more slowly now, 'that there is a whole world of sound about us all the time that we cannot hear. It is possible that up there in those high-pitched inaudible regions there is a new exciting music being made, with subtle harmonies and fierce grinding discords, a music so powerful that it would drive us mad if only our ears were tuned to hear the sound of it ...'

Later, after further fiddling with the wires and twisting the knobs on his machine, Klausner drags it outside, puts on the earphones and tries his invention. He listens just as his neighbour cuts the stem of a rose: 'suddenly he heard a shriek, a frightful piercing shriek'. As she cuts another stem, he hears it again: 'a throatless, inhuman shriek, sharp and short, very clear and cold'.

In addition to the thoughtful description of ultrasound, which occurs at frequencies higher than the human hearing range, the piece also contemplates the nature of pain, as Klausner considers the strange noises he has been hearing.

It wasn't pain; it was surprise. Or was it? It didn't really express any of the feelings or emotions known to a human being. It was just a cry, a neutral stony cry – a single emotionless note, expressing nothing ... A flower probably didn't feel pain. It felt something else which we didn't know about – something called toin, or spurl, plinuckment, or anything you like.

The noise that comes from a large beech tree as Klausner cut into its base with an axe was particularly haunting:

a harsh, noteless, enormous noise, a growling, low-pitched, screaming sound ... drawn out like a sob lasting fully for a minute, loudest at the moment when the axe struck, fading gradually fainter and fainter until it was gone.

The implication that humans might be inflicting cruelty on plants is mind-boggling. The next day Klausner's doctor is about to test the machine for himself, to verify his findings, but Dahl intervenes with one of his typical twists of fate, and we are left wondering whether the machine really did capture these sounds, or if the obsessed little man had simply lost his marbles.

This was not the first sound-machine story by Dahl. Twenty years earlier as a schoolboy he wrote an essay, 'The Kumbak II', along the same theme. The narrator goes to stay with his uncle Aristotle, 'a particularly learned man who was keen on wireless and all such inventions', who has invented a new instrument with which one can hear the voices of people from the past. The uncle explains that 'sound travels in waves, and those waves go further and further away and eventually nearly disappear into space, where, although no atmosphere or any kind of gas exists, there is still a glimmer of sound'. Using the machine, they hear the voices of people speaking in 'olden-day language' from hundreds of years ago. The pair then use the sound machine to investigate an unsolved murder, visiting the crime scene to listen to the desperate appeals of the victim which reveal her killer. The villain is convicted and 'the next day the papers were simply brisling with the invention'.

This unpublished piece by the ten-year-old Dahl is a remarkable foreshadow of what would characterise much of his future writing: a crackpot inventor working secretly out of view; a scientifically plausible story; a mystery to be solved, and a heroic act which would be feted and recognised by the world.

The idea of extraordinary senses appealed greatly to Dahl. Decades later he would endow the BFG with superhuman hearing:

Sometimes, on a very clear night ... if I is swiggling my ears in the right direction ... and the night is very clear, I is sometimes hearing faraway music coming from the stars in the sky.

And soon after *The Witches* would have 'the most amazing powers of smell':

'An absolutely clean child gives off the most ghastly stench to a witch,' my grandmother said. 'The dirtier you are, the less you smell ... The smell that drives a witch mad actually comes right out of your own skin. It comes oozing out of your skin in waves, and these waves, stink-waves the witches call them, go floating through the air and hit the witch right smack in her nostrils. They send her reeling ... to a witch you'd be smelling of fresh dogs' droppings.'

An extraordinary sense of taste was important in *Charlie and the Chocolate Factory* as well as the adult story 'Taste', in which a wine expert is challenged to name the exact vineyard and vintage of a claret he is served at a dinner party.

Dahl was fascinated by a Pakistani mystic, magician and fire walker he met in 1952, called Kuda Bux who could apparently see 'without the use of his eyes'. Dahl wrote an article about him for *Argosy* magazine; along with his editors he watched with 'mingled wonder and scepticism' as Bux could apparently copy sketches and read newspaper articles despite the dough and cotton pads placed over his eyes, and extensive bandages wrapped round his head. The episode was adapted to become 'Imhrat Khan, the Man Who Could See Without His Eyes' in *The Wonderful Story of Henry Sugar*. In this tale Dahl provided an intriguing explanation of how such vision might be possible, by swapping the sensory abilities of the eyes and skin.

> *Even the doctors who blindfold me in the most expert way refuse to believe that anyone can see without his eyes. They forget there may be other ways of sending the image to the brain.'*
> *'What other ways?' I asked him.*
> *'Quite honestly, I don't know exactly how it is I can see without my eyes. But what I do know is this; when my eyes are bandaged, I am not using the eyes at all. The seeing is done by another part of my body.'*
> *'Which part?' I asked him.*
> *'Any part at all so long as the skin is bare. For example, if you put a sheet of metal in front of me and put a book behind the metal, I cannot read the book. But if you allow me to put my hand around the sheet of metal so that the hand is seeing the book, then I can read it.'*

The possible implications of such a feat were not lost on Dahl:

> *This man would have doctors all over the world turning somersaults in the air! He could change the whole course of medicine ... ! We must find out exactly how it is that an image can be sent to the brain without using the eyes. And if we do that, then blind people might be able to see and deaf people might be able to hear.*

Credibility was important in Dahl's short stories, and he would go to great lengths to be sure he got as close to the scientific truth as possible. For 'Taste', Dahl read extensively about clarets, even visiting the author of the leading guide, *A Wine Primer*, to check the details. For 'Lamb to the Slaughter', he quizzed Charles Marsh's cook all about freezing and defrosting meat. 'Everyone thought he had gone mad,' Marsh's daughter recalled.

Ophelia remembers him grilling Brian Higgs, the surgeon and family friend, over dinner about what exactly would happen if you swallowed some jewellery: would it get stuck? How long would it take to come through? She later realised he was researching for 'The Surgeon'.

Dahl did not mind borrowing ideas off others: 'Dip in the Pool' is based on a cunning plan Charles Marsh devised to try to win the bet on how much progress an ocean liner would make in one day. 'The Way Up to Heaven' was also inspired by Marsh's misadventure when he got stuck in a lift. Marsh seemed not to be bothered, but others were. Douglas Bisgood was a fellow RAF officer who had swapped gremlin stories with Dahl as they crossed the Atlantic together. He was aghast to see his terms for gremlin wives and children, *Fifinellas* and *Widgets*, used by Dahl and Disney without acknowledgement.

The 'Imrat Khan' story was also remarkable in the extent to which it demonstrated one of Dahl's favoured literary devices: the story within a story. Dahl often adopted this approach, which would allow an extra layer of narrative, and also scope for the tale to be interrogated to ensure it was being understood: 'Do you mean to tell me that ... ?' the narrator checks. 'That's precisely what I am saying!' comes the reply.

In 'The Wonderful Story of Henry Sugar', Henry Sugar, a wealthy and idle gambler, stumbles across 'A Report on an Interview with Imhrat Khan, the Man Who Could See Without His Eyes' by Dr John Cartwright. Within the report Cartwright relates Khan's life story word for word as told by the man himself. And at the end of the wonderful story we discover the whole tale has been recorded by the narrator, a professional writer; thus Khan's account is a story within a story, within a story, within a story! Henry Sugar's adventure is also typical of many Dahl stories in that the protagonist ends up performing marvellous deeds that benefit thousands around the world.

Guinea Pig

After their wedding in New York in 1953, Dahl and Pat honeymooned driving through Europe in a Jaguar convertible before ending up in Great Missenden where Dahl's mother and sisters all lived within a few miles of each other. This was the first time Pat had met them – the wedding had been friends only. She was surprised that no one gave her a hug, and even more surprised that the family entertainment included Dahl's brother-in-law Leslie rolling on to his back, legs in the air, breaking wind, and setting fire to the gas.

The newlyweds were keen to start a family, but struggled initially. A gynaecologist diagnosed blocked Fallopian tubes, probably related to the abortion Pat had undergone after becoming pregnant during an affair with the film star Gary Cooper. She was treated with 'air blown through my tubes' and in the summer of 1954 was delighted to discover that she was pregnant.

Dahl's family found them a house, Little Whitefield, on the edge of Great Missenden, which could be their base in England. Its name was changed to Gipsy House in 1963 when Dahl discovered this had been an earlier name. Their first child, Olivia Twenty, was born on 20 April 1955 in New York and named after Pat's first stage role at Northwestern Theatre, and the day of her birth. Chantal Sophia was born soon after on 11 April 1957; her parents changed her name to Tessa when they realised Chantal rhymed with Dahl and worried she would be teased at school. Their son, Theo Matthew, was born on 30 July 1960.

The growing family spent the next few years careering back and forth across the Atlantic, dividing their time between New York and Great Missenden. When he was not tucked away in his writing hut, Dahl would restore furniture, collect paintings and grow prize-winning orchids and onions, interests about which he was passionate for much of his life. He also renovated an old gipsy caravan he had bought off his sister Alfhild; it became a playroom for the children, and featured in *Danny, the Champion of the World*.

In the States, Dahl spent time with Dr Ed Goodman, a gastrointestinal surgeon at the New York Presbyterian Hospital, who was married to Marion Goodman, a close friend of Pat's. At one stage they lived in the same apartment block. Goodman had helped invent the electrogastrograph, a device that could measure electrical activity in the stomach. He had just published in *Science* and was looking for volunteers on which to test his new apparatus. Dahl was happy to offer himself 'as a guinea pig', he told his mother. 'They are trying out a new machine for plotting electrically what goes on in the stomach. They stuffed the tube up my nose and right down into the stomach and left it there for two hours.' Dahl's gastrointestinal rumblings may well have been included in Goodman's paper on 'The Clinical Significance of the Electrogastrogram' that he published in *Gastroenterology* in 1955.

Through his medical contacts, Dahl also researched one of his most famous and macabre medical tales, 'William and Mary'. Landy, 'a magnificent neurosurgeon, one of the finest', proposes to save the brain of William Pearl, a Philosophy teacher at Oxford, who is dying of pancreatic cancer, by surgically removing it just after Pearl's death; he will preserve the brain's blood supply through the arteries and veins by means of an artificial heart.

'I should immediately open your neck and locate the four arteries, the carotids and the vertebrals. I should then perfuse them, which means that I'd stick a large hollow needle into each. These four needles would be connected by tubes to the artificial heart.

'Then, working quickly, I would dissect out both the left and right jugular veins and hitch these also to the heart machine to complete the circuit. Now switch on the machine, which is already primed with the right type of blood, and there you are. The circulation through your brain would be restored.'

'I'd take a small oscillating saw and carefully remove your complete calvarium, the whole vault of the skull. This would expose the top half of the brain ...'

From the description it is clear that Dahl had done his neuroanatomy homework. The plan is for the brain to be kept alive in a basin of Ringer's solution. One eyeball, still connected to it via the optic nerve, would float on the surface of the liquid so that William could see his devoted wife, Mary, smiling down at him. This image of a brain, still alive in a basin of fluid, with just one eye bobbing above it staring up at the ceiling, is one of the most chilling from all of Dahl's fiction.

'William and Mary' was included in Dahl's third collection, *Kiss Kiss*, the tales of which continued in the same vein of short, tense, unsettling plots, many with sinister endings. He wrote approximately two short stories a year, but by the 1960s was worried that it was increasingly difficult to come up with good ideas. Several of the tales in *Kiss Kiss* involved children, perhaps reflecting the greater role they were taking in Dahl's life.

'Genesis and Catastrophe' centres on a mother's worry that her newborn son will not survive longer than her other three children who had all died soon after birth; 'Royal Jelly' builds on parental anxiety that a child is not feeding properly and losing weight. Both stories have rather disturbing twists. The collection also included 'The Champion of the World', which later developed into the children's book *Danny, The Champion of the World*, with much of the same plot.

Dahl's children were becoming very much the centre of his life. Although they had hired help, Dahl was a very 'hands on' father, who at first even refused to leave Olivia alone with the nanny. For weeks at a time when Pat was away filming, he was the sole parent. Like many parents, at bedtime he would tell the children stories to help them get off to sleep.

'There was one particular story,' Dahl told me one evening in Oxford when all was quiet on the wards, 'about a peach that grew and grew.' He stopped and reached into his bedside cabinet to pull out a bottle of whisky and a glass. He carefully poured himself an inch, offered the bottle towards me with raised expectant eyebrows, shook his head sadly when I refused, then popped the bottle back in the cabinet. 'You see,' he continued, 'I would notice the apples in the orchard outside my hut growing bigger every autumn, and I wondered what would happen if one kept growing. But for the story I decided on a peach, with its nice big stone in the centre.' I could see where this was going. 'Anyway each night the children seemed to like the story and wanted more, so I kept going.'

James and the Giant Peach was published in 1961. Dahl always considered this, rather than *The Gremlins* as his first children's story. It set the tone and style of much of his children's literature, with its orphaned child, cruel adults, magical creatures and fantastical plot. It is hard to imagine now but this book, like many of Dahl's subsequent ones, was initially banned from libraries and schools. His writing was seen as seditious, with cruel adults, disobedient children and gruesome plots.

Dahl was unrepentant. 'If you are a child, the adult world can be a cruel, dangerous and confusing place,' he told me, 'and the nippers enjoy it when terrible things happen.' His writing was funny rather than sadistic, he felt, and his view was that children are the toughest readers to keep happy. 'The greatest fear is that they will get bored. So you have to keep things moving all the time.'

Just as Dahl's literature had many cruel quirks and twists of fate, so too would his personal life. In an amazing coincidence that could have come straight from one of his short stories, just a few months after 'William and Mary' was published, he would find that his knowledge of intricate brain anatomy and neurosurgical treatments would prove crucial for a much more compelling and tragic reason.

Chapter 7

Threats and Dangers

'How is your article coming along?' Dahl asked me as I was tapping away on the ward computer one evening.

'Slowly,' I complained. 'We have all the data, but the journals are very fussy about how you write it.'

'Where will you send it?'

'We'll probably try the *Lancet*.'

'Ah yes, it's a good journal. We published there many years ago ...'

'Really?' From the sparkle in his eye I thought he was probably trying to get a rise from me.

'Yes, we invented a valve for hydrocephalus.' He started fiddling self-consciously with the pens on the work station. 'Well, I was only the go-between really.' He looked slightly embarrassed. 'Look it up if you like, the *Lancet*, 1964. We were living in New York at the time, and Theo got hit by a taxi ...' I could see him thinking back. 'He was only four months old, in the pram, you see, and, well, it was a terrible business ...' He wandered back to his side room.

From the mid 1950s, Dahl, Pat, and their children were typically spending spring and summer in Great Missenden and autumn in New York. In England Dahl would write in his hut, and in Manhattan he borrowed an empty room of their neighbours, the Goodmans. Because his back ached, he preferred to work in a large armchair; he had the green beige writing board made, which he would use for the rest of his life. It was important for Pat's acting career to be in America, but Dahl was finding the peace and quiet of the British countryside better suited his writing. Besides, he was becoming increasingly disquieted by New York, which he thought a violent city filled with threats and dangers, not the place to raise a young family. His feelings were encapsulated in the gruesome short adult story 'Pig'. In this ghastly tale, an orphaned boy, brought up in the countryside, heads to New York to claim the fortune left for him by his aunt. Unfortunately, ill prepared for the tough and unforgiving reality of city life, he is swindled out of his inheritance by corrupt lawyers, and meets his end in a most unpleasant way.

Dahl's anxiety that New York posed a danger to the young and uninitiated would soon prove to be sadly prophetic. Pat who had just finished filming *Breakfast at Tiffany's*, recalled the fateful day in her biography, *As I Am*:

It was a crisp December morning. The fifth ... I left with Susan [their English nanny] to pick up Tessa. I had quite a lot of shopping to do, so Susan, walking Theo in his pram, went on ahead to collect Tessa. I was in the A&P on Madison when I heard the shrill blast of a siren.

Susan had fetched Tessa from nursery school at lunchtime, and was returning down Madison Avenue, pushing the pram, with a friend's dog in tow. Olivia was doing full days at the nursery by then. Approaching 85th Street, Susan waited for the light to turn green then started to cross. But as they stepped out a taxi sped round the corner and collided with Theo's pram. The panicking driver stepped on the accelerator, rather than the brake, and propelled the pram forty feet through the air until it smashed against the side of a bus. The baby was rushed by ambulance to the nearby Lenox Hill Hospital. This was the siren Pat had noticed. Dahl had also heard it, as he sat writing, but had paid no attention. By the time they had been called to the emergency room, things were looking very grave, as recorded a few days later by Dahl:

Theo was in the examination room with two doctors. Susan, Tessa, Stormy (the dog) were in small waiting room with policeman who drove squad car and policeman in charge of school crossing. Things looked grim. They were giving plasma to Theo ... He was in a state of deep shock, colourless, high pulse, temp 102. They didn't dare move him for X-ray. I suggested portable X-ray. They did this. Also arranged round-the-clock special nurses. But this was a general paediatric ward, and none of the nurses nor the floor doctors were trained in neurosurgery ... Multiple skull fractures were revealed by X-ray. But there were no signs of other bodily injury.

Dahl's extensive 'Note on Theo's Accident' was written in one of the 'ideas' books that he always carried with him. The baby's skull had been shattered, but there was disagreement among the medical team about whether or not to perform a subdural tap: inserting a needle into the anterior cranial fossa, the baby's soft spot, could remove excess fluid, and relieve the pressure on the brain, but it had associated risks.

Dahl was horrified that the doctors were arguing publicly in front of him about what should be done. However, part of the problem was that in addition to the paediatrician and surgeon on call at the hospital, Dahl had called in three other doctors for their opinions within just a few hours of Theo's admission; this included the family paediatrician, Milton Singer, and their friend the gastrointestinal surgeon Ed Goodman from the Presbyterian Hospital. In the end, the tap was performed, drawing off 18 ml of cerebrospinal fluid and blood. However, the hospital paediatrician was incensed that his decisions were being vetoed by a family friend who happened to be a doctor.

As Theo's condition fluctuated over the next two days, Dahl became increasingly unhappy with his care. In his 'Note on Theo's Accident', it is revealed that at one point he had to advise a nurse on how to fix a catheter tube:

> First she strapped it to his kicking leg! Then she strapped it upwards to the side of his cot. I said, 'Lay it on the mattress!' Eventually she did.

Dahl stayed over that night and the next 'watching the inefficient antics of the nurses, trying to advise them when I could'.

Then he observed as another nurse gave Theo a massive overdose of the anticonvulsant drug, Dilantin, for his seizures. This was despite Dahl asking her to check the amount: she had given half an ounce instead of half a cc. Thankfully the hospital paediatrician arrived in time to aspirate the excess drug from Theo's stomach. But the incident triggered a huge row. The local clinician pointed out the nurse had misunderstood the chart because the drug had been written up by one of the visiting doctors. It sounds as if it were chaos, and not what any parent would want for their child.

Complex Anatomy

By this stage Dahl had had enough. 'His general attitude is too much to stand,' he commented on the paediatrician. Theo was wrapped in a blanket and taken by car to the neurological wing of the Presbyterian Hospital, where he would be cared for by Milton Singer, Ed Goodman and their colleague the neurosurgeon Joseph Ransohoff. Over the next few days Theo was kept in an oxygen tent, and had the excess fluid causing the hydrocephalus drained off with a needle several more times. Dahl, of course, understood all about the cerebrospinal fluid and its flow around the cerebrum and spine, following his research for 'William and Mary'. In that story, the neurosurgeon Landy describes some quite complex anatomy:

> You may or may not know that there are three separate coverings around the brain itself: the outer one called the dura mater or dura, the middle

one called the arachnoid, and the inner one called the pia mater or pia. Most laymen seem to have the idea that the brain is a naked thing floating around in fluid in your head. But it isn't. It's wrapped up neatly in these three strong coverings, and the cerebrospinal fluid actually flows within the little gap between the two coverings, known as the subarachnoid space. As I told you before, this fluid is manufactured by the brain and it drains off into the venous system by osmosis.

This cerebrospinal fluid is a salty solution that contains a few white cells and creates a kind of soft shock-absorbing cushion, as well as providing immunological protection against infection. The term *hydrocephalus* is used to describe a build-up of fluid (from the Greek *hydro*, water; *cephalus* brain), either because too much is being produced or because it is not draining properly. And because the brain and fluid surrounding sit within a fixed box – the skull or *cranium* – this excess fluid causes the pressure inside the head to go up: raised intracranial pressure. In young children, the box is not completely fixed, and so over time, if hydrocephalus is not treated, it causes the skull to enlarge. Descriptions of children with enlarged heads due to hydrocephalus can be found in ancient Greek texts from 2500 BC. Nowadays in developed western countries such children are rarely seen because it is always treated. However, in parts of Africa and Asia, where neurosurgical treatment is less readily available, we still see children with this condition, most often secondary to neonatal infections such as meningitis. In Theo's case, several processes probably contributed to the raised pressure: the swelling of the damaged brain tissue, bleeding from the ruptured blood vessels and impaired flow of the cerebrospinal fluid.

By Christmas 1960, Theo's excess fluid appeared to be settling down and he was well enough to be allowed home, but over the first days of January Dahl noticed that his eyes were becoming 'groggy and unfocused'. He was quieter, his reactions were dulled and he no longer smiled. They called Singer, and Theo was rushed back to hospital where they discovered he had lost his vision due to raised pressure in his head again – the optic verves are especially vulnerable to this condition.

For a week they repeatedly tapped off the excess fluid, but it showed no sign of abating. In addition, an X-ray revealed further bleeding below the dural membrane, a subdural haematoma, which needed a craniotomy. And so on 5 January Dr Ransohoff inserted a tube to drain fluid from one of the fluid-filled cavities deep in the brain, the ventricle, to the right atrium of the heart – a ventriculo-atrial shunt. Luckily Ransohoff, whose initial neurosurgical experience had been with the military, was especially interested in hydrocephalus and its treatment; he had published his first paper on the subject a few years earlier. Although in theory the treatment of hydrocephalus is simple – if there is a build-up of fluid causing pressure, just let it out – in practice things are not so straightforward. The main issues are where the excess fluid should drain and how to minimise the complications, such as infection and blockage.

The Arab physician and surgeon Abu al Qasim al Zahrawi first described in his tome *Al Tasrif*, a classic of Arabic medicine written in AD 1000, drainage of superficial intracranial fluid in children with hydrocephalus. In the 1880s, the German physician Carl Wernicke showed how to insert a sterile needle directly into the ventricle and drain the cerebrospinal fluid off into a container, but this was not really a permanent solution – no one wants to walk around with a beaker on their head. The German surgical pioneer Mikulicz hit upon the idea of draining the excess fluid from the ventricles to the soft tissue outside the skull just under the skin; from here fluid is absorbed into the veins. However, as you will know from every time you clonk your head on a cupboard, there is not much soft tissue between the skin and the skull, and the procedure had limited success.

Since then surgeons have developed a range of shunts that drain into the large veins (venous sinuses) in the head, or the pleural cavity in the chest, or the abdominal cavity, or even directly into the right side of the heart, as Theo experienced. As long as the pressure in these spaces is lower than in the ventricles of the brain, then the excess fluid should flow in the right direction. From the 1940s onwards, however, valves were added to the shunts to ensure one-way drainage. The shunt inserted into Theo's head included a Holter valve, which coincidentally had first been developed by John Holter in the 1950s to treat his own son's hydrocephalus.

A Small Pale Face

Theo's symptoms improved rapidly with the shunt and valve in place; his vision returned and he perked up. But two days later he deteriorated and was back in hospital again – the shunt had blocked. Ransohoff replaced the shunt, but it failed again. Over the next nine months Theo's shunt blocked six times. Each time he lost vision, and became quiet; with some episodes he also had convulsions. Dahl and the family were exasperated, as he later wrote in the *Ladies Home Journal:*

> *It is a long fight and a hard one to keep a hydrocephalic child going.*
> *The shunt blocks, the pressure builds, the eyes go groggy. Then comes the*

drive to hospital, the walk through the snow (it was always snowing) to the hospital entrance, the swift elevator ride to the neurosurgical floor, and suddenly there you are again, standing in the pale yellow corridor with the child in your arms, handing him over, consigning him, trusting him to the ruthless but precise alchemy of the neurosurgeons: the subdural taps, the lumbar punctures, the manometers, the myelograms, and finally, inevitably, comes the operation itself. When it is over you go into the ward and you see upon the bed a great turban of white bandages and below it a small pale face and two huge blue eyes that are wide open, desolate, bewildered. The eyes look at you, and they are saying, 'Why did you let them do this to me again?'

Ransohoff explained that the problem was not so much the shunt, but the valve at the end of it. The small slits within the valve kept blocking up with debris that had accumulated in the ventricles. This is especially common in patients like Theo where there has been trauma and bleeding contributing to the hydrocephalus. The shunt 'had a terribly demanding life of its own', Pat recalled. 'Three times daily, the little pump under the scalp had to be pressed twenty times to ensure it had not clogged, and the fluid was flowing.'

'I couldn't believe that with everything science had come up with, they couldn't produce one little clog-proof tube.' Dahl and I were chatting about the valve a few nights after he had mentioned the *Lancet* article. He contacted the hydrocephalus and spina bifida charities in the United States; children with spina bifida often have hydrocephalus as part of the condition. Dahl was horrified to learn that so many children suffered with exactly the same problem, and no one seemed able to do anything about it. 'Infants all over the world were being subjected to all these traumatic brain operations,' he exclaimed in frustration, 'simply because surgeons had to accept what they were given. There had to be something we could do, some way of improving on this slit thing.' So he learned everything he could about hydrocephalus and its treatment.

Meanwhile Theo's valve had blocked again, resulting in another operation. This time a ventriculo-pleural shunt, draining fluid from the brain into the lung cavity, was inserted, but this failed too.

'Very distressing, the whole thing,' Dahl wrote to his mother.

The escalating medical costs were a cause of anxiety too. The bill for Theo's first two days at Lenox Hill hospital was US$408 (more than US$3,000 today) and Dahl noted they had not even been charged for the doctors' time. By January 1961 the medical fees were 'running well over $10,000' (US$80,000 today), but family and friends helped out. Cary Grant's wife, for example, sent a cheque for US$1,000.

I don't think much of the tubes that they use here for this work [Dahl wrote to his mother] *particularly the valve at the lower end which is meant to open up between 40mm and 80mm water column pressure. This valve is literally nothing but a slit in the plastic tube ... Do they have anything better in England, something less likely to block and clog?*

There was an alternative in England. The family returned to Great Missenden in May 1961 and when Theo suffered a further relapse the only alternative valve, the Pudenz, was fitted. The operation was performed by Wylie McKissock, a famous neurosurgeon at Atkinson Morley Hospital in Wimbledon. However, this too failed and so a Holter valve was used once more. McKissock was not interested in trying to improve the valves; he was an adult neurosurgeon whose expertise was in war-related brain injuries and frontal lobotomies. He suggested Theo's care be taken over by Kenneth Till, Britain's first dedicated paediatric neurosurgeon, who was newly appointed to London's Hospital for Sick Children, at Great Ormond Street.

Till later described Dahl as being different to the usual distraught parents with whom he dealt. He noted Dahl had already spent a lot of time in hospital, was interested in everything that went on and read much of the literature for himself. When they discussed Theo's care, Till found 'he had the coolness – I think this perhaps is the word – the coolness to want to know the pros and cons, the whys and wherefores.' Dahl didn't mind admitting the limitations of his knowledge, and when he did not understand the procedures that Till proposed he would make him draw it for him.

The two men got on well. Like Dahl, Till had been with the RAF, though after the war had ended. He could be obsessional, and didn't suffer fools gladly, but he was also kind and compassionate, and was said to have a twinkle in his eye and a ready smile. At Great Ormond Street he is remembered as the man who introduced brightly painted walls into the children's hospital to replace the drab grey. He was also known to be an exceptionally rapid surgeon, perhaps he had to be, given the fact that he was the only neurosurgeon in the hospital until 1970.

A Toymaker

Like Dahl, Till was keen to try to improve upon the current valve technology, inviting Dahl into the operating theatre to see shunt operations and discuss alternative strategies. Dahl had two ideas for Theo. The first was to simply remove the draining system, which seemed to be causing so much trouble, and see what happened. Till doubted this would work. Dahl's second suggestion was to develop a better device. They were in touch with Ransohoff in America, who agreed it was worth moving away from the current slit-valve technology, but the question was who would build such a device?

Dahl had an idea: A toymaker!

Just as the toymaker saves the day in *Chitty Chitty Bang Bang*, for which Dahl would later write the screenplay, it was a toymaker on whom Dahl called for help. He had known Stanley Wade for many years, from when they would make and fly model planes together on a hillside near Amersham. In reality, Wade did more than make toys. He was a highly skilled hydraulic engineer who crafted miniature engines for model planes as a hobby.

'He was a beautiful turner of metal.' Dahl enacted this with his hands. 'He could make anything ... turn a tiny steel component to an accuracy of ten thousandths of a millimetre. And he was a lovely chap.' He smiled slowly. 'An eccentric, retired fellow with nothing much to do.' Wade was invited to watch the operations so he could understand exactly what was needed. Dahl saw Wade almost daily for three years, liaising with Till, and also keeping in touch with Ransohoff in New York, as well as Kenneth Shulman, a new member of the American team.

'We produced this splendid little valve. Most precise. It had to be non-return, open at a certain pressure, not clog up ... you understand?' I nodded as Dahl drew a sketch for me on the back of the day's *Times* newspaper. 'Of course it was Ken and Stanley who really did it all, not me. Till worked tremendously. I did not really do much. I was just the go-between, finding out what he wanted and letting Stanley know.'

At the time I took what Dahl said at face value. I later heard him say very similar things in recorded interviews. It was only more recently, when trawling through the notes from the time, that I realised Dahl wasn't being completely straight. With his war-time exploits, the plane coming down in Libya and the invention of the gremlins, Dahl was inclined to overplay his part, painting himself as something of a hero, whereas with the shunt and valve he seemed to be minimising his involvement. In reality he was the driving force behind the whole venture, and documentation in the archive reveals he had actually been intimately involved in the inventing process. For example, when they needed a way of checking the pressures at which the valve would open, the papers show he devised a series of water tanks to create pressure differentials, with the valve sitting in the middle. A sheet of his yellow legal paper displays his calculations for the length and diameter of a stainless steel capillary tube to allow CSF to flow. Another shows Stanley Wade's prototype sketches of the valve itself. Dahl was also concerned about how the valve would be decontaminated before being inserted. 'The bacteriologist considers that the most satisfactory way of sterilising will be by sending the valve to Harwell for irradiation,' Till tells Dahl in one letter.

Whilst the Americans experimented with the valve in dogs, Till felt happy enough with the design to try it in his own patients. In August 1962, he wrote to Dahl: 'I expect to do two more patients this week, and would like a few more valves if possible.' Dahl arranged a travel grant from England's Central Council for the Care of Cripples to allow Till to visit the American team, and the following year Ransohoff made the return trip hosted by the Dahls.

Originally the valve was designed to shunt cerebrospinal fluid into the brain's small cortical veins, but realising these tended to collapse the team decided to implant the device directly into the larger sagittal sinus. Their final product, the Wade Dahl Till (or WDT) valve was registered with the British and US Patent Offices in 1963. It consisted of a small flexible tube, seven millimetres in diameter, and four centimetres long, something like a cross between the valve of a bicycle tyre and a small fuse from a plug. Inside it were two non-return valves arranged in series, essentially tiny discs housed in cages that allowed fluid and small bits of debris to flow across them without jamming. The system was very sensitive, however, with the valves closing rapidly if the pressure changed and fluid attempted to flow in the wrong direction.

'A Valve for the Treatment of Hydrocephalus' was published by Kenneth Till in the *Lancet* in March 1964. At the end of the article, Till acknowledged Stanley Wade for the design 'with the assistance of Mr Roald Dahl and myself'. Nowadays both Wade and Dahl would likely be credited as authors on the article, but back then it was unusual to include those who were not medical.

One afternoon as I was leafing through the Dahl archive I came across three sides of the famous yellow notepaper, with the characteristic slanted Dahl pencil handwriting: *'The basis of many operations designed to relieve hydrocephalus is the diversion of cerebrospinal fluid to a vein, a venous sinus, or the cardiac atrium.'*

It took me a moment to place this familiar text, but when I did the significance of this document became apparent. This was the first draft of the *Lancet* paper: Dahl had actually written it himself. In the archive there is also a pile of correspondence between Dahl and Till finalising the manuscript. 'I think the end result is something reasonably suitable for the journal,' wrote Till.

Dahl's contribution would certainly merit authorship today, but more importantly this confirmed that he was much more involved in the whole venture than for which he would later take credit.

Perhaps surprisingly, the Americans Ransohoff and Shulman were also absent from the list of authors of the paper, despite their significant contribution to the valve's invention. If they felt aggrieved, they did not mention it in any subsequent correspondence. Indeed, Shulman congratulated Dahl on the *Lancet* publication, and remained friends with him for many years. He moved, soon after, to become director of neurosurgery at the Children's Hospital of Philadelphia, where he confirmed the WDT valve would be 'first choice in treatment of hydrocephalus'.

Ransohoff, whose correspondence with Dahl had been at times rather quarrelsome, went on to develop his own system to treat hydrocephalus. This consisted of a tiny pump, just below the skin, coupled magnetically to an external motor, held over the skin. Perhaps not surprisingly it never went into mass production. The WDT valve, in contrast, was produced in its thousands, through engineering firms with which Wade had connections. One of the problems for any valve or shunt was that there was a chance it would become blocked by fragments of brain tissue or debris as it was inserted. It was, after all, being pushed through nervous tissue into the lateral ventricle. So Wade also designed an introducer for the valve, the details of which were published alongside the main paper. It consisted of a thin hollow steel tube, with a flexible extractor that would remove any organic material before the permanent tube was introduced down the centre.

The speed of progress with the WDT valve was remarkable. Within a year of the family's return to England, the patent application had been lodged. Wade had given all his time for free, and the three men agreed early on that this was not to be a profit-making venture. Instead they established the Children's Research Fund at London's Hospital for Sick Children that would own the exclusive rights of manufacture. Dahl was keen that the valve should be available to children with hydrocephalus all over the world.

Thousands Across the World

'The valve was taken up, and used in all sorts of places – India, Kenya and Tanganyika,' he told me with a faraway look. 'We charged more for the rich countries – America and England – so that it was cheaper for the poorer ones.' In the West the valve cost US$21 (about US$130 today), but Dahl thought this was just too low a price: 'I am still worried about the psychology of customers, virtually all of whom think that something inexpensive is inferior,' he wrote to Till.

Dahl made sure that the British and American advertising emphasised the non-profit nature of the valve's production, and gave advice on how it should be promoted in the United States. 'America is America, and many advertisers have discovered to their cost that Americans are not impressed by understatement. It is not in their character. And all the American surgeons I know, with the exception of Charlie Carton, are flamboyant and rather loud. They sell themselves in the most aggressive manner and they expect others to do the same.'

Dahl was also keen to promote the valve in the UK, not because he was interested in sales, but because he wanted to share its benefits. He attended the annual meeting of the Society for Research into Hydrocephalus and Spina Bifida in York in 1964, and the following year was invited to the Parents' Association for Spina Bifida and Hydrocephalus Northwest Group.

'I would like to have it out in front of parents etc.,' Dahl wrote, urging Wade to accompany him on the trip, 'and show them our valve and discuss its merits.'

Dahl was especially concerned that the parents of children with shunts never seemed to be instructed to pump the valves that had been inserted. He felt this was critical to ensure that they did not block, and wanted to survey the parents. 'We were not instructed to pump the valve at any time,' one parent told Dahl, 'and indeed were not told anything about the valve.'

Dahl invited the Northwest Group's treasurer, Ian Wilson, with whom he had been corresponding, to visit them at Gipsy House. This group was one of several across England, Wales and Northern Ireland that joined together in 1966 to form the national Association for Spina Bifida and Hydrocephalus (ASBAH). This was renamed as Shine (Spina bifida, Hydrocephalus, Information, Networking, Equality) and celebrated its fiftieth anniversary in 2016.

Altogether somewhere between three and five thousand children across the world had had a Wade-Dahl-Till valve fitted. My neurosurgical colleagues in Liverpool still occasionally come across them today, operating on adults who had them inserted as children. By the time the valve had been developed, Theo had outgrown the need for a shunt. His was removed by Till when they realised it was actually causing him to be febrile and groggy.

Dahl and his wife had a nervous few days after the device was taken out, carefully watching the child to see if the old signs of raised pressure would recur. Thankfully they did not. Theo's eighth craniotomy was his last, and by the time I met him, more than thirty years later, he was a happy, healthy and gentle young man. But in a bizarre twist of fate, the WDT valve was used on Dahl's godson, the child of his British literary agent, Murray Pollinger, who had also been injured in a car accident.

Although Theo grew up to be a fine young man and Dahl tried to put the dreadful accident behind him, even decades later his writing would have vestiges of the trauma: the archive reveals that in an early draft of the 1986 book *Matilda*, the heroine and her teacher encounter a 'nightmare scene' on a by-pass, where a container truck has crushed a minibus full of schoolchildren. It appears that some of the children are dead, whilst others remain trapped: 'You could hear the kids screaming inside it,' an onlooker observes.

The incident did not survive into the book's next revision. However, English Professor Damian Walford Davies, who has studied the drafts in detail, suggests that 'the butcher with bloody lumps of meat on display and naked chickens hanging up', which Matilda and Miss Honey pass en route to Miss Honey's cottage, may have been an echo of this earlier carnage.

Until recently I had struggled to see a link between Dahl's adult *Tales of the Unexpected* and his children's books – it almost felt like two different writers were at work – but when you start looking into it the hilarious calamities that occur in many of Dahl's children's books often started in earlier drafts as rather gruesome horrors, which are not all that different from his adult short stories.

'I don't know why I write such nasty things,' Dahl said to me. 'I don't know why they come into my head. I'm not a nasty person.'

'He was not cruel or nasty at all,' Ophelia later concurred. 'When one of Theo's chickens was sick and needed putting out of its misery, Dad couldn't even bring himself to wring its neck.'

'I have a theory about surgeons,' Dahl commented one night after we had been talking about Theo and the WDT valve. 'It seems to me surgery is about fifty years behind the times.' He settled himself back on his pillow as he warmed to his theme. 'You see, the average surgeon is far too busy in the operating theatre to have any time to think about new developments. And the good ones, the top men, are even busier. They are brilliant in theatre, but they have no time to experiment.' I thought about the professors in Oxford. It was true there were many more professors of medicine than of surgery. 'If you think about the car industry – Jaguar, Rover, BMW – they have whole teams of people on the development side, fine-tuning, and improving. The same in the drug industry – whole departments working on new medicine. But what do you have in surgery? When I first asked Kenneth Till about making a new valve, do you know what he said?' I shrugged. 'He said, "I wouldn't have the foggiest where to begin. And I wouldn't have the time anyway." Mind you, he was delighted to cooperate, and of course spent a lot of time on it in the end.'

'I don't think surgery is quite so bad now,' I interjected, but Dahl was on a roll.

'What about my hip? How many hips do you think I have had replaced?'

'Two?' I offered.

'No, you are wrong,' he chortled. 'I've had three. This one done once and the other twice. It's a simple operation, but nobody thought of it until Charnley, in Lancashire in the 1960s. You know most people think it is glamorous to be a surgeon, but I am not so sure.'

In Dahl's childhood daydreams, he had imagined himself as a great surgeon, or a brilliant medical inventor. The idea of the naturally gifted amateur rising to the occasion and outperforming the professional was still one of his fantasies in his idle moments. Indeed, Liccy had to restrain him once on a flight to Australia, when a call was put out for a doctor.

'What would he have done if you'd not stopped him,' I asked her.

'Oh, I don't know. Probably have tried something. He really did have a lot of medical knowledge, and sometimes thought he wasn't far off being a doctor.'

Curiously, though, with the WDT valve, when Dahl clearly had a major role in a new medical invention that was used on thousands of children around the world, he seemed to shy away from the limelight. On many occasions afterwards, he described himself as simply the go-between for Wade, the brilliant engineer, and Till the highly skilful surgeon. Yet in reality it was Dahl's idea to develop a new valve. He studied the problem himself, put the team together and raised funds for the American and British surgeons to meet. He developed a system for testing the pressures at which the valve would open, and even wrote the first draft of the paper for the *Lancet*. Like a real life Henry Sugar Dahl decided it would be a non-profit venture, and that the wealthier countries should subsidise the shunts for the poorer ones. Yet, like a shy Mr Hoppy in *Esio Trot*, Dahl seemed reluctant to claim any credit for this marvellous medicine.

'*Those who don't believe in magic will never find it.*'

– The Minpins

PART THREE

AN ENORMOUS SHADOW

Chapter 8

'It'll Be Good for Them'

Although it is less than an hour on the train from London, the village of Great Missenden has not changed much since I first visited it twenty-five years ago. From the station I walk down the high street, past banks, shops and pubs, some of which have been there for hundreds of years. There is red brick, lots of Tudor timber, some tasteful blue and green washes. And what is that up on the left? A house with a huge and strange shadow on it. Wait a minute … it is not a shadow. It's a pale outline that I recognise: a tall figure, very tall – the size of the house; he is draped in a great coat, holding a case and trumpet-like tube. It's the BFG, lightly sketched on the front of the building. Below him are the words: 'IT IS TRULY SWIZZFINGLY FLUSHBUNKINGLY GLORIUMPTIOUS.' But this is no crude graffiti, and no normal building. It is an old coach house converted in 2011 into the Roald Dahl Museum and Story Centre. It tells Dahl's amazing life story, showcases much of his memorabilia, and inspires children to create stories of their own. The interior of Dahl's legendary writing hut was carefully moved here, piece by piece in 2012, to preserve it and make it accessible to viewers. However, the museum is not my destination today. I resist the enormous temptation to pop in, for I know if I do I will be there for hours, lost in another world.

I continue past the museum and down the high street. A couple of miles further is St John the Baptist Church at Little Missenden. It is a beautiful Saxon building, dating back more than a thousand years. Inside, I see pale twelfth-century frescoes on the walls, and the original Roman bricks can just be discerned, incorporated into later arches. My eye is drawn towards a wooden puppet-like statue, brightly painted and sitting incongruously just above the front pew. I go to take a closer look …

Although the Dahl family were not ardent churchgoers, St John the Baptist Church at Little Missenden is where all the children were christened. The Norman church of St Peter and St Paul in Great Missenden was closer to the family home, but for Dahl the petite and pretty building at Little Missenden, with its extraordinary frescoes, held a greater attraction.

In the early 1960s, the family had settled into a comfortable, if unconventional, routine. Most of the time they would be based in the quiet English countryside of the Chilterns; it made sense to be here because of Theo's health needs. However, for a few weeks every year, Pat's Hollywood career would take them off to America for filming. By the autumn of 1962 the two-year-old Theo had been well for nearly twelve months, and his speech and mobility were improving. Tessa, aged five, was in a local nursery school, and Olivia, who was two years older, was at Godstowe Preparatory School in nearby High Wycombe. She was growing up to be the apple of her father's eye, a happy and carefree girl who loved to paint pictures, and write poems. She seemed to have Dahl's imaginative streak, making up stories for her dolls and the little glass animals her parents bought her. She had learned the names of all the flowers and birds, and her parents converted a summerhouse into an aviary for her. There were around seventy homing budgerigars or parakeets, which would come and go as they pleased. Dahl loved to see them 'sitting in the trees or strutting on the lawn or flashing overhead with their brilliant blues and greens and yellows and mauves and whites'. Olivia's job was to look after them, and she spent more and more time with the birds, even writing little stories about them.

James and the Giant Peach had been published the year before, and Dahl was working on *Charlie and the Chocolate Factory*. By this stage its main characters, Willy Wonka and Charlie Bucket, had been fleshed out, though the book was still called *Charlie's Chocolate Boy*. The Dahl children were affected by the usual coughs and colds, but Olivia seemed to be hit especially hard by anything that was going round. In November, a note came back from the headmistress at Godstowe notifying all parents that there was an outbreak of measles in the school.

In view of all their previous problems with Theo, Dahl and his wife took it seriously. There was no specific vaccine for measles in the early 1960s – it had not yet been developed – but you could protect children for a few weeks by giving them gamma globulin, which gives broad defence, boosting the immunity against a range of viruses. It also ensures that even if they do get measles it will only be a mild case. In America, gamma globulin was used like this quite routinely, but in England it was expensive and hard to procure. It was thus reserved for protecting pregnant women who had been in contact with German measles, caused by a different virus, Rubella. However, the Dahls had a contact. Dahl's half-sister Ellen was married to Sir Ashley Miles, head of the Lister Institute of Preventive Medicine. This was the same doctor whose pipe had been stuffed with goat droppings years earlier by the young practical joker Roald.

The institute had been established in 1891, later taking the name of Joseph Lister, the illustrious pioneer of antiseptic surgery, who used carbolic acid to sterilise equipment and clean wounds. As well as conducting microbiology research, one of the institute's key roles was to make vaccines, including gamma globulin.

Miles, who had been director for ten years, was reluctant to break the rules for Dahl, but did provide some gamma globulin for Theo.

'Let the girls get measles,' Miles laughed. 'It will be good for them.'

Most children who get measles have a nasty illness, feeling miserable for a few days, and then make a full recovery. The risks of it developing into anything more serious are very small.

Sure enough, three days after the note from school Olivia came out in spots. Dahl and his wife kept her away from her siblings, and after a couple of days she appeared to be on the mend. However, the next morning, all she wanted to do was sleep. The GP, Mervyn Brigstock, came to see her that afternoon, and reassured the family that although she was very lethargic this was quite normal; there was nothing to worry about. On the morning of the seventeenth Dahl tried to get her to play.

> *I was sitting on her bed showing her how to fashion little animals out of coloured pipe cleaners, and when it came to her turn to make one herself, I noticed that her fingers and her mind were not working together and she couldn't do anything.*
> *'Are you feeling all right?' I asked her.*
> *'I feel all sleepy,' she said.*
> *In an hour, she was unconscious. In twelve hours she was dead.*

This is how, twenty years later, writing an open letter urging parents to vaccinate for Sandwell Health Authority, Dahl summarised that dreadful day. These few shocking words glossed over a terrible ordeal from which he never really recovered.

'We thought she was over the worst of it,' he explained to me one evening in Oxford. 'One saw, you know, the usual sort of thing, the fever, the tiredness, the spots. We even teased her for her polka dots.' Dahl had a wan smile and his eyes began to well up. He looked so tired, and sad.

'Well, the rash is quite striking,' I said in an effort to distract him. 'It's usually centrifugal, spreading from the body out on to the limbs. Smallpox is centripetal, starting on the limbs and working in, not that I have ever seen it ...'

'She was very tired, but then she seemed to be improving.' I don't think he had heard a word of what I said. 'I taught her chess. In the morning, the day before she died. She picked it up so quickly, all the moves. I fooled around a bit, being careless, and she actually beat me. Huh! She had such a good brain, a good sharp brain.' I sat quietly and said nothing. 'We thought the measles was over. But that night she wouldn't have supper. She said she just wanted to sleep, and she didn't wake till the middle of the next morning.' He sighed slowly. 'She wasn't interested in the chess, so we played with some pipe cleaners; I think someone had brought them as a present. But she was fumbling and couldn't cut with the scissors where I showed her, and just wanted to sleep.' He paused and looked at me searchingly ...

Theo's Best Friend

After Olivia fell asleep over the pipe cleaners, the Dahls called the family doctor back, who came at 3.30 p.m. and woke the child to examine her. He checked her throat and ears, and listened to her chest, then reassured the family that this sleepiness was the normal after-effect of measles. Dahl went back to his writing hut to continue working on *Charlie.* At five that afternoon, just as dusk was falling, Pat went to check on Olivia in her bedroom and found she was having a convulsion.

'Olivia's body was still. Her eyes open in a fixed, wall eyed stare, her mouth gaping limply, oozing spit,' Pat recalled in her autobiography. She ran downstairs to a light switch that turned on a bulb in Dahl's hut. They had a code. One flash meant a visitor or phone call; two meant an emergency, usually a worry about Theo. Pat flashed the light four times, and Dahl came running, not even pausing to turn off the electric bar heater. They called the doctor urgently, and whilst waiting cooled Olivia's forehead with flannels, turning her head to one side to stop her swallowing her tongue. Brigstock arrived after thirty minutes, took one look and went deathly pale. They phoned for an ambulance.

'Fill this quick,' he said to Dahl, handing him a syringe and an ampoule of sedative to stop further convulsions. But there was nothing with which to break the ampoule open. Dahl tried unsuccessfully with his fingers, then rushed to the tool shed for a file. The ambulance men arrived with oxygen, and Olivia was wrapped in her eiderdown and carried out to the vehicle. They set off for Stoke Mandeville Hospital at a pace, with the sirens wailing. To Pat this seemed unnecessary for a Saturday evening on quiet country roads. Dahl followed in his car, and his sister Else brought Pat after she had settled the other children. In the hospital, Olivia was put into a side room, and after more sedatives to control further seizures she had a lumbar puncture.

'It's encephalitis, not meningitis,' the doctors said to Dahl. The virus had entered the brain causing inflammation and swelling. They said she had an even chance. Dahl went into the room and spoke Olivia's name. She raised her head slightly off the pillow, but the sister warned him not to disturb her. His brother-in-law bought some whisky and joined Dahl in a drink. Dahl instructed the doctor to consult with experts, call anyone. The doctor spoke with a man in Oxford, but there was not much that could be done. Pat was keen to get back to the other children, worried they would be terrified about what was going on. Dahl was initially going to stay, but then changed his mind, and they all went back to Gipsy House together. After a quick sandwich, Dahl called a distinguished paediatrician involved in Theo's care, Dr Phillip Rainsford Evans, who offered to go to Stoke Mandeville straight away. Dahl then phoned the doctor at the hospital.

> *He said I'm afraid she's worse. I got in the car. Got to hospital. Walked in. Two doctors advanced on me from waiting room. How is she? I'm afraid it's too late. I went into her room. Sheet was over her. Doctor said to nurse go out. Leave him alone. I kissed her. She was warm. I went out.*
> *'She is warm.' I said to doctors in hall, 'Why is she warm?'*
> *'Of course,' he said.*
> *I left.*

This harrowing description comes at the end of a heart-wrenching account Dahl wrote in a school exercise book soon after Olivia's death. He then buried it away at the back of an obscure drawer in one of the many filing cabinets in his hut, and never told anyone about it. It was only discovered by Ophelia twenty-eight years later, after Dahl's death. On a visit to the archive, I am privileged to be allowed to look at this most private of items. I open the first page of the green book, which says OLIVIA on the cover.

> *Theo's best friend.*
> *The best person in the world to go for walks with.*
> *Driving her to school was an enchantment. Her love of nature and of small animals and insects caused her to ask endless questions.*
> *About God, too, she kept asking.*
> *And about the stars, the moon, the planets*
> *She had a collection of hundreds of tiny toy animals and people. These she would spend hours arranging upon shelves in a cabinet that I bought for her.*
> *She went to bed with up to a dozen dolls and teddy bears. She thought it unkind to leave any out, whether they were Tessa's or her own*

Reading it, I feel an overwhelming sadness for this little girl, dead long ago, before I was even born; as a father of four girls I feel a terrible emptiness for her father too. Unlike 'A Note on Theo's Accident' in which Dahl set out to capture every detail of that accident and Theo's early treatment in one of his ideas books, I think Dahl's intention here was different. In this empty school exercise book he starts off recording everything he can remember about his treasured daughter. Why else dedicate a new book to it? Why else start with these wonderful memories? But his description of Olivia in bed with her dolls and teddies focuses Dahl's mind all too quickly on the horrors of her last few days, and within a couple of sides he is describing these grim recollections. As the story of her last few hours unfolds, the careful punctuated prose deteriorates into hasty notes, which become increasingly terse. The account peters out after a few sides, never to be revisited. The final words are so faintly written they are barely legible:

> *'Why is she warm?'*
> *'Of course,' he said.*
> *I left.*

Writing about this tragedy was beyond even the great storyteller.

Such Pretty Little Names

'I didn't even know measles could cause encephalitis,' Dahl told me, 'although I found out all about it afterwards.'

We were talking about the virus, and how it affects the brain. Measles is one of the most infectious agents known to man. When someone has the disease, the chance of others in the same household becoming infected is about ninety per cent, unless they have been exposed before and are thus already immune. In the pre-vaccine era, almost everyone had met the virus by the time they were a young adult.

Long before we could isolate the cause, or even knew what a virus was, clinicians distinguished childhood febrile diseases according to the pattern and spread of the rashes. The measles rash typically starts behind the ears and spreads across the face, down on to the trunk and then into the limbs. Measles, also called rubeola, is known as 'first disease'; scarlet fever is 'second disease', caused by the bacteria, *Streptococcus pyogenes*. The numbering reflects the order in which the diseases were first described. 'Third disease' is German measles, also called rubella; 'fourth' is caused by *Staphylococcus aureus*; 'fifth' is erythema infectiosum, due to the parvovirus B19; and 'sixth disease' is called *roseola infantum*, which we now know is due to human herpes virus six, or seven.

'Rubeola, rubella, roseola … Such pretty little names for such terrible diseases,' Dahl observed.

The night nurse, who had checked Dahl's pulse and temperature earlier, came back with two cups of tea.

'Sit down,' I suggested, 'why don't you join us?'

'Yes!' Dahl brightened up. 'Tell us what that no-good chappie of yours has been up to.'

'I don't have time to sit and gossip,' she chastised us with a laugh. 'I have far too much to do.' She playfully fluffed up Dahl's pillows and left.

Before we had vaccines for the viral infections and antibiotics for the bacterial ones, these childhood diseases were, to some extent, considered a rite of passage, as Ashley Miles had suggested. A day or two before the measles rash appears, patients may have white Koplik spots inside the mouth on the cheek. Identifying these can be helpful because they allow a child to be isolated as soon as possible. The rash is the most definitive symptom, but when children are sick with measles they also have a runny nose, and are full of cough and splutter. This is how the virus spreads, in respiratory droplets, and also by direct contact with infected saliva and snot. The tiny droplets containing the virus are inhaled into the chest of the unsuspecting next patient. Here the virus replicates within lung tissue, crossing into the bloodstream and then to the spleen and other lymph organs, all the time reproducing to increase the number of virus particles. Infected immune cells then carry the virus from the lymph tissue back to the epithelial cells lining the lung. Here it is shed back into the airways, where it triggers enough mucus secretion and irritation to ensure it is nicely packaged and sent on its way to somebody new: '*Atchoo.*'

None of this is an accident, I said to Dahl. The virus has evolved to develop this replicative cycle; it has precisely the right proteins on its surface to enter the different cell types, ensuring it survives and gets passed on to a new host. However the virus also ends up in other places it does not need to be, such as the skin, and even the brain. From the bloodstream the virus infects the capillaries, small blood vessels in the skin. This causes inflammation here: the body's immune cells detect infection and release chemicals such as nitric oxide and histamines. These destroy the viral invaders, but also cause swelling and damage to the host cells, which results in the red itchy bumpy measles rash that is so characteristic. There is no advantage to the virus getting into the skin. It doesn't help it spread to new people, which is all that it is trying to do. In some people, measles virus also crosses similar capillaries to get into the brain. Again there is no advantage to the virus in doing this. I paused to check that Dahl was still interested. He nodded thoughtfully.

'That's about one in a thousand,' he commented.

'Actually, it's a lot more common.' About one in one thousand develops encephalitis, meaning the virus has triggered enough brain inflammation to cause altered consciousness, but if you do a lumbar puncture you find that there is evidence of brain infection for about one in three patients. Dahl looked astonished.

'In the 1960s,' I went on, 'someone examined the spinal fluid of a large group of measles patients and found a third of them had an elevated white cell count. There was a mild degree of inflammation.' Many patients also have an abnormality on the electroencephalogram – the brain-wave test. We think the virus probably gets across the blood–brain barrier quite often. But in most people the infection is gently brought under control before it causes too much harm.

'Why do you say gently?' asked Dahl.

'Because if the immune system sends in the big guns it can cause damage itself: it's like a "friendly fire" incident. What you really want is some clever sniper picking out the cells infected by the measles virus, before it replicates too much.' If that fails, I explained, then the immune system's heavy artillery is sent in: a cascade of inflammatory neutrophils and lymphocytes, which destroy virus-infected cells, and probably anything else nearby. I sketched it out for him on a spare sheet of paper. In some patients this happens at the height of the illness, in others it can be a couple of weeks later when you think they have recovered. In some it takes even longer. I am reminded of a patient I saw at the Walton Centre in Liverpool, nearly ten years after Dahl died.

The Big Guns

The patient is a seventeen-year-old male called Keith. He has been in a psychiatric hospital for three months with depression and strange behaviour. His low mood is interspersed with periods of an odd happy manner, smiling inappropriately, and he is deteriorating intellectually. When he has convulsions, the team realises this is more than a psychiatric illness, and he is transferred to our care at the neurology centre. I take the history again from Keith and his mother. Keith is pleasant and engaging, perhaps inappropriately cheerful given the circumstances. He knows where he is, and understands why, but is unsure of the month or year. As a child, Keith had the usual vaccinations against diphtheria, tetanus and polio. He had measles aged two and was mildly asthmatic.

On examination, his vision is poor, six over thirty-six, in both eyes, and he has a left homonymous hemianopia: he cannot see anything to his left side, as if he is wearing glasses with half of each lens blacked out.

I ask him about his vision. 'Did you not notice?'

'Yer yes.' His voice is hesitant and slightly slurred. 'I erh, couldn't sign on, and, and, and my, mmm mum had to sign on f-f-for me.' He gives a little giggle. His left arm is held in an abnormal flexed posture, with increased tone. Every few seconds there is a very slight twitch, an irregular myoclonic jerking. I have listened to his chest, and now ask him to put his T-shirt back on. He pulls it over his head, places the right arm in the sleeve, but then gets stuck; where does the left arm go? He pulls the top off, looks at all the holes carefully then tries again, but again he gets in a tangle. Despite multiple attempts, he keeps failing. It is not weakness, or lack of sensation. This is a dressing apraxia, an inability to dress because of problems with spatial awareness.

Everything is pointing to pathology in Keith's right cerebrum: a dressing apraxia caused by parietal lobe damage, visual loss because of occipital involvement. Neurology is detective work, like a three-dimensional jigsaw puzzle. First, consider the neuroanatomy: could a single lesion explain all the clinical signs, or must there be multiple areas of damage? Then think about the disease process. Was this a sudden apoplectic attack caused by a stroke or a seizure, or has this developed insidiously over weeks and months? It is clear that Keith's problem is the latter.

We arrange an MRI scan of his brain, and I am not surprised to see a large abnormal area extending across the right parietal and occipital lobes. But it is not a tumour; instead there is a diffuse inflammation in the brain's white matter.

'There are not that many causes of white matter change with a movement disorder,' says one of the juniors as we huddle around the scans pinned up on a light box.

'PML, mitochondrial diseases, Hallervorden-Spatz,' calls a voice from the back – someone has clearly been brushing up for the membership exam.

'There is no eye of the tiger,' comments a third, referring to the characteristic MRI change in Hallervorden-Spatz disease. 'What about adrenoleukodystrophy or CJD?' Both are important causes of dementia and myoclonic movements, and reasonable suggestions. The rhythmic jerking has become more prominent over the last few days, and Keith has been sent for an electroencephalogram that measures the brain waves. Our discussions are interrupted by a call from the EEG department: 'You'd better come and see this.'

We find Keith lying on a couch, relaxed, dozing gently. Nearly two dozen electrodes are attached to his head, recording every cerebral impulse. On the monitor nearby, sixteen lines gently undulate across the screen in synchrony, with a fine high-frequency tremor superimposed – these are the normal alpha and beta waves we expect. Then suddenly Keith's left arm jerks, and at precisely the same moment the whole recording jumps: every line thrown up, then down, then up again, like a great tidal wave of electrical distortion. The recording settles after a few moments, but a few seconds later his body jerks once more, and the recording goes into spasm again.

'CJD?' the house officer mouths to me with raised eyebrows. But I don't think so. The dementia would fit, and the myoclonic jerks, but the scans are not right. There is too much white matter change. Besides, the jerks are more frequent in CJD. This is the late 1990s and we are beginning to learn much more about this old disease with a new variation caused by eating contaminated meat. It is Friday afternoon, and I fret about whether to contact Keith's consultant who is doing a clinic in Wales. At this stage I am a registrar, and so expected to take a certain amount of responsibility. I decide to give him a quick call to update him, but there is nothing to be done over the weekend.

By Monday morning we have our answer. The protein in the spinal fluid was much higher than normal so we had sent it to the public health labs in Colindale to be tested: there are massively elevated levels of measles antibody. Keith has a very rare brain disease that occurs years after measles infection, called subacute sclerosing panencephalitis – SSPE.

Sometimes, instead of causing the acute encephalitis that affected Olivia, the measles virus hides away in the brain, causing no problems at all for many years. Then ten, fifteen, even twenty years later the virus slowly starts multiplying, triggering an immune response, and destroying brain tissue. I had encountered it before in Africa, but had never expected to see it in the UK. With the clinical presentation, the scan, the EEG and now the antibody testing, there is no doubt at all. This is SSPE, and sadly it is almost always fatal. With no treatment, there is an inexorable progression over months until the inevitable end.

'It was all so quick with Olivia,' Dahl recalled. 'She was getting better. Had a good lunch. Measles is over, we thought. But then ...' His eyes narrowed, and he was quiet for a few moments, stirring his tea aimlessly. 'We believed there was a clue from her smallpox vaccination.' He turned to me. 'She never reacted even though she had it many times.'

The doctors had tested to see if Olivia had reacted to the immunisation, developing an appropriate immune response, but Olivia never had. He wondered whether other children who developed measles encephalitis might not have had some similar abnormal reactions to the smallpox vaccine.

'I wanted to study it,' he went on, 'to set up a careful investigation. I was prepared to get in touch with every parent of every child in this country who had had severe complications from measles.'

'Like a case control study?'

'What do you mean?'

'Well, let's say you questioned everyone with measles encephalitis, two hundred families maybe, and found that in twenty children there had been a smallpox vaccination problem – that's ten per cent.'

'Of course.'

'Well, you wouldn't know whether ten per cent was just the normal rate. So you would also want to question two hundred control families where the child had had measles but no encephalitis. If ten per cent of them had had smallpox vaccine issues, then you have shown there is no link. But if it were just one per cent then that could really be significant.'

'Yes, I see. Well, anyway, we got started, and I think we were on to something, but then the new vaccine came in, so it looked like the problem had been largely erased, at least for the time being.'

I remember wondering back then how much work he had really done on all this. After a family tragedy, many people feel they want to do something, but to try to set up a national study off your own back looking for risk factors for measles encephalitis sounded pretty incredible.

Chapter 9

A Clue Here

Many years later, pouring through the archive at the museum, I found that Dahl *had* in fact been doggedly corresponding with scientists for years after, to try to discover a link between smallpox vaccination and measles encephalitis.

'There must be some clue or clues as to the susceptibility of a person to encephalitis from this vaccination business,' he wrote to Dr John Adams at the University of California's Department of Paediatrics in 1966. 'It is probably staring us in the face. In what way for example is resistance to encephalitis provided when immunity to smallpox is achieved? My daughter was congenitally immune to smallpox (no vaccination ever took) and being immune to smallpox she was susceptible to encephalitis ... has anyone checked up the smallpox vaccination history of recent cases of encephalitis not only for measles but from all sources? There is a clue here I'm certain of it.'

In 1972 Adams sent Dahl drafts of his manuscripts, later published in *Science* and *Journal of the American Medical Association* suggesting that vaccinia, the strain of virus modified to make the smallpox vaccine, may become a slow virus and cause encephalitis years after the inoculation. Dahl thanked Adams for a publication that 'breaks new ground', but questioned him about 'one fact important to my mind that is missing from your report': had the child affected, who had been vaccinated twice against smallpox, had any reaction to the first vaccination? 'My guess is there was not.'

The next year Adams sent Dahl an article he had written on a child who developed neuromyelitis optica, another inflammatory condition of the central nervous system, years after primary smallpox vaccination. A decade later Dahl was still pursuing the same theory, sending a copy of this neuromyelitis publication to Professor Neville Butler at the University of Bristol, whose new charity he was supporting. Butler's reply describes why he thinks there are difficulties with Dahl's smallpox theory, but he does not come up with any better explanation as to why a virus sometimes causes such severe disease.

Improving Outcomes

Through my work with the Encephalitis Society I know how important it is for families to understand 'why?' even if it is too late for their loved one. It helps them come to terms with the disease, and of course may prevent others suffering the same devastating illness.

More than fifty years after Olivia died, we now are beginning to get answers as to why so many viruses that cause mild disease in most patients can occasionally lead to encephalitis in others. Herpes simplex virus is one such virus we are studying in the Brain Infections group in Liverpool. It is best known as a cause of the common cold sore, and is not quite as infectious as measles, being passed between people through kissing, and similar close contact, rather than the respiratory route. The majority of herpes simplex virus infections occur during childhood, and do not cause any illness at all. However, just like measles, herpes virus sometimes causes a very nasty encephalitis. Indeed, it is the most common sporadic cause of viral encephalitis worldwide.

Some recent ground-breaking work by the Frenchman Jean Laurent Casanova and colleagues supports the ideas I discussed with Dahl all those years ago, that those who develop encephalitis may have a failure of the body's initial response to the infection, so that it gets out of control. Casanova and his team studied two unrelated children who both had herpes encephalitis, and found they had a defect in a gene coding for a protein critical in the early response to virus infection, called 'toll like receptor 3', or 'TLR3'. They didn't find this mutation in any of fifteen hundred unrelated healthy controls who had all been infected with herpes virus at some stage but never developed encephalitis.

This is the kind of case-control approach I was discussing with Dahl.

Next they looked at how cells from the affected children responded to herpes virus infection when tested in the laboratory; compared with cells from healthy controls, those from children with the abnormal gene failed to produce the interferon proteins whose job it is to stop an invading virus from reproducing. Because this initial part of the body's response is ineffective, the virus can multiply in an unrestricted way, damaging neuronal cells. This continues until the back-up team in the form of inflammatory neutrophils and lymphocytes, part of the adaptive immune response, arrives. The cascade of inflammatory proteins, called cytokines, that these cells release to kill viral-infected cells also causes damage to neighbouring neurons, which can make things even worse. This inflammation is a key cause of damage in herpes encephalitis, and many people think the corticosteroid drug dexamethasone might be beneficial by controlling this damaging response. In Liverpool, we are currently leading a national study to see if the drug improves outcomes overall.

Darwin's Finches

You might wonder why people have this genetic susceptibility in the first place. The reason is that it is a simple, and unfortunate, consequence of Darwinian evolution. You may have heard of Darwin's theory about survival of the fittest by means of natural selection; he described finches that had evolved different beaks adapted for feeding on different islands. Darwin did not know it at the time, but this selection pressure that results in a physical difference is acting at the level of the nucleotides. These are the building blocks that carry the letters of the genetic code and make up the DNA; they form the genes that sit within our chromosomes. A random change in one of the nucleotides, if it happens to be in a gene that controls beak length, might make it easier for that bird to feed, so that on average it has more offspring to whom it passes on this fortunate nucleotide alteration. Helpful mutations thus get passed on. But the downside, since the mutations are all random, is that unhelpful ones can occur too. And if this mutation happens to be in the TLR3 gene of a young child, then it means they cannot control herpes virus infection and could develop encephalitis.

When the genetic studies into herpes encephalitis were first conducted, just over a decade ago, scientists had to take an educated guess about which genes might be important, and focus on those. Now we have much better ways of looking for genes that confer susceptibility to a particular disease. We can examine the whole human genome, approximately 20,000 genes, comparing people who have the disease with those who are unaffected, to identify the critical genes that might be important. The sequencing of the first human genome was a massive undertaking. It took two hundred scientists more than ten years, and cost three billion dollars. However, the technology has improved so much that it currently costs about a thousand dollars to sequence an individual's genome, and it can be done in a few hours. The TLR3 gene mutation is just one of a whole series that has been identified as rendering individuals susceptible to severe viral or bacterial infections, depending on what the gene defect is. Whether a similar genetic change is responsible for measles virus sometimes causing encephalitis is not yet known, but it is likely to be the case.

As to Dahl's theory about a failed response to smallpox vaccine being an indicator of an immune impairment that might leave one susceptible to severe mealses, it was never thoroughly investigated, but based on our current knowledge it is not totally inconceivable.

A Mountain Garden

When I spoke with Dahl about Olivia, I had no idea that this was a subject he never normally discussed. Only later did I discover how privileged I had been. I suspect the gentle, innocent questions of someone unaware that this was a taboo subject helped him open up. The day after Olivia's death, Theo's paediatrician, Dr Phillip Rainsford Evans, came to see them. He'd driven to the hospital the night before, but had arrived too late to help. He told Dahl that large doses of gamma globulin could well have saved her life. This would torture Dahl for many years, the fact that he could have done something; if he had pushed harder for Olivia to have the gamma globulin, she might never have contracted the measles that ultimately killed her.

According to Pat, Dahl all but lost his mind after the loss of their daughter. Nothing in his life had ever hit him so hard. Since his father and eldest sister Astri died in 1920, he had been the one always directing the family. She was aged seven, as was Olivia, and Dahl was haunted by the coincidence. His father Harald's death was said to be due to pneumonia, but everyone felt he died from a broken heart. Feeling unwell, Dahl took to his bed, and wondered if there was a pattern, and he would soon follow Olivia. Pat felt he wanted to die like his father had. She would try to get him to talk about his pain, but the deep Nordic restraint within him stopped him from reaching out. Fifteen years earlier, Dahl had presciently explored the fear and misery of losing a child in two of his short wartime stories. In 'Only This' a mother sits anxiously staring out of the window as she waits for her son's plane to return from battle.

> *The emptiness when he was not there and the knowing all the time that something might happen; the deep conscious knowing that there was nothing else to live for except this; that if something did happen, then you too would be dead ... there would be no use in living ... She could think of nothing at all except that she must see him and be with him, that she must see him now because tomorrow would be too late.*

In 'Yesterday Was Beautiful' a pilot stumbles across an old Greek man who is so dazed by the loss of his daughter in a German air raid that morning that he barely knows who he is.

> *The old man looked up slowly, turning his head but not moving his shoulders ... He looked at the pilot and he was like a blind man who looks towards something but does not see ... There was a pause, and*

when he spoke, the old man seemed to be talking in his sleep. There was no anxiety in his voice. There was no expression whatsoever.

During his most sombre moments Dahl worried that some kind of bitter fate hung over the family. Two years earlier in New York a white-faced boy in the street seemed to be an omen foretelling Theo's disaster. Dahl had moved the family to the safe haven of rural Buckinghamshire, and this very move had been responsible for Olivia's death. If they had stayed in America, she would not have been at the school with the measles outbreak. Even had she caught measles in America, gamma globulin would have been available. He wondered if the family was cursed. He even discussed with his mystically inclined mother, Mormor as she was known, the possibility of getting a male witch to come and exorcise evil spirits from Gipsy House. Poor Tessa, who at age five barely understood what was going on, asked if she could now have all Olivia's toys. Dahl put the toys, along with Olivia's books, in a polished oak chest in his bedroom. In his writing hut he kept a portrait of his daughter facing his chair where he could always see her. On the wall just above his head was a framed contact sheet with forty-eight photos of her in various poses, taken when she was just three. When travelling, he would always take with him a small photograph of Olivia, which he would place by the bed. Liccy recalled that a few days after they returned from a holiday in Turkey she noticed he had somehow left it behind. With amazing luck the next guests in the same hotel room were friends who recognised the picture found under their bed, and returned it to Dahl before he even realised it was missing.

Dahl was too distressed to cope with Olivia's funeral arrangements, so his three sisters took care of everything, choosing the coffin, the flowers, the music, and seeing the little body prepared and dressed. Pat felt the Dahl family had taken over and was dissuaded from getting involved. She never saw Olivia's body after death, something she would always regret. Olivia was buried as the snow fell in the village graveyard just opposite St John the Baptist Church in Little Missenden. It was a private family affair, and afterwards Dahl's sister Else wrote a poem comparing the blanket of snow with the love enfolding the little girl's grave.

As the small coffin was being lowered into the soil Pat wished she had ripped off the lid to hold her daughter close one last time. Even three years later she still wondered might it be possible to see the body.

'How long are you buried … before you … come apart?' she asked visiting journalist Barry Farrell over dinner one evening. 'How long are you in the grave before you're just a … you know, just bones.'

He hadn't realised she was thinking of Olivia, and to her great distress explained the body would decompose in just a few months. Pat chose a headstone for the grave, with the inscription: 'She stands before me as a living child' from

Yeats's poem 'Among School Children'. But when the stone was delivered to Gipsy House she and Dahl could hardly bear to look at it. It remained facing the wall at the back of the garage for many years and was eventually discarded.

Instead Dahl decided to build a rock garden on the grave, a living memorial that would replace the horror of a gravestone. They had bought a double plot, thinking they would ultimately be buried with their daughter. Dahl spent weeks visiting quarries and nurseries to select the rocks and miniature plants for the grave. Nearly two hundred specimens were chosen – Japanese evergreens, tiny hybrids and wild mountain flowers, many that Olivia knew by name. They then added a dozen or so small porcelain animals from her collection.

When he had finished, Dahl had built a small mountain, a rare and affecting garden to gaze at for hours. For many years a small metal tag with Olivia's name, like those used for labelling plants, was the only indication of who lay there. Eventually a stone was laid discreetly under a bush. The garden project at least gave Dahl something therapeutic on which to focus during those first few difficult weeks and beyond. The plot would always require his care and attention, and he visited often, even keeping an old lawnmower under a tree. To Ophelia and her younger sister Lucy, it seemed perfectly normal to spend part of their early childhood playing regularly in a graveyard. For Tessa, her father's delicate weeding of the garden ensuring the growth of the plants made her wonder if he was 'frightened to let go of the last living part of her'.

Dahl did not refer directly to Olivia's death from measles in any of his books. However, in his late sixties, he wrote *Boy: Tales of Childhood*, and looking at the book now, I suspect he wanted to tell children about measles and his own loss, but somehow couldn't. Instead, among the reproduction of his letters home which are interspersed through the book, he included the following:

Thanks for your letter. There are exactly 23 !!!!!!!! boys with the measles! and all the other schools in Weston have got it.

On the next page there is another snippet:

Do you know that a chap called Ford has got double pneumonia on top of measles!!!!!! We've all got to be like mice going up to bed.

And on the following page:

Ford is still very bad, he got better on Friday but has again got very ill.
PS we have just been informed that poor little Ford died early this morning.

A Sham

'It happened so swiftly that one didn't have time to prepare for it,' Dahl reflected. 'I was in a kind of daze, I suppose, and morbid thoughts kept after me.'

After Olivia's death, he became depressed, drinking more, and increasing the daily dose of painkillers for his back. His great vitality was gone, and he would spend hours at the cemetery or with his mother. He often hid away in the comforting embrace of his little hut, though he was unable to write much for a year or so. Pat was able to express her feelings, talking openly about her loss, but Dahl wouldn't speak about Olivia, finding it unbearable to even hear her name mentioned. All those close to him agreed that he never got over the loss of Olivia, and always missed her.

Dahl and Pat differed in their spiritual response to the bereavement. Pat's 'mystical self' found a sense of 'deep purification' through the bitter pain, bringing her closer to God. At times she tortured herself with the thought that God was punishing her for taking the life of her first baby, a terminated pregnancy with Gary Cooper. She became closer to Dahl's mother, a religious and mystical women, whose spirituality also included elements of Nordic folklore.

Mormor often amazed the family by foreseeing future events: she had predicted Dahl's family would be like her own: two girls, then a boy, then two more girls. More than anyone, she could empathise with Pat, having also lost her oldest daughter, aged seven, to a tragic illness. Mormor herself died on the fifth anniversary of Olivia's death, a synchronicity that would have pleased her. Many years later she would appear as the Norwegian grandmother in Dahl's 1983 book *The Witches*: 'a wonderful storyteller ... tremendously old and wrinkled, with a massive wide body ... smothered in great lace'.

Whilst Pat found succour in religion, Dahl was at a loss. He wanted to believe, but found his faith was severely tested. Pat's conviction that she would meet Olivia in heaven seemed like trashy sentiment. He needed to be convinced. Less than a month after Olivia died, he and Pat went to visit his ex-headmaster from Repton, Geoffrey Fisher. 'The boss' as Dahl called him, had just retired as the Archbishop of Canterbury, and should know more about God than anyone.

'I would love to embrace the Christian belief in an afterlife,' Dahl said later, 'but common sense tells me this is wishful thinking ... Nor do I subscribe to the Christian creed that of all animals in the world only the human is a candidate for an afterlife.' Fisher assured Dahl that his daughter was in heaven.

'What about Rowley?' Dahl asked the archbishop about a favourite dog of theirs that had died the same week. 'Is he also in heaven?'

The archbishop threw up his hands in horror and was genuinely shocked by this suggestion. Dahl found it impossible to believe Olivia would be happy in heaven without the animals for which she loved and cared so much. Dahl later claimed the conversation with Fisher finally convinced him that Christianity was a sham.

Although he no longer believed in God, a few years later when journalist Farrell was staying with them, Dahl declared that there might still be a value in praying to a spirit, or at least communing.

'Commune! I didn't know that you communed,' Pat teased him, 'who is it you commune with?'

'None of your business,' Roald told her. Pat sprang on to his lap, with tickling fingers digging into his ribs to tease it out of him.

'All right! All right!' Roald said. 'I'll tell you. Olivia.' The whole dinner table went quiet. 'That is ... I try to. I tried to when we used to go to church.' He smiled softly. 'Well, that's just what I do. You have to do what you can.'

In some respects Olivia's siblings lost their father too for a while, Tessa, especially, finding her father distant and cold. Eventually he fought off the depression, which he viewed as a great self-indulgence. In his view the only way to deal with these things was not to wear your emotion on your sleeve, but to roll those sleeves up and get on with putting things right.

'You try to make something out of it, and actually you nearly always can.'

There was nothing he could do to help Olivia. He never had the chance to fight for her, but he was going to do everything possible to stop others going through the same hell. Dahl liked to tell the wartime story of Lady Rachel Workman MacRobert, a widow who lost her three sons in the RAF, two of them just a month apart. Her response was to give twenty-five thousand pounds, nearly one million pounds today, to pay for building a new Stirling bomber; *MacRobert's Reply* was the name she had painted on the front. This indomitable spirit, which could not be defeated, was what Dahl admired most in others and aspired to in himself.

Within days of losing Olivia, Dahl had ensured two of her school friends, who had also come down with measles, were given gamma globulin. And once the specific measles vaccine became available a few years later Dahl would do all he could to ensure its uptake.

'If only we'd had the chance to fight for her, but it all happened too quickly.'

I hear Dahl's grief-stricken voice echoing in my head as I am telling Keith's mum and dad about SSPE and what will happen to him – he will steadily get worse and die, probably over the next few months. But maybe there is a chance to fight for Keith.

As part of my PhD a few years earlier, I looked at the effect of an antiviral drug, interferon alpha, in a different form of encephalitis – Japanese encephalitis. I remember reading something about its effects on measles virus. I look up the scant literature on drugs that might work against SSPE. There is no known treatment, but there are hints that a new combination of drugs might work. Some have been tried in animal models or isolated cases. With the support of Keith's family, we come up with a plan: a cocktail of three drugs – one oral, one intravenous and one given directly into his brain via an Ommaya reservoir. This is similar to the valve on which Dahl worked. It sits just under the skin of the scalp, with a tube leading into the brain, and we use it to inject drugs directly into the ventricle.

In the couple of weeks it takes to get hospital approval for these expensive drugs, and to get the neurosurgeons to insert the device, Keith has deteriorated. He can now barely see, the jerking movements have become more frequent and have spread to his left leg, and he has become bed-bound. But once the treatment starts he improves remarkably. Within a few weeks he can see again, the jerks have settled, and his strength has returned. All the objective measures of his condition, the visual acuity, and neuropsychological testing have also improved.

Keith returns home, and continues his treatment as an outpatient, but we have problems with the Ommaya reservoir. Having silicone inside the head can lead to all sorts of difficulties, as Dahl found with Theo. For our patient it is not blockage, but infection with *Staphylococcus*, a skin organism. Despite weeks of treatment with a strong antibiotic, we cannot clear the infection, and eventually have to remove the reservoir. Keith continues to progress on oral treatment alone, but I worry that it was the intra-ventricular treatment, the drug going directly into his brain, that was really making the difference. Ten months later he deteriorates suddenly, becoming unsteady, incontinent and confused. He is admitted to hospital, and whilst we are making plans to insert a new Ommaya reservoir so we can restart the treatment he deteriorates suddenly and dies.

Like his family, I am devastated. I wonder if it was worth putting Keith through all this, the long hospital admissions, the operations, for just ten extra months of life; his family reassure me they are grateful for every single day. Medical history is full of pioneering patients who were willing to try. And even if they only benefited a small amount, the collective build-up of knowledge pushes forward our understanding in small increments, so that one day great things are possible. I share my frustrations with Mr Conor Mallucci, the neurosurgeon who inserted the Ommaya reservoir.

'If it wasn't for the infected silicone,' I rant, 'Keith would probably still be alive.'

'I know, but we see this all the time, not just with reservoirs, but with shunts too.'

'The shunts you use for hydrocephalus?'

'Yes, even today about one in three shunts has to be replaced because it is infected or blocked.' It seems little has changed since all the difficulties with Theo's shunt.

'And you neurosurgeons accept that?' I challenge him, remembering Dahl's comments about surgeons being too busy operating to spend time on research and development.

That was back in 2000. In March 2014, I am delighted to find myself as the guest speaker at the British Neurosurgical Research Group's annual meeting. I stand at the podium and peer through the lights at the crowd. I talk about our research on brain infections and how we have worked with the neurosurgeons over the years. There is a fair amount of good-natured banter – only to be expected give the rivalry between neurologists and neurosurgeons. In the previous few years, shunts impregnated with antibiotics or with silver had been developed, which are supposed to be more resistant to bacterial infection, but no one knows for sure.

From the podium I describe the work I have been doing with Conor and his colleague Mike Jenkinson, who are leading a national study to see if the new shunts really are better. Twelve hundred patients are being randomised to receive one of the three types of shunt, and we are counting the numbers getting infected. In a couple of years we will know which shunt should be used in the future. This is just the sort of high-quality research by surgeons that Dahl wanted to see.

As I finish my talk, I fancy I see a shadow of him at the back of the room, nodding sagely with approval, encouraging us in our work to reduce these terrible diseases that cause such devastation for patients and their families.

Chapter 10

A Shot in the Arm

In 1796, physician Edward Jenner inoculated a young boy with pus extracted from a cowpox sore on a milkmaid's hand. His action not only protected eight-year-old James Phipps from smallpox, but ushered in the era of vaccination. It was a slow start; it would be one hundred years before Pasteur spearheaded the development of vaccines for cholera and anthrax that got things going properly.

Cowpox is principally a disease of cattle, but Jenner noticed that milkmaids, who were liable to get the lesions on their hands, seemed not to be affected by smallpox when it ravaged communities. He was not the first to inoculate with cowpox; a Dorset farmer had safeguarded his family against smallpox twenty years earlier. But Jenner gets the credit for convincing the world. He showed, experimentally, that the recipients of cowpox vaccine were immune to subsequent smallpox inoculation, and published the results leading to its widespread introduction across the world. The word *vaccination* actually derives from *vache*, the French for cow. Dahl knew a bit about Jenner, telling me he thought he was 'a thoroughly good egg'.

In his spare time Jenner experimented with hot-air balloons, and studied nature. Even before his vaccine studies he had become a Fellow of the Royal Society for his work on cuckoos. It was Jenner who described how newly hatched cuckoo chicks are responsible for pushing the eggs and young chicks of their host out of the nest.

'I didn't know it was Jenner,' exclaimed Dahl, who had a bit of a thing about cuckoos. 'Nasty creatures. Did you know they are very particular about which nests they use? It is nearly always the hedge sparrow. I'm not sure why.'

Jenner also showed that cuckoos even have a concave back to help them shift the eggs.

The cowpox virus worked as a vaccine because it is similar enough to smallpox to generate a response that protects against both viruses. The body's initial defence against an infection is the non-specific innate response described earlier for herpes simplex virus: toll like receptors recognise something abnormal, the nucleic acid of a virus, without being sure exactly which virus it is. This is called the innate response, because it is built-in, primed and ready to go. But it is not very strong – only a short-term measure to try to keep the invading microbe under control whilst the full immune defence develops.

This later reaction is called the adaptive immune response; it takes time because it is very specific, adapted to the surface proteins on each individual microbe. All microbes – viruses, bacteria, parasites, fungi – are coated in proteins that are unique to them. The corners of protein sticking out of the surface, called antigens, are like Lego bricks, all shaped differently. The body's white bloods cells, which patrol the blood and tissues looking for invading bugs, have similar Lego bricks with complementary shapes on their surface called receptors. If the white cells find a match, i.e. the bricks interlock, then it knows it has found an invader. One white cell on its own is not much use, so the next step is to make more of them, all with the same surface receptor. This army of white cells, T-lymphocytes, can then attack the virus. The whole process is called cell-mediated immunity.

The other arm of the adaptive immune response is antibody-mediated immunity: B-lymphocytes do not attack virus directly, but produce lots of antibodies, like Lego bricks floating free in the blood. These can then attack the microbe too, remotely. The adaptive response takes a few days to develop, but, once the invader has been fought off, your immune system remembers it for ever. Memory T cells and antibodies specific for that virus continue to circulate in the blood. This is where the gamma globulin that could have protected Olivia comes from. Gamma globulin is just a cocktail of antibodies taken from the blood of people who have met, and so are now protected from, a whole range of microbes such as measles, German measles, mumps and many others. Adaptive immune response explains why for many infections you only get them once. After you have had measles or chicken pox, for example, your body remembers it; if you meet the virus again, your immune system deals with it before you even know anything about it.

The Golden Age

Vaccines are usually a tame version of the virus; they have enough similarity to the real thing to trigger the adaptive immune response, but are not so similar that they cause disease. Cowpox worked as a vaccine for smallpox because the viruses are so closely related and share enough of the same antigens, the Lego bricks, that once you have been infected with cowpox you are protected against smallpox too. The fact that cowpox and smallpox are so similar was a piece of biological good luck: they evolved from a common ancestral virus. This was way before the golden age of vaccines when rationale design began.

Dahl interrupted my monologue. 'The golden age of vaccines?'

'Yes, from about 1945 onwards, for thirty years; more than a dozen vaccines were developed.'

'What about the golden age of microbiology?'

'That was earlier, from about the 1860s. It came with the development of better microscopes and the realisation that microbes cause disease; Pasteur, Koch and all the others seemed to describe a new bacteria every year.'

'And the golden age of chocolate?'

I'm confused. 'The what?'

'Yes, why not a golden age of chocolate? Did you not know all the great chocolates were created in the 1930s?'

I looked at him askance, expecting another of his usual teases. 'Really?'

'Yes, of course they were: Cadbury's Whole Nut, 1930; Mars Bars, 1932; Black Magic 1933 ... Surely you knew this?' His face was something between puzzled, surprised and hurt, as if I had admitted to not knowing the dates of World War II.

I laughed. 'But why should –'

'Aero, 1935; Maltesers, 1936; Rolo, 1937 ...' Dahl went on to tell me that almost every one of the great chocolate bars that we eat today was invented in the 1930s; in fact, in just seven golden years. I learned later it was an argument he rehearsed many times. 'Everyone should know these dates. Don't they teach you this in medical school ... ?'

He laughed so loudly that one of the nurses popped her head in to check everything was all right. Dahl went on to tell me about the ball of silver paper that he kept in his writing hut, made from the crushed wrappers of hundreds of chocolate wrappers.

The golden age of vaccinology saw the development of vaccines against all the major viral killers of the day: influenza, polio, small pox, yellow fever, measles, mumps, rubella. They contained either killed or live modified virus. The polio vaccine developed by Jonas Salk in the 1950s, for example, contains polio virus killed by formalin, so that it cannot replicate, but with the surface antigens intact, so they trigger the protective immunity. A live attenuated vaccine was created by Albert Sabin soon after, by growing the virus in different cell types until it was so altered that, although it could reproduce in the gut and thus trigger an immune response, it could not replicate in the nervous system to cause poliomyelitis. Neither Salk nor Sabin received the Nobel Prize, but John Franklin Enders, who had first isolated the poliovirus, which thus allowed the vaccines to be developed, won the award in 1954. In that year he also cultured measles virus for the first time, and in the early 1960s developed a live attenuated measles vaccine. Following its introduction in the United States, the number of cases of measles fell from hundreds of thousands to tens of thousands, and by the 1980s this was down to just a few thousand cases. In the UK there were around half a million cases annually before the vaccine was introduced in 1968, but, although there was a steady decline since then, by the late 1980s there were still more than 80,000 cases a year.

'That bothers me, you see,' said Dahl. 'No need for it. Why do we have so much measles in Britain, when the Americans have virtually got rid of it?' Dahl was becoming indignant. 'Do you know why?' I shrugged. 'I'll tell you why. The Americans took action where the British did not. Apparently, you can't force a parent to stick their child with a needle, or even take the oral polio. But what the Americans did was absolutely delicious. They said that no child could go to school without a certificate of measles immunisation. A beautiful sort of blackmail. No immunisation, no school.'

Dahl had offered his services to the British government in 1985 to 'assist in the campaign to increase measles vaccination uptake'. His first letter to the Department of Health and Social Security was met with a lukewarm response, but Ophelia remembers her father describing meetings with Jeffrey Archer, the Conservative Party Chairman, who seemed interested. However, soon after their discussions, a political scandal involving a prostitute and two thousand pounds put paid to Archer's political career and so too Dahl's aspirations for supporting a nationwide measles-vaccine campaign.

A Dangerous Illness

Dahl had more success in the Midlands. In December 1985 Dr Barry Smith, a consultant physician and member of Sandwell Health Authority, gave an interview on Radio Four's *Today* programme. He discussed the importance of measles immunisation, the misery of the disease and the difficulties in persuading parents to get their children immunised. The programme was heard by Dahl who immediately contacted Smith, offering to write a letter addressed to children. Smith agreed and invited Dahl to launch the letter the following year. Dahl was surprisingly reluctant at first, claiming it would only have an impact if he visited many schools, and at nearly seventy and recovering from recent illness, he felt too frail for this. He seemed charmingly unaware of the publicity his appearance would generate. Nevertheless, at the beginning of July 1986, Dahl travelled with his wife, Liccy, to launch the measles vaccine letter at the Midlands Centre for Neurosurgery and Neurology.

'A pop star has teenage appeal and power,' Dahl explained to the press, radio and children invited from local schools. 'I have great child power. I understand how a child's mind works – that's how I can help and influence.'

His open letter to parents, 'MEASLES: A Dangerous Illness', described his own experience: 'Olivia, my eldest daughter, caught measles when she was seven years old. As the illness took its usual course, I can remember reading to her often in bed and not feeling particularly alarmed about it.' She began to have difficulty playing with the pipe cleaners, he continued, and was unconscious within an hour, then tragically 'in twelve hours she was dead'.

Dahl explained how the doctors could do nothing to treat Olivia's measles encephalitis in 1962, but even now if a child develops the same deadly reaction from measles there would still be no therapy. 'On the other hand, there is today something that parents can do to make sure that this sort of tragedy does not happen to a child of theirs. They can insist that their child is immunised against measles.'

He compared America, where measles has been virtually wiped out, with Britain, where 'because so many parents refuse, either out of obstinacy or ignorance or fear, to allow their children to be immunised' there are still a hundred thousand cases of measles every year, of whom more than 10,000 will suffer side effects. 'At least 10,000 will develop ear or chest infections. About twenty will die. LET THAT SINK IN.' He emphasised the point. 'Every year around twenty children will die in Britain from measles.'

Dahl acknowledged that parents have concerns about side-effects, but described the risks as almost non-existent. 'Listen to this. In a district of around 300,000 people, there will be only one child every 250 years who will develop serious side-effects from measles immunisation! That is about a million to one chance.'

The probability of a child choking to death on a chocolate bar is probably greater. As far as Dahl was concerned, it was criminal not to immunise your child. He appealed directly to schoolchildren who have not yet had a measles immunisation to 'beg their parents to arrange for them to have one as soon as possible'.

He concluded the letter by talking about Olivia, advising the reader to look for her name in the dedication of two of his books, *The BFG* and *James and the Giant Peach*; he urged readers to think about how happy Olivia would be 'if only she could know that her death had helped to save a good deal of illness and death among other children.'

Dahl had composed the letter carefully, running drafts by Dr Smith. He had to mention his personal involvement, he explained, otherwise it would just be another technical circular. He made a point of keeping the language simple *caught measles* rather than *contracted*, or *got infected by*, and he himself calculated the odds of a serious adverse reaction to the vaccine, based on the evidence that Smith had given him; 'Do correct me if I am wrong,' he asked, checking his figures with Smith.

In Sandwell, the letter was sent to GPs, health visitors, school nurses and other healthcare professionals involved with children, as well as to parents of babies and young children. It was also distributed nationally to all district health authorities for them to use as they saw fit.

Dahl the amateur epidemiologist encouraged the Sandwell health authorities to determine whether the letter had any impact. 'If I was you and I was going to give it a try I know what I would do.' They should ask the schools to ensure the letter went home to each parent, then in about a year's time measure the response, by once again getting the cooperation of the schoolteachers. *'Please take this letter home and give it to your parents'* is written across one draft of the letter in the Dahl archive.

It was worth all the effort. In Sandwell special immunisation clinics after school hours were set up to cater for the increased demand. At last Dahl had the results that he had sought from a campaign. The impact proved even longer lasting. Dahl's letter was published again two years later in a pamphlet from the Sandwell Health Authority, and is still quoted in British and American newspapers whenever there is a measles outbreak, more than thirty years after it was written, a legacy he 'would have been proud of'.

In 1988 the measles vaccine was combined with that of mumps and rubella to create the triple MMR vaccine, which was easier to administer. Dahl was invited onto a Thames TV programme called *The Treatment* to talk about his experiences. The introduction of the triple vaccine was led by health minister Edwina Currie and, intriguingly, during a measles outbreak in south Wales in 2013 she declared that compulsory vaccination for nursery and school-age children should be introduced. So perhaps Dahl's interventions at government level had more influence than he realised. Regular outbreaks in the United Kingdom and the United States serve as a reminder of the ongoing challenge in convincing parents whose fears over the very rare side effects of vaccination override concerns about the disease itself. In both countries, measles control was set back decades by the subsequently discredited work of Dr Andrew Wakefield, published in the *Lancet* in 1998, which attempted to link the MMR vaccine to autism. There is no such link, and Wakefield was later struck off by the General Medical Council for his fraudulent work.

'Dad would have been appalled at the irresponsibility of Wakefield,' said Ophelia, when I asked what Dahl would have made of it all. Of course the measles vaccine, just like all vaccines, does have extremely rare side effects, but none of those that Wakefield asserted were linked. One of the ironies is that the more successful a vaccination programme, and the less of the disease there is, then the more the very rare side effects of the vaccine become an issue, especially to those who have never seen the full horrors of the disease. Even though there may be thousands of children dying from measles elsewhere on the planet, parents sitting comfortably in the West can ignore this, and obsess about very rare vaccine side effects instead of appreciating the value of protecting their children from deafness, blindness and even death from measles.

A Wonderfully Gigantic Concept

Dahl's vaccine advocacy was not limited to measles. In 1988 he was asked to help raise funds for a 'Europe for Children' campaign that aimed to support the worldwide elimination of polio. He was invited to Brussels to talk to a small group of big businessmen 'from leading industrial companies' like Phillips, KLM and others. A rather curious film, which accompanied the campaign, shows Dahl, depicted as the quintessential Englishman, driven from Gipsy House to Brussels in a Rolls Royce. En route he talks about the language barriers that keep the world apart, and the desire of this campaign to overcome those barriers for health reasons. He then appears on the stage at the Hyatt Regency Hotel, Brussels, dressed in red cardigan, thick stripy tie and green trousers, with his stick at his side and glasses perched on his forehead.

'I have been invited to come here this afternoon, not as a politician or an organiser or anything like that,' he begins. 'I am simply here to speak for the children of the world.' He described himself as amazingly fortunate to have been able to reach so many millions of children in so many countries and being 'able to speak to them with books. Now I want to speak for them as best I can'. He was a 'very unofficial children's ambassador'. The focus of the campaign was underdeveloped countries, like Nigeria, India, Indonesia and China. Although his books were published in forty-seven countries, this did not include any of these four countries until recently. Appealing to these industrialists to be generous, he explained how he received no royalties for his publications in countries like China, despite a recent first print run of two million copies for *Charlie and the Chocolate Factory* – 'far and away a world record', he could not resist mentioning as an aside. 'Nobody should be trying to make money from the underdeveloped countries for a long time yet,' he said.

The idea of eliminating polio entirely throughout the world, he explained, was a 'wonderfully gigantic concept', one hundred per cent possible and one that should appeal to the industrialists who were used to thinking in global terms on a grand international scale. He compared polio with measles, mentioning his family's own tragic experience, and explaining how both are preventable. He criticised the British government for failing to act, and lauded the American approach, suggesting something similar might work for polio. The delegates then watched a short film, which explained how the money from donors would be used to establish a European lottery, which would then raise the funds needed by the World Health Organisation to eradicate polio.

The Europe for Children project never really progressed beyond this stage; it was perhaps an idea too far ahead of its time. It was not until 2004 that the EuroMillions fundraising lottery was established along similar lines.

Poliovirus is a target for eradication because it only circulates among humans, and there is no animal host. So, if the world's population is vaccinated, there is nowhere for the virus to go, and it will die out. This is how smallpox eradication was achieved in 1977. Despite Dahl's modest involvement with the global polio eradication campaign, and subsequent major World Health Organisation initiatives, and more recently considerable investment from the Bill and Melinda Gates Foundation, polio has not yet been eradicated, and is still endemic in Afghanistan and Pakistan. The ninety-nine per cent reduction from more than 350,000 cases in 1988 to 74 reported cases in 2015 is remarkable, but a sustained final effort will be needed to finally rid the world of this disease.

A Little Henry Sugar Now and Again

Dahl's involvement with charity grew steadily after Olivia's death. He and Pat had set up a trust fund at her birth, as they had with the other children. After she died they wanted to do something useful with the money. Prompted by one of their neighbours they decided to support a new charity, International Help for Children, set up by Father Mario Borrelli in southern Italy. After the Second World War many abandoned and illegitimate children ended up on the streets. Borrelli, who was quite a character, dressed as a 'street urchin' and mingled incognito with them to gain their trust. Then he revealed his identity and convinced them to leave the streets and move into a dormitory, which grew to have hundreds of youngsters, and become known as the Casa dello Scugnizzo: the House of the Urchins. It was not just somewhere to sleep – it also supported education and training.

Around the time Olivia died Borrelli's autobiography was released, and his work featured on British television. International Help for Children brought these youngsters for short visits to the UK to support their education. Dahl became a very active chairman in the Great Missenden branch, which grew to more than three hundred members.

'All she'd needed right from the beginning was a good hard job of work to do, and plenty of problems to solve – other people's problems instead of her own,' Dahl wrote in 'The Last Act' of a recently bereaved woman who had been grieving heavily for many months.

Supporting the charity became a big part of his and Pat's life. The film, *Hud*, for which Pat won an Oscar, had its British premiere in nearby Aylesbury, a fundraising event which generated almost £1,000, nearly £15,000 today. The money supported the visits of thirty Italian children to English families for up to three months. Ophelia remembers a childless couple in the village ending up adopting an Italian girl. 'I think Dad would have loved the fact that you and Rachel adopted your two girls,' she told me. 'He loved all acts of kindness.' We adopted Leah and Daisy when we lived out in Vietnam, then had two of our own, Rosie and Eva, when we returned to England.

Ever since he was a young man Dahl had worked for Charles Marsh's charity, the Public Welfare Foundation, he had always been interested in supporting charities. In addition to Dahl's well-known charitable work with the Italian Orphans, there were other causes he helped discreetly over the years with donations, time and effort. These were private, not much talked about. In the 1970s at the behest of Theo's neurosurgeon, Kenneth Till, he became involved in raising funds to get one of the recently invented EMI computer tomography brain scanners for Great Ormond Street Hospital.

'I myself have seen the machine in operation and it is magically impressive,' he wrote to potential funders. 'It is a British invention. Medical men are saying it is the biggest breakthrough since Roentgen discovered X-rays, and, having seen the machine in action myself, I'm inclined to agree ... It will locate any tumour or cyst in the brain, diagnose hydrocephalus, demonstrate the size of the ventricles, locate a cerebral haemorrhage, locate an infarct stroke, reveal atrophy of the brain, whether a tumour is responding to treatment ...'

The scanner cost £140,000, just over a million pounds today, and there were just five in British hospitals at the time. Meanwhile Pat was donating money towards a similar machine for the hospital in her home town of Knoxville, Tennessee.

A flick through the archive shows the wide range of other charities they helped. In 1981 Dahl became patron of the International Centre for Child Studies at the University of Bristol, working with Professor of Paediatrics, Neville Butler. He also helped the neurosurgeon at the Radcliffe Infirmary in Oxford, Michael Briggs, raising funds for a new seminar room for the trainees. There is money for a scanner appeal at Wycombe Hospital, and a request to support Repton School's one million pound appeal. Ten thousand pounds is donated to the Handicapped Children's Trust, and there is support for Partners in Health, the organisation set up by Dr Paul Farmer, and Ophelia: 'He would pack me off to Haiti with thousands of pounds in cash for new schools or clinics.' There is a donation to The Sick Children's Hospital in Edinburgh, and Birthright, and Helen House Children's Hospice in Oxford. It seems that every letter is met with some kind of response. But these were not just thoughtless donations from a wealthy man with plenty to spare. Dahl would also spend time thinking about the fundraising.

'Now I have a problem and to tell you about it clearly, I must be completely frank,' he wrote to Neville Butler at Bristol. The planned International Centre for Child Studies, Dahl felt, was too diversified and lacked focus. It was 'all too nebulous', rather than concentrating on one or two specific things. 'I have studied the prospectus. I have even tried writing a draft letter. But in the end I could not find anything that I could really bite on.' Dahl suggested something more specific such as a scanner for every major hospital in the country. Despite Dahl's reservations, Butler's International Centre for Child Studies did get established the following year. He studied children over the next four decades, examining inequality, social exclusion, problems of literacy, numeracy and health. I am sure this would have appealed to Dahl, had he been able to grasp it. 'This one has got me beat,' he wrote, but decades later the centre has proved its worth, impacting on national and international policy.

Dahl's last significant involvement in medical charities was with dyslexia. In 1990, the International Literacy Year, he was delighted to be helping with the British Dyslexia Association's Awareness Campaign. In an open letter Dahl described the horrors of not being able to read or write properly.

'As an author, the written word is my livelihood and I know what an endless source of pleasure and interest it can be.' He pitied anyone denied one of life's great joys, unable to take part in the fun and education afforded by words and books. 'Let's do all we can to make the precious window of words and books available.'

At the time, Dahl was writing what would be one of his last books, the *Vicar of Nibbleswicke*. This is about a reverend who suffered severe dyslexia as a child, 'but guided by the Dyslexia Institute in London, and helped by some excellent teachers' he could now read and write more or less normally. However, with the stress of his first appointment as a vicar, something had gone '*click* in his brain and stirred up in some way vestiges of the old dyslexia'. But it is a peculiar form of dyslexia, which only Dahl could have come up with; thankfully there is a cure. The rights from the book were donated by Dahl and his long-time illustrator, Quentin Blake, to the institute.

Liccy continued the charitable work after Dahl's death, setting up the Roald Dahl Foundation. The original focus was on children's neurological and haematological conditions, as well as children's literacy. In 1991 the charity appointed the UK's first paediatric epilepsy nurse specialist at Alder Hey Children's Hospital in Liverpool, where she has worked with my wife, Rachel, for many years. She was the first of more than fifty Roald Dahl nurses around the country. The charity's interest in haematology came from an illness that Dahl suffered later in life. At the Royal Liverpool University Hospital, where I am a visiting consultant, I still get a thrill when I walk past the Roald Dahl Haemostasis and Thrombosis Centre. In 2010 the charity became Roald Dahl's Marvellous Children's Charity, which has more recently moved away from supporting particular diseases to concentrate on those with the biggest need, whatever their diagnosis, that aren't being fully supported by anybody else. This change recognises the fact that children with some serious life-threatening illness, for example cancer, have access to lots of support, but those with rarer diseases, or even undiagnosed conditions, may have none.

'Liccy has done a wonderful job,' said Donald Sturrock, Dahl biographer, family friend and now a trustee of the charity. 'I think some people were a bit doubtful at first, because she had no experience of this kind of thing. But she's proved highly effective. She's passionate, a great team-builder and brilliant at getting things done.'

Liccy also led the way in creating the Roald Dahl Museum and Story Centre. An old coaching inn and yard came up for sale on Great Missenden High Street in 1996 and she bought them 'on instinct'. Her family and friends were worried about how she would ever raise the funds to restore them and fit them out, but with her 'gentle and charming persistence' she enlisted the help of all sorts of people, even convincing Tony Blair to host a fundraising dinner at nearby Chequers – the prime minister's official country residence. Film star Johnny Depp was among the guests.

A Puppet-like Statue

Back at St John the Baptist Church in Little Missenden I think again about Dahl's attempts to strengthen vaccination campaigns for measles. I cannot help reflecting ruefully that this is one area where the world of marvellous medicine still has not quite met the ideals he'd had. Dahl certainly had an impact locally on measles vaccination in the Midlands, and the incidence of measles in the UK has dropped dramatically since the mid-1980s, but we still have outbreaks in the UK and America, countries in which the disease should long since have become a distant memory. Through his famous essay Dahl continues to provide advocacy, twenty-five years after his death, to fight this appalling situation.

There are now aspirations for global measles eradication, but the difficulties with finally ridding the world of polio have shown just how challenging this will be.

I peer at the frescoes Dahl loved so much on the church walls and go to take a closer look at the little wooden statue with its sad, plaintive face and bright red robe. '*In Loving Memory, Olivia Twenty Dahl*' reads the inscription at its base.

'Beautiful, isn't she?' One of the churchwomen who earlier was dusting the pews is at my side, gazing up wistfully at the statue. 'St Catherine. The Dahl family gave it to the church after the young girl died. The original statue was Spanish medieval; Dahl restored it himself.'

'The original?'

'Stolen, many years ago. This one's a reproduction.' My sadness deepens. 'Liccy had it made,' the woman continued. 'Mind you, it's a very good one, even down to the woodworm.'

'Was this before or after Dahl died?'

'Afterwards, thank heavens. It would have destroyed him all over again.'

I leave her to the dusting, and wander a hundred feet up the lane to the graveyard. Olivia's double plot is not hard to find.

'What I want to know, what I *really* want to know is why did God allow her to die if he could have saved her?' the seven-year-old Ophelia had challenged Dahl when they'd visited the grave one Christmas many years ago.

'Have you ever thought,' he answered slowly, 'that there might not be a God at all? There's sure to be something,' he continued, 'but I don't think the church people have got it quite right. I think they are too exact about it all ... But they honestly don't really know anything about Him for sure. So the only thing to do, I think, is to live a good life and be kind and generous, and try to make other people happy, and after that you just hope for the best.'

Dahl later recorded the details of this conversation in a draft *Christmas Message to Children*, which was later published as *What I told Ophelia and Lucy about God*.

'During our childhood Olivia was like some mystery and sainted presence in the family,' Ophelia told me years later. 'Always there, but never spoken about.'

At Olivia's grave, I find the rocks are still in place, though the plants are overgrown, dominated by three or four ferns, which have become bushes. Tucked under one of them lies a small gravestone: *Olivia Twenty Dahl, 20th April 1955 – 17th November 1962.*

The porcelain animals from her collection have long disappeared, but I have four little figures, one for Olivia from each of my girls, and I place them carefully among the rocks.

> *'It doesn't matter who you are or what you look like, so long as somebody loves you.'*
>
> – The Witches

PART FOUR

GOBBLEFUNKING

Chapter 11

A Bubble Bursts

For thirty-nine years, Patricia Neal's brain had successfully coped with about 750 millilitres of blood pumped up through her cerebral arteries every minute of every day. But on 17 February 1965 things went disastrously wrong. Neal had won the Oscar, the Academy Award for Best Actress in *Hud*, the year before, and was back in Hollywood working on her next movie project, *Seven Women*. She was three months' pregnant with her fifth child, Lucy, and was at home giving seven-year-old Tessa a bath when suddenly a pain shot through her head. Initially she wondered if she had just overdone it at work. It had been a long day. Filming had only just started, and she had spent most of the day on the back of a donkey. Dahl came upstairs with a Martini for Pat to find that she was staggering around the bedroom, clutching her head.

'I've got the most awful pain,' she told him. 'I think there's something wrong.' She was swaying and wincing in agony, pressing the palm of her hand against her left temple. 'I've been seeing things too.'

'What sort of things?'

'I don't know. I can't remember.' She lay on the bed. 'The pain is terrible.'

'Is it only in one place?'

'Yes. Right here.'

In his bed at the John Radcliffe Hospital, Dahl sat up, showing me exactly where she had pointed – the left temporal bone. I'd had a busy day, and was glad to settle into the chair by his bed and listen; the soft folds of Dahl's large dressing gown, draped across the chair, had a faint sweet smell of pipe tobacco, and I wondered what Dahl had been up to in the day.

'The pain was here.' He gestured again, his face alert. 'It happened in an instant. Suddenly Pat's head jerked back and she lost consciousness. I just knew she was in trouble. She looked like she was dying right in front of me.' Although he had been trembling with fear, Dahl didn't panic. Instead, his calm, calculating, problem-solving mind took over, the one that had seen him coolly extricate himself from a crashed plane as it exploded around him, the one that had methodically created a new device to solve the problem of hydrocephalus, the one that had systematically reviewed publications looking for a link between severe measles and smallpox vaccination.

Dahl hurried from Pat's side to the study where pinned to the wall was the phone number of a local neurosurgeon, Dr Charles Carton. Pat had met Carton in Hollywood when she was working on *Breakfast at Tiffany's*, and Dahl had recently been showing him the new Wade-Dahl-Till valve, with a view to bringing it to America. Dahl rushed back to the bedroom with the phone number, getting through to Carton on the third attempt. At first Dr Carton thought it must be Theo that Dahl was calling about. Dahl described Pat's symptoms.

'Is her neck rigid?' asked Carton, who was already formulating a diagnosis over the phone. 'I'll send an ambulance and meet you at the hospital.'

Whilst he was waiting for help to arrive, Dahl wrapped a teaspoon in a handkerchief and put it in Pat's mouth; the conventional wisdom at the time was that this would stop someone biting their tongue during a fit, though we now know it can do more harm than good. Within minutes Dahl could hear the wail of the ambulance. Theo wanted to know what the noise was.

'It's an ambulance coming for Mummy,' said Tessa, shivering in her towel. As a three-year-old, Tessa had seen the ambulance that had rushed her baby brother, Theo, to hospital with a head injury. When she was five her sister Olivia was taken away by ambulance never to return. Now, aged seven, the arrival of this ambulance heralded another calamity in her troubled childhood.

As the ambulance men were carrying her out, Pat regained consciousness, but realised she couldn't remember the names of her children. It was a foretaste of what was to come. She was taken to the medical centre at UCLA, the University of California Los Angeles, just ten minutes away. The time from the onset of the headache to the hospital admission was barely half an hour. Dahl described the events in a letter to his mother:

> Dr Carton examined her. He said he found no real evidence of cerebral haemorrhage. Perhaps she has had a migraine. The fact was we had got her there so quickly that the real signs (stiff neck etc.) had not had time to develop.

'What's wrong with me?' Pat asked Dahl.

'Nothing much,' he replied.

She sat up. 'My God,' she said, 'I've got an early call tomorrow morning. I've got to be at the studio at seven thirty.' As she spoke, her hand went suddenly up to her left temple once again, and she called out with pain. Dahl imitated the doctor, taking Pat's head in his hands and moving it sideways. He found that her neck was now stiff.

Whilst I was there, she had another haemorrhage and passed out. I called in Dr Carton. He did a Spinal Tap on the spot. It showed the spinal fluid scarlet red with blood.

Textbook History

'The history was absolutely classical for a subarachnoid, you know.'

Dahl nodded. 'Subarachnoid, bleeding below the arachnoid membrane that covers the brain.'

'That's right,' I continued, 'a sudden severe headache with vomiting, neck stiffness, and a brief loss of consciousness is typical.'

Pat's initial symptoms were probably a sentinel headache, a warning from a tiny leak of blood. Then she had the big one. People usually say it is the worst headache they ever had, like being struck on the back of the head with a bat. This is not just a lyrical description. Patients will literally look round behind to see what has hit them. Dahl loved this aspect of medicine, taking the history, the story of the illness; the fact that an eloquent description could nail the diagnosis even before the patient has been examined. In medical school we were taught that eighty per cent of diagnoses are based on information contained in the history alone, with the examination and investigations each adding a further ten per cent. That is why the best doctors are great listeners. Like detectives sifting for clues, they sense which bits of the story are irrelevant dead ends, and which should be pursued, teasing out a bit more in the patient's own words, without leading the witness on.

Dahl understood the anatomy very well: a subarachnoid haemorrhage is a bleed beneath the pia arachnoid, the innermost of the three layers covering the brain, as so beautifully described by Dahl in *William and Mary*. Bleeds can also occur within the brain itself, intracerebral haemorrhage. Altogether, bleeds account for about a fifth of all strokes; the remainder are due to a sudden blockage of an artery. The Greek physician Hippocrates, the 'father of medicine', is credited with the first descriptions of stroke more than two thousand years ago. He used the term *apoplexy*, meaning 'struck down with violence', but did not know the cause, and was probably describing strokes and any number of other attacks.

In the mid 1600s the Swiss physician and pathologist Johann Jacob Wepfer showed that some patients who died following apoplexy had bleeding in the brain, whilst in others there was obstruction of the blood vessels. The term *cerebrovascular accident*, CVA, is now widely used in medical parlance, recognising the sudden disruption to the brain's blood supply, be that due to bleed or blockage. Without oxygenated blood, brain cells can only survive a few minutes. In recent years some neurology textbooks have discouraged the use of the term 'cerebrovascular accident', arguing that the word *accident* ignores the modifiable risk factors such as smoking and diet, i.e. a stroke is not just an accident, people can do something to reduce their chances. They suggest 'cerebrovascular *insult*' is better. Personally, I doubt people who smoke, eat poorly and do no regular exercise spend much time fretting over such medical pedantry. And for the medical profession, there are far more effective public health interventions than fussing over the semantics; banning smoking in public places, for example, has had an enormous impact.

Having determined that Patricia Neal's collapse was due to a subarachnoid, the next step for Dr Carton and his radiology colleagues at the UCLA medical centre was to determine the source of the bleed. Back in 1965 there was no magnetic resonance or computer tomography scanning, but vessels could be examined by injecting a radiopaque dye into the bloodstream, and then taking an X-ray a few seconds later. Because Pat was pregnant, lead aprons were used to protect the baby. As they began the investigation, Carton could see, immediately, two areas where the blood had escaped from an artery. During the procedure a third much larger bleed occurred. After three hours they had taken enough images from every angle to pinpoint the exact cause of the leak.

Dahl described to me how Dr Carton had invited him into the viewing room. 'It was eerie. A dark room with large X-rays of Pat's skull hanging – still wet – on the viewing screens: grey shades of brain with chalky white streaks, a tree of arteries reaching up into the skull; and there in the centre of it all, a small dot, the size of a farthing, over the left temporal lobe.'

This was the cause of all the trouble. Pat had an aneurysm.

Materia Medica

An aneurysm is a ballooning out of an artery, caused by a weakness in its wall. Over the years the aneurysm stretches, becoming thinner and thinner, until eventually it leaks blood. The arteries undergo a hell of a pounding, especially those in the head. Although the brain accounts for only two and a half per cent of the body's weight, it receives fifteen per cent of the total blood volume pumped out by the heart. Every minute about three quarters of a litre of blood is forced up the two internal carotid and two vertebral arteries at great pressure, bouncing from about 80 to 120 millimetres of mercury. If you want to know what that feels like, it is the tightness of the cuff when a doctor measures your blood pressure. Inside the head, at the base of the brain, these four great arteries are joined together by smaller connecting ones to form a rather complicated, beautiful and elaborate ring of vessels, *the Circle of Willis*. The great English physician, anatomist and professor of natural philosophy Thomas Willis was not the first to identify this structure that bears his name. However, he gave one of the best early descriptions with illustrations, and recognised its physiological importance. Willis was a busy man. He was a founding member of the Royal Society, Britain's preeminent scientific organisation that exists to this day, and he coined the term *neurology* in his 1664 book *Cerebri anatome*. His death on St Martin's day, 11 November, has been commemorated since 1734 with the firing of Fenny Poppers, a sort of medieval party popper that looks a bit like a large beer tankard. In 1920, the exclusive 'Circle of Willis' medical dining club was established in Oxford; it was still running some seventy years later when I was a houseman.

Dahl, with his insatiable appetite for new knowledge, especially *materia medica*, absorbed these facts quietly. I suspect if he'd had his Ideas Book to hand he would have jotted a couple of things down.

'And are you a member of this famous dining club?' he enquired.

'No, but a friend of mine, another house officer, tried to join.'

'And ... ?'

'He was given short shrift. Apparently it is very exclusive, and only for the most distinguished neuroscientists.'

'Ah.' Dahl had faced this kind of snobbish exclusivity all his life, never quite being accepted as part of *the establishment*. He would have been amused to know that my friend, rejected by the Oxford neuroscientists, subsequently became Professor of Neurology at the University of Cambridge.

Dahl knew quite a lot about aneurysms, but wanted to understand why the Circle of Willis is so vulnerable.

'It is like a rather elaborate garden irrigation system,' I explained.

In most of the body, blood flows from arteries to capillaries to veins, dropping pressure along the way. However, in the brain the vessels join up to form this ring with one high-pressure artery connecting directly to another. This circle then gives rise to all the major arteries supplying different parts of the brain – the anterior, middle and posterior cerebral arteries, the cerebellar arteries, and smaller vessels that sink into the brainstem. But, unlike inert plastic hoses, the arteries are dynamic responsive vessels. They have a sensitive inner layer of endothelial cells, wrapped in muscle and an elastic lamina, which is contained within a tough outer layer of connective tissue. This elasticity allows arteries to cope with the variations in blood pressure; the smooth muscle contracts and relaxes to control the tension and flow of blood. In people with high blood pressure the tension is generally too high, but captopril, the drug based on snake venom, eases the muscles to reduce the pressure. However, there are weak points in the system. Just as garden pipework is most likely to leak at the joints, so the Circle of Willis is vulnerable where the arteries connect. In some people the elastic lamina is too thin here; the vessel begins to stretch and extend, like an inner tube billowing from the edge of a badly fitted bicycle tyre. Eventually it stretches so thin that it can contain the blood no longer.

Dahl interrupted me. 'That's all very well, but are there any ideas about why this happens in some people and not others?'

I stopped a moment to think. On the floor I noticed Dahl's enormous shabby slippers. I could probably fit my feet into them without even taking my shoes off. I wondered how long Dahl would be in hospital this time, and whether we would get to the bottom of his anaemia. I thought I would probably miss him, once we got him home; Liccy too, whom I was also getting to know.

'Tom ... ?' he interrupted my reverie. 'Are you okay?'

'Yes ... Fine ... What were we saying?'

'Why don't you go to bed?' he smiled kindly. 'You look exhausted.'

'No I'm okay, honestly. I have to wait to do the evening drug round, anyway.' I checked my watch; it was only quarter to ten. 'You were asking about aneurysms ... ?' I helped myself to one of his wine gums. 'There are a few rare genetic conditions where people have connective tissue that is too flexible, which allows the aneurysm to form' I explained. 'Ehlers-Danlos is one. Some patients with this disease have very extendable joints, and hyper-elastic stretchy skin. The collagen in their blood vessels is also too stretchy, hence the aneurysms. In other cases we don't know what the gene defect is, but the risk does seem to run in families.'

'Yes, Pat's sister had an aneurysm too, years later. But hers was less severe.'

'It's a common dilemma in the neurology clinic. A family member has had an aneurysm; do you screen the others in the family, or not?'

'Of course you do,' insisted Dahl in his forthright manner.

'Are you sure?' I pushed him. 'Aneurysms are very common, you know, between one and five per cent of people have them, and the vast majority don't rupture.'

'Hmmm.'

I could see him reconsidering. 'And what would you do if you found one?' I continued. 'The operation to clip them has risks, often greater than the chance of the aneurysm bleeding.'

'Ah, it's like playing blackjack –' his forehead creased – 'weighing up the odds, and deciding whether to *hit*.'

'Exactly. So if you were not going to do anything about it, would you really want to know?'

'Hmm.' His eyes were darting as his mind wandered. 'Would you want to spend your whole life, knowing you had one of these balloons in your head, which might pop at any moment, but until it did, there was nothing you could do ...' It was the sort of delicious conundrum that had helped make his name, decades ago.

Thankfully in the last twenty-five years the odds of this game of blackjack have improved somewhat. We now have better ways of screening for aneurysms, with magnetic resonance and computer tomography imaging. We know that small aneurysms, less than a centimetre, are unlikely to rupture, and can be watched with annual scanning to see if they grow. The risk of a bleed for larger aneurysms is about one per cent per year.

The procedures to treat them have also become safer. So, nowadays, if two or more family members have been affected, we will offer screening to any first-degree relatives. But when I discuss it with people in clinic I make absolutely sure that they really want to know if they have an aneurysm, and have thought what they would do if we discovered one. If the answer is they wouldn't risk the operation, then there's usually no point looking for trouble.

A Brave Operation

Patricia Neal was lucky to have got to hospital as quickly as she did. It was only through Dahl's quick thinking and good connections that she got such prompt attention. Just a few hours after admission the neurosurgical team had pinpointed the problem. Her aneurysm was at the junction of the internal carotid and posterior communicating arteries, one of the most common sites for this aberration.

> 'Her condition is very critical,' Dr Carton told Dahl.
> 'Are you going to operate,' he asked.
> 'I doubt she would survive an operation.'
> 'What will happen if you don't?'

'If I don't, then she will succumb for certain.'
'In that case you must operate.'
'Yes. All right. But please don't be too hopeful.'

'No doctor likes to lose a patient on the table,' Dahl reflected years later, 'and a Hollywood doctor certainly doesn't want to lose a Hollywood film star on the table. So he was very brave to perform the operation.'

Dr Carton talked Dahl through the procedure afterwards. Pat's head had been shaved, the skin cut across the temple and peeled back, and two burr holes drilled through the skull. I described for Dahl the first time I made such a burr hole. My patient was an elderly man who had fallen and banged his head. His was a chronic subdural haematoma – a less severe bleed than Pat's. We were operating under local anaesthetic, and he chatted merrily as I drilled through his skull. The process differed very little from a DIY task with the Black and Decker I had been using at home the evening before. For my patient a single hole was all that was needed: we sucked out the clot of blood, and he was on his feet again a few days later. Pat had a more serious problem and so a square of bone was cut out, and folded back across the scalp to create greater access. The clots were removed from below the arachnoid mater; the largest was several centimetres across, and one was extracted from within the temporal lobe itself. This third bleed would prove to be the most damaging. I have seen patients with a minor subarachnoid who are fine afterwards. But Pat's left temporal lobe had been damaged, along with part of the frontal lobe. The third cranial nerve, which controls eye movements, and lies very close to the posterior communicating artery, was also affected. The brain tissue was gently lifted by Carton to expose the aneurysm lying below; as indicated by the X-rays, it was ballooning off the arterial junction.

The aberrant structure was clipped and a plastic adhesive spray used to hold everything in place. Although this would stop further bleeding, the damage had already been done.

Neurosurgery has advanced enormously in the last fifty years. We still clip some cerebral aneurysms, more or less like the surgeons who treated Patricia Neal. However, most are now treated endoscopically by neuroradiologists without the need for a craniotomy. A long silicon tube, a catheter, is inserted into the femoral artery in the groin. Under X-ray guidance it is fed all the way through the abdomen, chest and neck into the head. Contrast dye is injected to help localise exactly where the aneurysm lies. Thin platinum wires are then teased up the catheter, and directed into the aneurysm from the inside. As they become free from the silicon constraint, they coil up inside the ballooned section of artery where they promote blood clotting to close the aneurysm off.

More recently glue-like substances have also been squirted into aneurysms, with the same result. These are high-risk procedures demanding skilful expertise; if you get it wrong, the coil can go shooting down the wrong vessel and end up causing a much bigger stroke.

Pat's operation lasted through the night. Although the procedure had gone well, Carton told Dahl the chances of her surviving were slim. The newspapers reported there was little hope, and one magazine mistakenly announced *Film Actress Patricia Neal Dies at 39.*

'Reports of my death are greatly exaggerated,' Pat later quipped, Twain-like.

But as she lay in a coma after the operation, Dahl felt Pat just *had* to survive. If only he could work out what was needed, surely he could make things better as he had done with Theo a few years earlier. With Olivia it was different; it had all been too quick, no time to intervene. But here was Pat, lying in a coma ... if only he could get through to her.

'Pat, this is Roald. Roald, Pat. Tessa says hello. Theo says hello. Don Mini says hello.' *Don Mini* was the family nickname for young Ophelia. Sometimes Dahl shouted in Pat's ear, at other times he just whispered. With his research for *William and Mary*, and all his time working with Till on the valve, Dahl knew quite a bit about the brain, but he did not know what was the right thing to do here. He carefully observed the doctors assessing her. He copied them, peeling back her eyelids to check for a response. To visiting friends it looked obsessive, frightening even. He was like a man possessed.

'The key thing,' Dahl told me, 'was not to get depressed and feel sorry for yourself. You had to rise to the challenge. Do something. Anything was better than nothing.' He wouldn't leave her in peace. He would harass her until she improved. This was war, he felt, and you had to fight it with all your resources.

Danced All Night

Pat lay unconscious for nearly three weeks on intensive care. For visitors it was a worrying sight. There was a nasogastric tube through her nose into her stomach for feeding, a catheter to drain her bladder, and a tracheostomy in her throat for easier breathing and suction of chest secretions. At least she was breathing spontaneously and did not need ventilating. She lay on a cooling mattress; keeping the body temperature down was thought to help reduce the extent of brain damage. More recent studies have shown that it helps for some forms of brain insult, for example after a cardiac arrest, and maybe in traumatic brain injury, but does not appear to make a difference after aneurysm surgery.

Dahl was enormously impressed with the nursing staff who cared for Pat. 'It was wonderful to watch them work. They were swift, adroit and calm. These girls didn't make any mistakes, and except when they were writing their reports they never sat down.'

He was sure that without their extraordinary skill and loving care Pat would not have survived the early days. Dr Carton continued to warn Dahl that Pat's chances of survival were poor. The longer she remained unconscious the worse was the outlook. But Dahl wouldn't believe it. He carried on looking for evidence of recovery. A sign, any sign. As he stared at her face he tried to visualise what was happening just centimetres below: the squashed brain tissue, and the angry distorted blood vessel clipped to prevent more destruction. But what would it take now for this brain to recover? At times Dahl would harangue her; at others he was quiet, pensive, thoughtful, gazing into her face, carefully stroking her hand.

Gradually things began to improve. 'I witnessed the slow, mysterious recovery of a brain that had been severely insulted,' Dahl recalled thoughtfully, 'and the steady return to consciousness of the owner of that brain.' During the second week, though still unconscious, Pat's coma was becoming lighter, and she was moving about on the bed. Her left hand had to be tied down to prevent her from pulling the tubes out. This was a good sign. Worryingly, there was no need to restrain her right side. And then suddenly and dramatically came the first evidence of a reaction. Dahl squeezed Pat's left hand and it began responding. 'The squeezes were good and strong, and there was little doubt that in her semi consciousness she was trying to communicate.'

'She's going to live!' he exclaimed to Carton, rushing out to him in the hospital car park. 'I'm absolutely sure of it.'

'Yes, she is,' Carton replied. 'But I'm not sure whether or not I've done her a favour.'

That gave Dahl pause for thought.

One day in the third week, Pat's right eye popped open, staring at Dahl for five seconds, before dropping shut again. Dahl was elated. Soon the right eye was opening quite often. A couple of days later both eyes opened together. Then all at once she smiled!

'It was one of the first things she did after becoming conscious of her surroundings. She was smiling long before she could utter a word of any kind.' It soon became clear she could understand everything going on around her, but still there was no speech. Pat later recalled trying to get words out: 'toilet', 'pee', 'potty' when she wanted the loo. Although she knew what she was trying to say, nothing would come.

One afternoon as Dahl stood smoking by the window he realised that Pat was reaching out to him. He was calling Pat's nurse to come and witness this great advance when he realised Pat was not reaching for his free hand, but was after his cigarette – she wanted a drag. This caused him great hilarity and excitement. If the first thing she wanted on recovery was a cigarette, then perhaps the old Pat was in there after all. It is hard to imagine now, but back in the 1960s smoking was not considered the unpleasant, unhealthy and dangerous habit that it is today.

'At the end of the third week, words were beginning to come,' Dahl remembered. 'Not many of them meant very much, and few of them were in the dictionary, but they were words nonetheless. Then she began to sing.'

Her favourite nurse, Jean Alexander, was washing Pat's feet and singing 'I Could Have Danced All Night' when suddenly Pat joined in, just for one word. However it was a start. From there Jean would sing more and more, and Pat would chime in whenever she could. Pat couldn't remember the names of people visiting her, or even those of her children or husband, but she knew the lyrics of songs she had learned twenty years before.

Chapter 12

The Mysterious Joy of Language

'It was an extraordinary sight.' Dahl was recalling Pat's slow recovery from the stroke. 'Extraordinary to walk into the intensive care, with all its intravenous drips and tubes and oxygen tents, to see Pat propped up in her bed with the nurse beside her singing songs, and yet she could barely utter a word.'

'It's an example of localisation of function.' I drew a sketch on a scrap of paper. 'The speech centres are here on the left side of the brain ...'

'That's Broca's area.'

'Yes, exactly, and music and singing are on the right.'

Early on as a medical student you learn about Wernicke's area in the left temporal lobe, and the fibres that pass forward, connecting it to Broca's area in the frontal lobe. Damage to either site can cause aphasia, difficulty with speech and language. If Wernicke's area is damaged, then patients have a receptive aphasia – they can't understand what is being said. In contrast, when Broca's is affected people can understand clearly – they know exactly what they want to say – but they have expressive aphasia, and just cannot get the words out.

'That's what Pat had, of course,' Dahl said, 'expressive aphasia. But she also struggled to understand what was being said, especially if many people were talking at once.'

'She probably had elements of both. But clearly the right side of her brain was fine. This is where music and melody are based, and also foreign language.'

Years later I saw a patient, a young man, whose case would have fascinated Dahl.

Near the North Pole

Darren is in his twenties and doesn't remember much about his illness. He remembers being a bit unwell, and the doctor diagnosing flu. He remembers being at his girlfriend's house, and the food smelling disgusting and making him sick. He goes to bed feeling tired and with a headache. When he wakes, his speech isn't making sense. He thinks he is talking normally, but he isn't.

He cannot understand why everyone is looking at him strangely. He doesn't remember much after that.

His dad, Raymond, realises that this is more than flu because Darren is mumbling incomprehensibly. They get him to hospital. A young doctor rushes into the accident and emergency department, and Raymond fears the worst.

'It's either meningitis, a growth on the brain, or encephalitis,' says the doctor.

It turns out to be encephalitis caused by herpes simplex virus. He is treated with aciclovir, but the brain scans show extensive damage to the left temporal lobe. For a couple of weeks Raymond fears his child will not survive, but when he does nobody can tell him what sort of person his son will be when he recovers.

Bizarrely, he cannot speak any English at first, only French. He had studied French at university and spoke it fluently. But his parents don't speak French, so cannot converse with him.

'We had to have a translator to talk to our own son.'

Things improve and he is allowed home for a weekend. But he does not know where he is, and at the end of the weekend when it is time to go back to hospital Darren very politely thanks his mum and dad for having him to stay.

'It was heart breaking at the time,' Raymond recalled later.

Each day in hospital Darren is asked to name things in English. He can describe how a fountain pen works in minute detail, and what it was for, but he can't actually tell you what it is called. The doctor asks him who the prime minister is. Hour after hour his dad drums it into him: 'Tony Blair, Tony Blair.'

But he still can't remember. He has to relearn everything.

'A woman, blonde, pearl necklace, always wears blue and carries a handbag,' Darren answers one day. Everybody laughs. He has given a perfect description of a prime minister, but the wrong one. She'd been succeeded in office ten years earlier.

Darren remembers being shown all the pictures. But he cannot name the objects. Some he still struggles with all these years later.

'For example, the thing you get near the North Pole – it's made of ice; like a circle; it has a door on it; you can go inside; all the blocks of ice are put together; it has to be cold there, otherwise the ice melts. I can tell you all about it, but can never remember what it is called.'

He watches French DVDs with English subtitles, to help him relearn the English words; then he watches the film again in English to see if he can understand it. He read books, especially children's books, by authors such as Roald Dahl. Unlike adult literature, books for children, especially younger children, often repeat the same words, which helps you remember them.

'Sometimes if I can't remember an English word, I'll think of the French, and that helps me get there.'

Darren has probably been infected with herpes simplex virus for years. In most people it hides away in the trigeminal and olfactory nerves at the back of the face, causing no symptoms. Every now and again the virus travels down the nerves to be shed from the nose and mouth, sometimes causing ulcers. However, in a small number of people, for reasons we don't understand, the virus heads off in the wrong direction, up the nerves into the brain, to cause inflammation here – herpes encephalitis. Because the olfactory nerve has branches leading to the brain's temporal lobe, this is where it causes damage, especially on the inside where lies the hippocampus, which is important in laying down new 'anterograde' memories. So however many times his dad tells him something, Darren cannot hold on to it. His semantic memory is especially affected, causing a striking inability to recall the names of common objects.

Perhaps most extraordinary of all, though, is that despite his difficulties with English, Darren's French language skills are relatively preserved. Whereas verbal memory is strongly focused on the left, learning of foreign language is thought to reside in the right hemisphere, and clearly in Darren's case it was spared. The fact that some language functions, like foreign language and singing, operate through the right side of the brain offers fascinating possibilities for new treatments.

Dr Nancy Helm-Estabrooks and colleagues in the United States started developing melodic intonation therapy in Boston in 1972. Working with a patient who could only say 'nee nee nah nah', but who could sing along to the piano, like Pat, they realised that simply singing familiar songs would not do the trick. Through trial and error, they discovered that if they took everyday phrases such as 'open the window' and added a little tune, and got the patient to tap out the syllables with their fingers, the patient could sing along too. After some practice the patient could manage with just a little starter prompt, and eventually they could do it all on their own. From this small start the whole field of melodic intonation therapy developed.

More recent functional MRI studies have confirmed the role of the right hemisphere in this response, though there is controversy about how much it is the music and how much it is the repetition and the tapping that are responsible for progress. Interestingly, in expressive aphasia, patients cannot write words either, and if they knew sign language before the stroke this is affected too. So it is clearly more than just getting the mouth to move in the right way: aphasia is about formulating the language you want to express.

In addition to Pat's speech problems, it became clear as she improved that her right side was paralysed, and she had double vision. Both of these could also be explained by the location of the damage. Just above Broca's area in the frontal lobe, sits the left motor cortex; this is the part of the brain that controls movement of the right side of the body. Large pyramidal cells run from here, down through the internal capsule into the brainstem, where they slip past the Circle of Willis and into the spinal cord. The large bleed into the left side of Pat's brain clearly impinged on these nerves, though thankfully the damage was not permanent.

The underside of the brainstem is also the exit route for the twelve pairs of cranial nerves, which convey the special senses, and other functions unique to the head and neck. We still number them as did the great anatomist Thomas Willis, centuries ago. At the top of the brainstem the first cranial nerve emerges, the olfactory nerve, which conveys the sense of smell. Behind it the second, the ophthalmic, carries vision; and then the third, the oculomotor, which as its name implies is critical for eye movement, and this was damaged by Pat's bleed. As Pat discovered when she awoke, if your eyes cannot move in synchrony you see double of everything. She found this infuriating until it was easily solved by wearing an eye patch. The weakness in her right leg was addressed with a brace.

In hospital, Dahl was acting as chaperone, secretary, general fixer and security. He controlled the visits, allowing some friends, including Cary Grant, to visit, but not others. He organised everything from cleaning up, sorting out flowers, emptying the ashtrays and responding to letters. He screened the correspondence. Some of the get-well cards that he thought were overindulgent were thrown away before Pat saw them; he did not want his wife dragged into a mire of self-pity, which would distract her from the notion that recovery was in her own hands. He also had no time for overbearing religious messages. Pat's views were the same. She felt angry that after all she had been through God had done this to her. Against the hospital rules, Dahl sneaked the children in to cheer her up. She was still struggling to get the right words out, and seven-year-old Tessa looked frightened and hurt. However younger Theo, who himself had suffered such terrible brain injury, smiled shyly; he seemed to know intuitively what his mother was going through.

Jake My Dioddles

Pat went home one month after being admitted to hospital. It took more than an hour to say her goodbyes to all the nurses and other staff. When they arrived home, Dahl carried her up the stairs, despite his constant back trouble.

He would ferry her up and down at least four times a day, until she got some strength back in her right leg. As she improved, she became increasingly frustrated by her limitations, as she recorded in *As I Am*:

After a stroke, anger grows with awareness of what you have lost. The fog of unconsciousness that held you prisoner from the outside world was, in fact, a blessing in disguise. First you're like a soul with no body, but the soul is drugged. Then the soul awakens into a body you cannot command. You are a prisoner in a private hell. Everybody is just pushing you around. They push your arms and your legs, your body. They say things, shout things, look at you with expectation, and you don't know what they want.

Despite the frustrations, her speech was beginning to improve, and Pat started to manage simple sentences. 'My mind is wrong,' was one of the first, and she would repeat it many times in the months ahead. However, as is often the case in aphasia, it was the names of objects and people that she really struggled with. Dahl kept careful notes of her progress, and later that year wrote 'My Wife, Patricia Neal', published in *Ladies Home Journal*. Although initially reluctant to air this private matter in such a public way, the healthcare in America was proving horribly expensive and the cash would help them get back home to England, plus he wanted people to see what progress she had made.

Her speech is coming back now, but she still has plenty of trouble finding the words. When she can't find the ones she wants, she invents others. Some of them are better words than the ones we use ourselves, and I have been noting them down very carefully. Here is a typical conversation:

The time is 6 p.m. Four or five of us are sitting around having a drink, smoking.

Pat: 'Listen, will someone get me another ... another sooty swatch.'
'A what?'
Pat: 'Oh, you know? A soap driver.'
'You want a big soap driver or a small one?'
Pat: 'Oh, come on! You know quite well what I want.'
'What?'
Pat: 'A red hairdryer.'
'You want another drink, don't you?'
Pat: 'That's right! A drink! A drink!'
'Why didn't you say so?'
Pat: 'You make me skitch, that's what you do. You give me the sinkers.'

Those around would giggle and laugh, and eventually Pat's serious face would crumple and she would give a big grin. Dahl felt she was a decent sport, and the teasing did her good. Others were not so sure, and thought it was cruel to torment her like this. One friend who visited soon after Pat left hospital described how Dahl stood watching over them, like a stage manager, or someone about to direct the traffic. Pat took a sip of tea and made a face as though it was very bitter. She reached for the sugar, but Dahl interrupted. 'What do you want, Pat?'

She shrugged her shoulders. Dahl asked again with a hard, emotionless tone, '*What* do you want?'

The visitor wanted to intervene, but Pat cunningly sipped the tea again, and smiled as though it were just perfect, and put the cup down as if she did not want for anything.

'Do you want sugar?' Dahl finally asked.

The visitor admired Dahl's fierce unrelenting approach, but could not help thinking it was how you might train a dog. Stroke rehabilitation did not really exist at the time, but, amazingly, many of the approaches that Dahl felt instinctively to be right have subsequently gained favour. In constraint-induced movement therapy, a patient's good arm is restricted with a sling or glove, forcing them to use the weaker one affected by the stroke. This is to avoid 'learned non-use', in which any abilities that are still there after the stroke deteriorate, rather than improve.

The same approach is also now being tried on patients with aphasia – constraint-induced language therapy. Patients are not allowed to point, gesture, write or draw, but have to use their voice. It appears Dahl was fifty years ahead of his time.

'I want a … a …I want an oblogon,' Pat said one day.

'Somebody get Pat an oblogon,' Dahl responded.

'Now stop it! I don't mean an oblogon. I mean a … a … a crooked steeple. God! You know!'

'A cigarette?'

'Ah! I love you! A cigarette. A cigarette. A … what did you call it? What word did you say?'

'Cigarette.'

'Yes, cigarette. I'll go crazy if I don't have one. I'll jake my dioddles.'

Dahl's careful notes of Pat's neologisms, her new words, would help with the article he was writing, but also perhaps they might come in use elsewhere. It would be more than fifteen years before the BFG would greet little Sophie with a bellow of laughter and the words:

*Just because I is a giant, you think I is a man gobbling cannybull ... !
Please understand that I cannot be helping it if I sometimes is saying
things a little squiggly ... Words is oh such a twitch tickling problem to
me all my life ...*

Dahl spent hours creating new words for the BFG, a whole language, many
of which, as Dahl said of Pat's neologisms, were better than the originals. He
described *human beans* that taste *scrumdiddlyumptious* or *uckyslush* ... and
worries about being locked up in a zoo with all those *hippodumplings* and
crocadowndillies ... the *telly telly bunkum box*.

The BFG is an extraordinary collection of clever witticism, which has given
rise to many famous quotes; most are funny, some are quite profound. No
wonder it was Dahl's favourite of all his books.

'Don't gobblefunk around with words.'

*'Meanings is not important, said the BFG. I cannot be right all the time.
Quite often I is left instead of right.'*

'You is getting nosier than a parker.'

'Two rights don't equal a left.'

'Human beans is the only animals that is killing their own kind.'

The book also has some hilarious ideas, such as *frobscottle*, the fizzy drink
with bubbles that move downwards instead of up, causing whoever drinks it to
produce *whizzpoppers*:

*'Us giants is making whizzpoppers all the time! ... Whizzpopping is a
sign of happiness. It is music in our ears! You surely is not telling me that
a little whizzpopping is forbidden among human beans?'*

A Symphony of Words

However, *The BFG* was not the first time Dahl had used neologisms. Like many
children's authors, from Lewis Carroll onwards, Dahl had always relished
creating new words. But as Dominic Cheetham, a specialist in children's

literature at Sophia University in Japan, points out, *The BFG* had many more neologisms than any other Dahl book: Cheetham counts 472 'non-standard lexical inclusions' as the linguists call them, including completely new words, new uses of existing words and new phrases.

From his very earliest book, *The Gremlins*, Dahl enjoyed using neologisms. The term *gremlin* itself was not widely used before this piece. *Fifinella*, the name of a popular racehorse at the time, was repurposed to mean a female gremlin, and *widget*, a small gadget, became a gremlin child. *Curlicue* is another word purloined by Dahl; for him it is not a fancy artistic twist or curl, but a monster in *Charlie and the Great Glass Elevator*. Some of Dahl's best neologisms are completely new words: *Spandules* are gremlin-like creatures that cause ice to form on a plane's wings; *Wipple Scrumpet*, is a gremlin song, though it sounds like something delicious you might eat at a West Country fête. Indeed, Dahl used the term twenty years later when he cooked up Wonka's Whipple Scrumptious Fudgemallow Delight in *Charlie and the Chocolate Factory*.

Just like his ideas, many of Dahl's neologisms would recur throughout his works. For example, the *whangdoodle* is some kind of mythical beast in *James and the Giant Peach*, both *Charlie* books and also *The Minpins*; the word lost an 'h' in *The Giraffe and the Pelly and Me*, to become a *wangdoodle* sweet. *Vermicious Knids* are another Dahl beast that appear in many books.

At least one new word even made the transition from his children's to his adult literature. In *Charlie and the Chocolate Factory*, the snozzberry is a strawberry-like fruit on the wallpaper that the children lick, but it is something quite different in *My Uncle Oswald*, the adult novel written fifteen years later. Oswald is quizzing his assistant, Yasmin, who has just returned from an amorous encounter with an over-arduous lover:

> *'How did you manage to roll the old rubbery thing on him?'*
> *'There's only one way when they get violent,' Yasmin said. 'I grabbed hold of his snozzberry and hung on to it like grim death and gave it a twist or two to make him hold still.'*
> *'Ow.'*
> *'Very effective.'*
> *'I'll bet it is.'*
> *'You can lead them around anywhere you want like that.'*

Some thought this was a great perverted joke of Dahl's, to have the children licking snozzberries. But I suspect he was just reusing a word that he rather liked. He had also used the term in his first adult novel, *Some Time Never*, where it was a sweet fruit.

Taken collectively, Dahl's writing is like a symphony of music, with recurring motifs, which might appear in early works as a *forme fruste*, before developing into a full melody, with perhaps distant echoes later on. This applies not just to his neologisms; characters, names and ideas weave in and out of his work, evolving over the decades. For example, a plot to poach pheasants using drug-spiked raisins initially appeared in the 1959 adult short story *The Champion of the World* before being developed further into the children's book *Danny, the Champion of the World*, sixteen years later. In this book during a bedtime story told by Danny's father we meet the Big Friendly Giant for the first time. At this stage the BFG works his dreaming magic, but it is not until seven years later, when he has a book of his own, that we hear him speak his strange Gobblefunk, and learn of his extraordinary hearing. The BFG's great ears can detect the scream of a flower being cut and the soft moan of a big tree being axed, concepts that first appeared in the adult short story 'The Sound Machine' back in 1949. Trying to keep track of all these ideas weaving in and out of Dahl's literature, backwards and forwards in time, can leave you dizzy.

In Dahl's early books, *The Gremlins, James and the Giant Peach* and *Charlie and the Chocolate Factory*, almost all the neologisms were for the names of creatures, people, ingredients or sweets. The sweets are not so surprising, given that as a schoolboy Dahl used to think up names for new chocolates delivered by the Cadbury's Bourneville factory. His next books, *The Magic Finger* and *Fantastic Mr Fox* had almost no new words. Then, as Cheetham's analysis shows, there was a dramatic change with the publication in 1968 of *Charlie and the Great Glass Elevator*. The number of new words increased from approximately twelve per book to a whopping seventy-three. Also for the first time in *Charlie and the Great Glass Elevator* the neologisms included new verbs, like *fottles* around, *lixivate* and *rumbilate*, new adjectives such as *quelchy*, *mashy* and *squishious*, and exclamatory phrases such as *whistling whangdoodles* and *Oh, skid and daddle!*

Stop Squibbling

Cheetham does not speculate as to why Dahl's new words increased so markedly at this time, but it is notable that the *Great Glass Elevator* is the first book he wrote after Pat had recovered from her stroke. Dahl had always liked creating new names for people, creatures and objects, but I think new adjectives, adverbs and verbs really only occurred to him after he listened to Pat struggling with her words.

Dahl's use of neoligisms continued after the *Great Glass Elevator*: in *The Enormous Crocodile* Humpy Rumpy calls the crocodile 'a greedy *grumptious* brute!'; in *The Twits* Mrs Twit shouts, 'I'll swish you to a swizzle!'; in *George's Marvellous Medicine* there is 'a grizzly old grunion of a Grandma'.

Then in *The BFG* there was a veritable explosion with hundreds of neologisms of every form, made possible, of course, because the BFG himself had such difficulty with words. The BFG's neologisms include new uses for existing words – *Golden Sovereign* [the queen], little earwigs [ears], two little winkles [eyes] – as well as a delightful tranche of completely new words – *repulsant, snozzcumber, whizzpopping, vegitibbles, norphan* ... For most of these words the sense is clear, either because of the word from which they are derived, or because of the context in which we read them. Mrs Clonkers, for example is described as 'a rotten old *rotrasper* ... a filthy old *fizzwiggler*'.

The neogolisms add great humour and atmosphere to the book. Although Dahl had concocted many neologisms before, what was different here was that the BFG, like Patricia Neal was trying to speak normally but couldn't. The giant sadly explains:

> *'There never was any schools to teach me talking in Giant Country.'*
>   *'But couldn't your mother have taught you? Sophie asked.*
>   *'My mother!' cried the BFG. 'Giants don't have mothers! Surely you is knowing that.'*

He gives an account of his difficulty, which could have come straight from the mouth of Patricia Neal:

> *'... you must simply try to be patient and stop squibbling... I know exactly what words I am wanting to say, but somehow or other they is always getting squiff squiddled around ... what I mean and what I says is two different things ...'*

Dahl was a bit vague when I asked him about the BFG's language and Pat's aphasia.

'Well, I'd always enjoyed making up new words. That's part of the fun, you know, that keeps the nippers interested ... But I suppose, yes, some of the trouble Pat had did work its way into *The BFG*; yes, it must have.'

It seemed so obvious to me that I was amazed to find in researching for this book it had never been explored before. Looking back, I wish I had probed Dahl a bit further. I now recognise his answer as the sort of nebulous response he gave to questions where he felt the truth of the matter was not exactly the story he wanted to tell, issues like the origin of the term *gremlins*, or how his plane had actually come down in Libya. Perhaps he felt some discomfort in that he had created the speech of one of his best-loved characters by using the after-effects of his wife's stroke. Or maybe he had never really recognised the link until I raised it with him. Neither Liccy nor Ophelia remember him ever discussing the origins of Gobblefunk with anyone in the family, but then he rarely talked about the books upon which he was working.

People have suggested Dahl was dyslexic, and indeed the vagaries of the modern internet era mean that once something like this is postulated it is often repeated unquestioningly, until it almost becomes fact. Dahl's name now appears on several lists of 'famous people with dyslexia'. Looking at Gobblefunk, you can see why people might think he was dyslexic. But you only have to read any of his original handwritten manuscripts to realise this is utter nonswallop!

'No, he was not dyslexic.' Liccy asserts. 'He had terrible spelling, and was bilingual. But certainly not dyslexic.'

Some experts have worried about the impact of all the new words in *The BFG* on children's reading, although the popularity of the book suggests these concerns are misguided. Children love new words, and are learning all the time. Much of what they hear sounds initially like gibberish, but they have to make sense of it all from the context. So in this regard Dahl's neologisms are nothing unusual for a child. And of course when learning to speak, toddlers produce a whole lexicon of wonderful neologisms. Among my own children, this included having *breakwoof* first thing in the morning, eating *fweeties* and *molives*, playing *usical minstruments*, and a new way of sharing out a plate of meringues – these are *my ringues*, you get your own!

The BFG regularly features in lists of the most popular children's books of all time. An extensive analysis of British children's reading in 1999 found it topped the list of most frequently mentioned titles. Twenty-five years after Dahl's death, a survey of two thousand children placed *The BFG* in the top ten children's books, along with *Charlie and the Chocolate Factory* and *James and the Giant Peach*. It is arguably his best work.

THE WAR YEARS

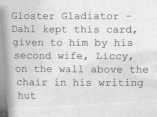

Gloster Gladiator –
Dahl kept this card,
given to him by his
second wife, Liccy,
on the wall above the
chair in his writing
hut

Crashed Vichy
French plane – Dahl
took the photo of
this plane, and
its pilot's grave
in Haifa

Dahl in safari gear –
collecting a coconut
from a palm tree in
Tanganyika

Dahl in
full RAF
uniform

THEO

Sleeping Theo, convalescing outside Gipsy House watched by (left to right) Olivia, Pat, Tessa and Roald

Theo with Pat, soon after his shunt operation for hydrocephalus at the Columbia Presbyterian Hospital

The taxi which collided with Theo's pram, in New York, 1960

Theo, in the early 1970s, enjoying his pipe - with (left to right) Tessa, Ophelia, Roald, Lucy and Pat, outside Gipsy House

THE WDT VALVE

Dahl and Stanley Wade - working on the Wade-Dahl-Till valve to treat hydrocephalus (above and below)

The 1964 *Lancet* publication on the valve (right) with Dahl's original draft manuscript (above) and an example of the valve itself (below) which Dahl kept on the wall of his writing hut

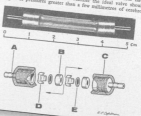

New Inventions

A VALVE FOR THE TREATMENT OF HYDROCEPHALUS

THE basis of many operations for relief of hydrocephalus is the diversion of cerebrospinal fluid to a vein, a venous sinus, or the cardiac atrium. In most of these procedures a one-way valve is required to prevent reflux of blood into the cerebral ventricle. Valves available commercially are expensive; they usually have components made of plastic; they depend upon the slit principle; and some of them are difficult or impossible to sterilise or resterilise after delivery from the makers. Quite often, too, they become blocked in course of time.

The valve here described is made entirely of stainless steel: it has no narrow orifices, and, instead of employing non-return slits, it carries cerebrospinal fluid over as wide a surface area as possible. It is self-flushing—i.e., it has a moving part which can be expected to dislodge and pass any particulate matter. It permits no reflux and opens at a pressure of 2-5 mm. water. Two valves in tandem, connected by a soft silicone rubber tube, are used to allow pumping, when required, by intermittent digital pressure through the scalp.

The valve was designed for the particular purpose of diverting cerebrospinal fluid to a cerebral sinus where the pressure differential is small, and its resistance therefore had to be minimal. This "free-flowing" characteristic has not limited its use. The valve has proved successful in otherwise conventional ventriculo-atrial bypass operations. Doubts have therefore been raised as to whether the ideal valve should open at pressures greater than a few millimetres of cerebro-

Dahl's daughter Olivia shortly before her death from measles encephalitis in 1962, aged 7

Dahl restoring the medieval Spanish statue of St Catherine (above right) before donating it in Olivia's memory to the Church in Little Missenden (right)

Dahl at the rock garden he built on Olivia's grave (left), and the overgrown ferns when the author visited fifty years later (right)

CHARITY

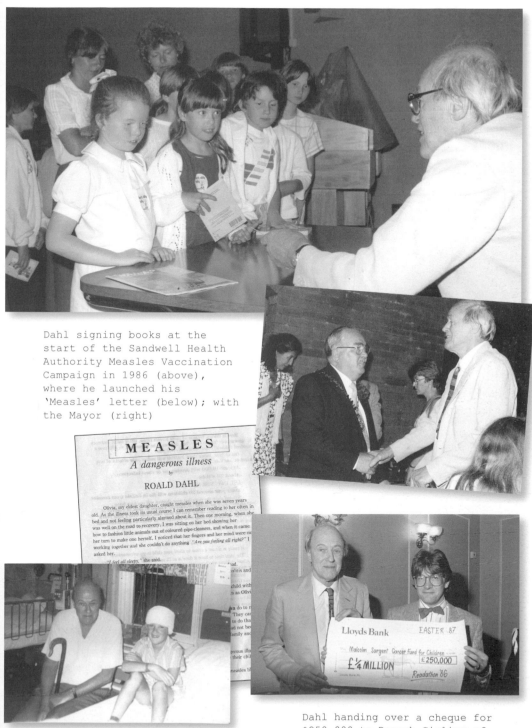

Dahl signing books at the start of the Sandwell Health Authority Measles Vaccination Campaign in 1986 (above), where he launched his 'Measles' letter (below); with the Mayor (right)

MEASLES
A dangerous illness
by
ROALD DAHL

Dahl visiting a child in a Sydney hospital during a tour of Australia

Dahl handing over a cheque for £250,000 to Brough Girling of the Malcolm Sargent Cancer Fund for Children following the 1986 Readathon

PAT'S STROKE

Patricia Neal at Gipsy House, soon after her stroke, with (left to right) Theo, Roald, Tessa, Ophelia and a nurse

Pat and Roald with Valerie Eaton Griffith, who worked on Pat's speech therapy

Physiotherapy at the RAF hospital, Halton

'Doctor' Dahl, Pat and newborn baby Lucy

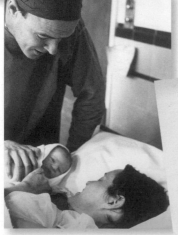

Dahl's notes of Pat's new words, and the BFG's Gobblefunk

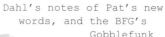

THE WRITER

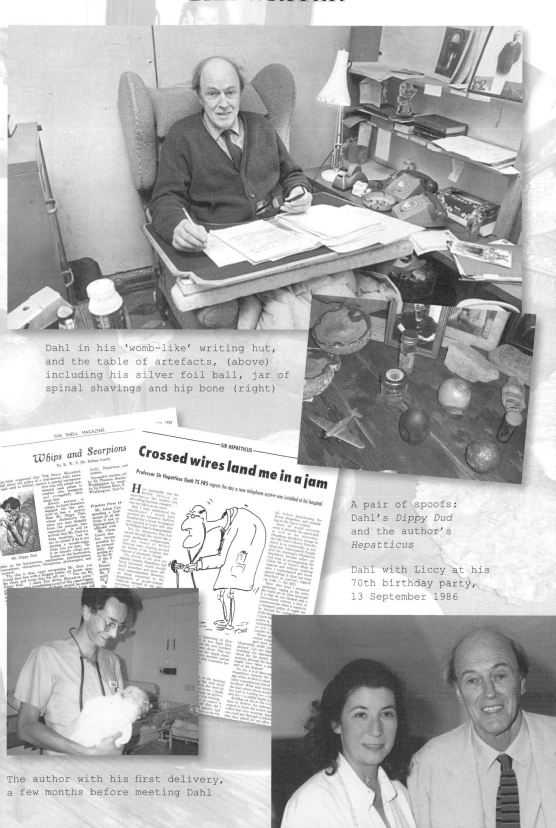

Dahl in his 'womb-like' writing hut, and the table of artefacts, (above) including his silver foil ball, jar of spinal shavings and hip bone (right)

A pair of spoofs: Dahl's *Dippy Dud* and the author's *Hepatticus*

Dahl with Liccy at his 70th birthday party, 13 September 1986

The author with his first delivery, a few months before meeting Dahl

Crossed wires land me in a jam

Whips and Scorpions

THE FINAL YEARS

Dahl's wedding to Liccy Crosland in 1983 (left to right): Sophie (Tessa's daughter), Lucy and Ophelia Dahl; Lorina, Charlotte and Neisha Crosland, Theo, Tessa, Liccy and Roald Dahl

Dahl outside his writing hut (above right), and Liccy showing the author's children the hut in 2007 (above)

Dahl's last photo, in bed with Chopper, 1990

Chapter 13

The Cabbage and the Giant

Before they left UCLA Medical Centre, Pat's neurosurgeon, Dr Carton, suggested to Dahl that immediate and intense stimulation might be the best chance for her recovery; they should start speech therapy and mental rehabilitation right away. Not a single day must be lost. This was just what Dahl wanted to hear, that you could actually do something to take control of the outcome. Carton arranged for a speech therapist to visit Pat daily at home. Dahl asked Jean Alexander, the nurse in whom they had such confidence, to also come as often as she could. Plus of course there were many friends who popped by. Well-wishers continued to send cards and flowers, including Frank Sinatra, whose chauffeur delivered a portable gramophone and a stack of records.

Pat found some of the guests were hard work. The worst would talk nonstop, allowing her no time to digest what was being said; or they would speak to her like a baby, assuming that she was simple. The more visitors there were, the harder it was for her to follow. Trying to listen to two people was like watching a tennis game, and a roomful of guests was like being on a firing range, words shooting past like bullets.

'Once in a while there would be a word I understood, and for a second I knew exactly what was being said. But before I could focus thoughts and trap words of my own, I would forget what I had heard.'

Pat learned that she could lean forward with her head at an angle, smile and nod occasionally, and everyone would assume she was taking it all in, though quite often she hadn't a clue who they were, let alone what they were talking about. Her best visitors would know intuitively when to talk, and when to shut up. The actress Anne Bancroft, who had previously been a rival for the top acting roles, and replaced Pat in *Seven Women*, now became a great friend. She visited often, and seemed to know instinctively when to hold back and give Pat a chance to speak a few words. Dahl described how Pat would watch his lips carefully. He would speak slowly: 'Tessa'; she would try, fail, try again and eventually succeed.

The speech therapist had warned Dahl that an hour of intense effort every day was enough, and beyond that it could be counterproductive.

'But I remember saying to myself, "Surely one hour a day is not enough,"' Dahl explained to me. 'I remember the precise moment. I was walking along Romani Drive, in Pacific Palisades, California, soon after Pat came out from hospital. I thought, What in the world are you going to teach a child if she only goes to school for an hour a day? That is what Pat was like then, a child. She didn't even know her ABC.'

The sight of Pat sitting in a chair staring vacantly at nothing horrified Dahl. In his view idleness was a greater risk than fatigue, and anything was better than vegetating. Theo, or *Titi* as he was known in the family, tested his mother to see if she could name the objects on his giant flash cards; the four year old was now reading well and did not need them any more. It was barely a year since his hydrocephalus had settled, and Pat drew great inspiration from the progress he had made. He seemed a living testament to the brain's ability to mend. Theo was not perplexed by Pat's garbled words. In fact, he took advantage of the fact she spoke less; for once he could do all the talking.

By now Pat was walking. Dahl recalled that 'she staggered and tottered like a drunken sailor'. Things were not helped by the fact that she was nearly five months' pregnant. She could also manage the stairs, with help. Despite Pat's remarkable progress, most in the medical team were guarded about her overall chances of recovery. Most except one, who considered himself to have an honorary medical degree, and told her with one hundred per cent certainty that she would get completely better. He knew the doctors thought this unlikely, but felt that you should at least aim for it. In his article for *Ladies Home Journal* Dahl described their tough stance.

> She had no self-pity, and she received no sympathy from us. We pushed her hard. She had to get up at 7.30 for breakfast, and get up alone. She had to put on her own shoes and brace, she had to find her own clothes, and make her own way downstairs. It was a rough school she was in.

There were differences of opinion, however, particularly with Pat's mother who was inclined to a more gentle approach. Dahl's *tough love* meant that Pat should get no special favours, and be treated like everyone else. Things came to a head over a fine cut of steak, which Pat's mother had prepared specially for her, whilst everyone else was eating pork chops. Dahl insisted the steak should be cut up and shared by all – and indeed it was. Pat did not resent his efforts at rehabilitation. Even twenty years later, after their marriage had ended, she recognised them as the 'heroic efforts of a genius'. Recent evidence continues to support Dahl's view: the earlier therapy starts, and the more intensive it is, the better.

England at Last

The brief press conference that Pat gave at Los Angeles airport just before the family flew to Washington on the way to England was an important landmark for the actress: her first public performance since the stroke. For Dahl too, who had been telling the papers Pat would make a one hundred per cent recovery, this event was important. Three months to the day since her stroke, Cary Grant drove them to the airport. Pat was thrilled by the turnout of reporters and photographers – far more, she noted, than when she had won the Oscar a year before. They all stood up and applauded as she walked in, unaided – her first steps towards resuming her acting career. Photographs show the family seated round the microphones, Patricia's head wrapped in an exotic turban to hide her scar, a patch on her left eye, little Ophelia on her knee; Dahl is at her side to take the initial questions, with Theo sitting on his knee, and Tessa standing behind.

Pat had rehearsed the likely questions with Dahl, and the interview went well.

'I'll be ... back at work in a year,' she told the reporters, 'the baby first.'

'And what have the doctors told you about the baby?'

'The prediction is ... the baby will be ... fine.' *Prediction* – where had that word come from? They had not practised it. Dahl was amazed to hear her drop it into the sentence with such insouciance.

When Dahl told the reporters that one day Pat would act again, the room became silent. 'I might just as well have announced that the woman was going to sprout wings and fly to the moon.'

There was a large reception of press and relatives to greet the family when they arrived at London's Heathrow airport after a few days in Washington. Hugged by Dahl's sisters, Pat found herself sobbing for the first time since her stroke. The entourage was greeted at Gipsy House by more family and neighbours. The village chemist had sent a bottle of champagne, and as Pat took her first sip she noticed her double vision had gone.

'Jolly good,' said Dahl, refilling her glass. 'I wonder if the medical profession would be interested in our cure.'

At Gipsy House there was no let up from Dahl's rigorous rehabilitation regimen. Pat grew weary of his plans, programmes and percentages – forty-two per cent better than yesterday, fifty-one per cent better than last week. She felt her motivation draining from her. At times she was beyond caring and wished she could be left alone, but Dahl would have none of it. Constant stimulation was the order of the day, or she risked just becoming 'an enormous pink cabbage'.

As he later wrote: 'By the time she arrived home in England, she was still about seventy-five per cent aphasic. She could neither read, write, nor handle numbers. She had no initiative. If left alone, she would sit and stare into space and in half an hour a great black cloud of depression would envelope her mind. Unless I was prepared to have a bad-tempered desperately unhappy nitwit in the house some very drastic action would have to be taken at once.'

He explained his approach to me one evening in Oxford, when we had been talking about stroke patients.

'I couldn't get this six-hours-a-day business out of my head. In America six hours of therapy a day would have cost more than £500,000 a year, so as soon as we were able, we flew home. The day we arrived back I asked about speech therapy and was told we could have an hour a week. I said to forget it, and started telephoning friends.'

Dahl arranged for friends from the village and relatives to spend time with Pat. In the morning there would be a reading and writing lesson, then she would be taken to the RAF military hospital, 'the boot camp', in nearby Halton for arm and leg exercises, before laps in the swimming pool at Stoke Mandeville. Back home for lunch, and then a relay of more neighbours, every hour through the afternoon, keeping Pat stimulated with dominoes, tic tac toe, number and word games.

No one knew what would keep her attention, so they just experimented. Books and poems were too difficult, but newspapers with their short punchy articles were good – especially since they kept Pat interested in what else was going on in the world. In total there were about fifteen amateur teachers on the rota.

'They honestly didn't care about my having been in films,' Pat recalled. 'Nobody in our village took much notice of that, anyway. They came because I needed help. They came for free. For love. And I'll remember them till the day I die.'

Dahl made a roster and stuck it on the kitchen wall. He arranged for Pat's American nurse Jean Alexander and her flatmate to come and work in England for a year. Living nearby, they would often visit for weekends, helping with the rehabilitation and keeping Pat's spirits up.

Pat had difficulty counting, and found herself easily overwhelmed. On her first trip shopping alone she stood in the grocery store, staring at all the labels on the shelves; there were just splinters of colour, and the writing had no meaning. Her higher cognitive functions were affected: she had difficulty interpreting cartoons, sometimes coming up with explanations that were more funny than the original ones. Although she was always with people, Barry Farrell, who was with them over several months writing his in-depth piece for

Life magazine, detected a great loneliness. Dahl took over the running of the house, and Pat started calling him *Papa*, as if she were another child.

At her lowest points Pat began thinking about suicide. It was not just the physical and language difficulties with which she struggled, but their impact on her whole life. She no longer had any responsibility for the household, or any role in it, and felt as if she were an irrelevance to the children. Even little Ophelia, by then just over a year old, did not seem to know who she was. Pat asked Farrell: 'How many sleeping pills or aspirin would you need to take?' He was worried and unsure whether to tell Dahl. However, soon afterwards, she half jokingly asked Dahl the same question over dinner. Farrell was surprised by the reply. Rather than being horrified, or concerned, or trying to dissuade her, the master of the macabre listed a whole catalogue of readily available methods she could use, such as a dagger from the kitchen, or the car-exhaust fumes.

Dahl did take her to see a psychiatrist soon afterwards, who reassured them both. The journalist kept such private details out of the article he wrote; the world wanted to hear the wondrous story of a film star's recovery from stroke, not the harsh reality of life after a devastating illness. However, when Farrell wrote his book four years later he was more expansive, giving details of the illness's impact on the complex relationship between Dahl and Neal as well as the toll it took on the whole family. The book was titled was *Pat and Roald*, though they joked that *The Cabbage and The Giant* might have been more suitable.

Slowly, Insidiously and Quite Relentlessly

The imminent arrival of her fifth child lifted Pat's spirits. With the birth just a few weeks away, Dahl allowed Pat a break in the intensive rehabilitation. Once the date for the induction was set, she was no longer anxious but felt happy and full of energy. Her speech was animated and her vocabulary was growing noticeably. Lucy Neal Dahl was born on 4 August 1965; *Lukie* would be her nickname. It was an easy delivery, over in four hours, and Pat declared she could not remember when she had last felt so good. Farrell was there, along with a photographer from *Life* magazine, to herald the arrival of this miracle baby. Dahl gave her an ancient gold ring of the Greek goddess Persephone, from Sotheby's, to celebrate.

Whilst Pat rested, Dahl took Farrell on a walk around Oxford, pointing out the colleges, with the 'accent and manner of an Oxford Don'. Farrell noted, as they toured the shops, that Dahl seemed to be interested in everything. In a pet shop he wanted to know how you could tell a male tortoise from a female –

apparently it is by their concave chests, which make mounting easier; he bought one for Theo. For Tessa, *Teddy* as she was known, he bought a witch ball, a hand blown glass ball hung from the ceiling to keep witches away. In a rare book dealer's they came across James Russell's 1833 treatise 'Observations on the Testicles'. I can imagine the mischievous glint in Dahl's eye as he bought it for Farrell. 'Take it. You never know when you might need to look something up.'

Before she left hospital with the newborn Lucy, Pat discarded the leg brace, and took her first hesitant steps. She walked like a puppet, lifting the right foot high before flopping it clumsily to the ground. Dahl stood behind her as she stumbled along the corridor, 'a drill sergeant urging her on'.

A fortnight after Lucy's birth, Pat and Dahl met Valerie Eaton Griffith for the first time. She would have a profound impact, not just helping with Pat's recovery but also ensuring Dahl's innovative regimen of high-intensity stroke rehabilitation delivered by volunteers become a national and then international movement, which would also lead to the formation of the Stroke Association.

Valerie was an energetic and kindly woman in her forties who had recently moved to Great Missenden to live with her sister and elderly father. Previously the manager at an Elizabeth Arden beauty salon in London, she had become unwell with thyroid problems ten years earlier, and retired through ill health. She herself had spent five months in hospital, still limped badly, and was taking many aspirins every day for pain. Although she did not know the family personally, like everyone in the village she knew about Pat's misfortune, but, as she later wrote, 'It never for a moment crossed my mind that I could help.'

However, as Dahl began to broaden the circle of volunteers enlisting the help of friends of friends, someone suggested that he call her. Valerie recalls that although she knew nothing about stroke, or rehabilitation, she was horrified to realise that instead of saying 'no' in response to Dahl's kind voice on the phone, she found herself saying 'yes'.

Val recalled the first time they met in a letter to Pat.

When I walked into the room, your face is what caught my attention. You were not going to get anywhere with that tragic face ... One of the first things you said was, 'My mind is gone.' That was not true ... My first lesson was to discover, bit by bit, what you could do and what you had to rediscover.

Rather than the stream of volunteers visiting Gipsy House, Pat would spend a few hours each morning at Val's, with some homework to do later in the day if she felt like it. Val had no formal teaching degree, or experience in rehabilitation, but she and Pat embarked on this as a journey together. She was very sensitive to Pat's needs, and could adjust accordingly. On some days they might be doing mental arithmetic, on others just drinking coffee, gazing out of the window and talking about the trees. They would browse through magazines, gossiping about other stars; they'd name coins; or solve jigsaw puzzles together. The key thing was that they built up a good relationship; Pat actually began to look forward to their sessions.

Valerie was careful never to overdo it: if Pat was too tired for a challenging conversation, they would go shopping together, and relearn the names of items on the shelves. Poetry was too difficult, but they hit upon the idea of reading plays. This would also help build Pat's confidence about possibly acting again one day. Occasionally Pat would snap and quarrel or become obnoxious, but she would soon want to make amends.

Important to the success of the whole plan, Dahl and Valerie also liked each other immediately, although they disagreed in their approach to the future.

'I knew that she could make a full recovery, and get back to acting,' Dahl told me in hospital, 'but Val was more cautious. She thought it was hard to look so far ahead, and put Pat under pressure.' However, the combination worked well. Dahl demanding that Pat reach for the sky, Val helping her get there. Dahl was happy to let Val take charge of teaching Pat. He realised his talents did not lie here, and worried it would alter his relationship with his wife. Besides, he was also busy running the house, and trying to work.

One of the key issues, Valerie realised early on, was Pat's dignity and self-respect. Her confidence was constantly being knocked back, usually unintentionally, sometimes even by her own children. At one stage Tessa confided that she wanted to get out of the house, because 'there are just too many babies here'. Pat wanted to take more responsibility in the household, but struggled even with the simplest things like making a dental appointment for the children. Some in the family wondered whether, if she put her mind to it, she could really do better. However, when the 'omnipresent, dependable and commanding' Dahl was away, Pat would come into her own. She spent two weeks running the house whilst he was in Japan filming the new Bond movie, *You Only Live Twice* – Dahl was finding screenplay writing a relatively easy way of making money. His sister Else looked in at Gipsy House every day and found that Pat was managing fine with the two au pairs from Europe. Indeed, having these two young women around, whose English was no better than Pat's, gave her an additional confidence boost.

Valerie recalled that in their interactions Pat would enjoy her small successes.

'Where is Washington?' she asked Pat. They were looking at a map of the USA. Pat pointed to the far western edge. 'No, no,' said Val pointing out

DC. But Pat kept insisting until eventually Val realised she was pointing to Washington State.

Most of Pat's recovery occurred in the first six months after her stroke, before she had the baby; that was when the obvious progress occurred, the return of walking and speech. After that was the true rehabilitation, which was much harder, the subtler long-term struggle to take her back to the person she used to be. She still had language difficulties, speaking slowly and using pet phrases – 'sorry to tell you' and 'a very good thing' – to buy time whilst she found the words for which she was searching: 'I am ... *very ... sorry ... to tell you ... that ...* I am going up ... to take a bath' or 'It would be ... *a very ... good thing ...* if ... we ... had a cup of tea.'

Left to her own devices, Pat's progress would have stalled, but it was the determination of Dahl, and others around her, who could see the slow changes, little by little, month by month, that were too subtle for her to notice herself.

'Slowly, insidiously, and quite relentlessly, Val coaxed her back to where she is now,' Dahl later wrote, 'virtually one hundred per cent recovered.'

A Missive from Great Missenden

With the publication of Dahl's article in *Ladies Home Journal* in September 1965, and Farrell's piece in *Life* magazine soon after, Patricia Neal became recognised not just as an actress but as someone who had survived against all the odds. Hundreds of letters poured into Gipsy House every week, and Pat teased Dahl that she had much more fan mail than him. Even an envelope simply addressed 'Actress Patricia Neal, England' found its way to her. Many letters were from movie fans wishing her well, but even more were from people seeking advice and help in recovering from a stroke.

'They wanted to know how we had done it,' Dahl told me, 'what the secret was. We knew we were on to something with this rehabilitation. So we began to answer the letters: Pat tapping away at the typewriter with just one finger, me helping when I had time.'

Just as Dahl had helped thousands with the development of the valve for treating hydrocephalus, he wanted to share this new approach to rehabilitation, in case it might be useful to others. The correspondence became overwhelming, so eventually, with input from Val, Dahl composed a long letter outlining their ideas on stroke rehabilitation. He added five pages of 'Notes by Pat's Teachers', and had everything copied by mimeograph. It was sent out by the thousands.

'A stroke patient who is having difficulty with speech, writing, reading, memory or concentration, and who suffers inevitably from inertia, boredom, frustration and depression, can be helped enormously by amateurs in his or her own home,' Dahl began. He went on to describe the roles of various people in the team. In his opinion the person on whom the patient is dependant – the husband, wife or other family member – will be too busy running the house, earning a living and above all keeping cheerful, to take on the onerous duty of rehabilitation. That should be done by close friends nearby. Make a list, and phone them up to ask if they can give a couple of hours a week, or, best of all, an hour a day, he advised. Then draw up the roster for the friends, now teachers, to fill two hours in the morning and three in the afternoon. The letter does not countenance the possibility that others may not be as fortunate as the Dahls, who had many friends in the village on whom they could call, and those affected by a stroke today might find it all a bit prescriptive.

'The friends will protest at first, saying they know nothing about how to teach people suffering from aphasia,' Dahl continued, qualifying this by saying they don't need to. 'The whole thing is common sense. All the patient wants is practice ... At the end of six months none of Pat's teachers were amateurs any longer. They were pros. They had become extraordinarily skilful.' Dahl would back them now 'to take on almost any case (which is not *too* severe) and show the patient how to live'.

The five pages of 'Notes by Pat's Teachers' outlined the problem areas where amateurs could be particularly helpful: trouble with speech and comprehension; difficulty in thinking or solving even the simplest of problems; lack of confidence in general; extreme inertia; and lack of concentration. Each of these could be addressed. Confidence could be boosted by teaching the patient that everything learned throughout their lives is still available to them; it is just a matter of accessing it.

To help with language, read children's books, especially those with pictures that help the story along, and encourage any gestures, stumbles, half words – any means of verbal communication – but don't treat them like a child. Play word games: what is the opposite of 'black', put the word in a sentence; give me a word that rhymes; jigsaws and simple arithmetic would help problem solving; play games like 'I Spy', dominoes and Ludo, get out a pack of cards and separate the hearts from the diamonds. On a car journey make up names to fit licence plates.

'Concentration and recall is what you are after.'

Quick, easy questions banged at the patient like a machine gun would deal with inertia and bad concentration. Any form of answer was acceptable – words, gestures, pointing, miming – as long as the patient was engaging.

'Push, push, push for answers. Make the patient sit up, try like mad, dig out something from somewhere, mangle out a bit of vitality, a laugh, an *effort*.'

Tackling apathy to keep the new student engaged and interested, was one of the greatest challenges.

'The frustrating thing' – Dahl became quite animated in his explanation to me – 'was that many of the letters came from families where someone had suffered a stroke years earlier. They were trying our approaches, but with no success because it was too late. You have to start straight away, but if you don't have a good doctor to advise you, how would you know?'

Dahl was right, of course, and we now know that rehabilitation should be started as soon as a patient has stabilised, often within a couple of days of hospital admission. Attempts at rehabilitation later are unlikely to be so successful.

In the Family

Valerie built on Dahl's letter and notes to produce a book, *A Stroke in the Family*, published in 1970. In his introduction Dahl explains that modest Val was initially reluctant to write a book at all, but when they showed her just one crateful of the 'stroke-patient letters' with their desperate pleas for help, she agreed. He noted her achievements – 'the more I think of it, the more I begin to doubt whether anyone else could have accomplished it' – whilst ignoring his own role. The book was essentially an expansion of the long notes on stroke rehabilitation that he had written, and could easily have been credited with both Valerie Eaton Griffith and Roald Dahl as authors.

As well as describing Pat's recovery, the book also talked about Val's work with Alan Moorehead, an author who had recently suffered a stroke. Moorehead, who was a few years older than Dahl, was a celebrated correspondent during World War II who went on to write history books. He won many awards for his work and was honoured with an OBE. He lived in London, and following his stroke in 1966 his wife sought help from Dahl. Val's initial assessment of him at Gipsy House provides a good insight into the methods she had developed:

'How are you, Alan?'
    'I am very well, thank you.'

(Good he can say these simple words perfectly. Let's stretch him a bit.)

    'Where do you live, Alan?'
    He points and makes gestures telling us his home is far away.

(Good, he has understood. Not so good, he could not answer in words.)

'Here are thirteen playing cards, Alan. Will you sort them in suits and seniority?'

Again, he has understood. But he only manages to sort them into reds and blacks with court cards at the front.

(So colours okay, pictures easily identified. Shapes and numbers not so ...)

The Mooreheads rented a cottage in the village so Alan could have a year of intensive therapy with Val. In the book she emphasised again the need to start rehabilitation as early as possible, and to keep trying different approaches until something works. Moorehead, for example, could not manage the alphabet in any format: spoken, written or learning by rote. However, great traveller that he was, they discovered he could find place names in the index of an atlas. This example also illustrated the need to moderate the approach to an individual's backgrounds and interests. Val also pointed out that four years after Pat's stroke she was still improving, despite the conventional medical wisdom that recovery only happened during the first two years.

Forty years after it was written, *A Stroke in the Family* is still available, the most recent reprint being in 2010 by the East Kent Stroke Association: 'We found that the book had gone out of print – yet it is still as relevant today as it was when originally published. So we decided to publish it ourselves.' In the preface Professor Tony Rudd, now NHS England's National Clinical Director for Stroke, points out that even today the amount of rehabilitation treatment Pat received in a week probably equates to the total amount received by the average UK stroke patient in a year. 'Perhaps the most important message that I have taken from this book is that we should not be relying on professional therapists to provide all the treatment that is needed.'

Chapter 14

Thousands Across the Country

Valerie Eaton Griffith's rehabilitation work with Pat and Dahl, and the book which described their methods, *A Stroke in the Family*, started a medical revolution in terms of stroke therapy; they were also key catalysts in the development of the Stroke Association of today from its predecessor the Chest and Heart Association.

The origins of the Chest and Heart Association can be traced back to the National Association for the Prevention of Consumption and other forms of Tuberculosis, which was founded in 1898. The organisation's evolution over the next hundred years, shifting according to the public health priorities, is reflected in a series of name changes. The term *consumption* was dropped once it became outdated; *tuberculosis* was switched for *chest and heart* as the relative importance of different diseases altered. By the 1960s the Chest and Heart Association was becoming increasingly interested in stroke, and the association's director general, Dr Harley Williams, read Val's book and invited her to their conference in 1970.

Three years later at their meeting on 'How to help the "Stroke" patient' both Dahl and Val spoke about their experience with Pat. Val also outlined her hope to expand what had worked so well in Great Missenden into a stroke service. She wanted to establish a programme of regular home visits by volunteers to help more people with stroke overcome speech and communication problems. In addition there would be weekly 'stroke clubs' organised locally, with outings and social events.

Volunteers would thus support the work of professional speech therapists whose time for each patient was limited. Her plans were already being adopted in America, but not yet formally in Britain. A meeting was arranged between Val, Roald, Pat and Sir John Richardson, President of the General Medical Council, who himself had suffered a stroke, with the hope of ultimately interesting the Department of Health and Social Security. The government could not help, but the Chest and Heart Association decided to support two pilot schemes, one in the city of Oxford, and a rural one in the Chilterns. They were run by Val, three assistants and two hundred volunteers. The programme was judged by the referring general practitioners to be very successful, and was written up in the *British Medical Journal*.

The Volunteer Stroke Scheme was thus established under the umbrella of the association, and by 1980 was supporting thirty-five individual programmes, with more than fifteen hundred volunteers, plus there were many more stroke clubs around the country. The scheme provided a framework within which volunteers were free to use their initiative, supported by Valerie's book.

The programme grew and by 1992 there were more than one hundred schemes across the whole of the UK. Through the 1970s Val worked independently, but in 1981 she became the official Volunteer Stroke Scheme organiser for the Chest and Heart Association. The changing emphasis of the association resulted in the addition of 'Stroke' to its name in 1974 to become the *Chest, Heart and Stroke Association*. As noted in Dr Anne Ritchie's 'History of the Stroke Association', 'Valerie Eaton Griffith's unflagging work on the rehabilitation of stroke patients over two decades laid the foundations for later stroke services.'

'She became a real expert,' Dahl remembered, smiling, 'and without any medical knowledge at all – just persevering, with common sense and good humour. An extraordinary achievement.'

Dahl spoke about the history of the Chest, Heart and Stroke Association at its ninetieth anniversary in 1989, emphasising the 'initiative of Valerie Eaton Griffith' for the remarkable stroke rehabilitation programme, and saying 'the results have, to put it mildly, startled the medical profession'. Dahl did not give his own role in initiating the whole scheme even a passing mention.

Films illustrating the work of the Voluntary Stroke Scheme were shown at Stroke Club meetings. In addition, a full-length movie, *The Patricia Neal Story*, covering her stroke and extraordinary recovery was made to help raise funds. With Glenda Jackson as Pat and Dirk Bogarde as Dahl, it was first shown in 1989 on Britain's ITV. Pat and Dahl continued with their fundraising efforts. She was at the forefront of the Chest, Heart and Stroke Association's 1986 National Stroke Campaign, which aimed to raise £2 million.

Between 1989 and 1992, the Chest, Heart and Stroke Association transitioned into the Stroke Association, recognising that this was now the major focus of its work, and that other charities targeted the heart and lungs. Valerie retired in 1983 and was made Honorary Vice-president of the association, along with Pat. Following Pat's death in 2010, the Stroke Association's Mo Wilkinson wrote a moving tribute to Pat and Val's work together: 'little did they realise as they stumbled through those gruelling and sometimes hilarious daily sessions that they were developing, by trial and error, a model of amateur rehabilitation that would be used in the future by thousands of stroke sufferers throughout the country.'

Tennessee Hillbillies Don't Conk That Easy

A glitzy gala dinner in aid of the Brain Injured Children's Charity at the Waldorf Astoria hotel in New York would mark Pat's return to the world of show business. Dahl had accepted the invitation on her behalf, volunteering that she would give the key speech at what became 'An Evening with Patricia Neal'. This was in February 1967, just two years after her devastating stroke. The cause of brain-injured children was close to their hearts after all their experiences with Theo.

In the months running up to the event, Pat was avoiding the whole thing.

'You'd better get on with it,' Dahl warned her. 'If you make a botch of it, it'll be curtains for you. All those film moguls in the audience will just say, "Well, that's it, she's through."'

With a few weeks to go, Pat mustered the energy to start rehearsing with Val's help.

'The old pro smelled the smell of battle once again,' Dahl recalled, 'and she sprang to life.'

After a dress rehearsal at St Martin's, the stately home where Val lived with her sister and father, they set off for New York.

At the dinner, Val gave a short introductory speech. She described the rehabilitation work with Pat, how they had struggled to get her talking properly, to move away from her pet phrases, with everything described as either *very good* or *evil*. Then it was Pat's turn. The thundering applause and standing ovation of the fourteen hundred people that welcomed her to the stage was like 'a warming blanket of love'. The guest list at this seventy-five-dollars-a-ticket event included Leonard Bernstein, Joan Crawford, Yul Brynner, Rock Hudson, Paul Newman, Alistair Cooke, Mel Brooks and her good friend Anne Bancroft.

'I thank you. I thank you. I thank you,' Pat began. 'I hope what happened to me never happens to any of you. It was *evil.*' This last was not meant to be part of the speech; it just slipped out, but to tremendous laughter. The rest of the speech was easy. Pat thanked the neurosurgeon Dr Carton, who performed the operation to save her life. 'I know very well that the doctor thought I would conk out in the middle of it. But Tennessee hillbillies don't conk that easy.' Again there was great laughter. Dahl had borrowed the phrase from a family friend, who was amazed at Pat's recovery. As people applauded the end of her speech, with cheering and weeping, Pat knew she had got her life back, and once again found a purpose. Having performed in front of all these people, she realised that a return to films might just be possible after all.

A few weeks later she was at the Oscars in Hollywood, presenting the award for the Best Foreign Language Film. The prolonged standing ovation that welcomed her was said to have cost forty thousand dollars in lost airtime revenue. From footage of the occasion you can see the mild sequelae of her stroke as she moves across the stage and is helped down the steps by Bob Hope: she has a slight limp, walking with reduced right arm swing, and there is a subtle facial asymmetry. Her brief speech announcing the winners is slightly laboured.

Pat's return to the world of show business would be complete in October 1968, when her first feature film after the illness, *The Subject was Roses*, premiered in New York. Again it was Dahl who pushed her into it. She needed to make another film for her own sake, he felt, otherwise she would never know the limits of her capacities; she would condemn herself to a smaller life than she had before the stroke. Pat had six months to prepare for filming. Rehabilitation continued in Great Missenden with Val, but there was no need for made up games: they had a script on which to work.

Val joined Pat in Hollywood where they rehearsed the lines the night before each day's shooting. This did not always go smoothly. One scene had to be shot twenty-seven times, and some of the monologues were especially challenging. But Pat was encouraged to hear she had struggled no more than Marilyn Monroe, who was notorious for difficulties with her lines. Dahl joined them on the set occasionally, and clearly took great pride in his wife's achievements: 'Marvellous, really quite marvellous.'

'I have this theory about Pat's speech recovery,' Dahl told me one evening when we had been discussing current treatments for stroke patients. 'You know how a baby with a left hemiplegia learns to use the right side of its brain for speech – it's called *shifted sinestral*, isn't it?'

'Yes, that's right. There is enough neural plasticity for the right side to take over the key language functions.'

'Well, I think with the pressure we put on Pat's brain, six hours a day, it reacted the same way: slowly, subconsciously, her brain switched the speech centres from the damaged left side to the uninjured right.' He could see I looked doubtful. 'Why not?' he laughed. 'It may sound like a crazy notion, but the world is full of crazy things.' I had to agree with that.

Dahl told me about a plan he had devised to test his hypothesis: the neuroradiologists would inject a little anaesthetic up Pat's left carotid artery. 'If her words started slowing we would know that her speech was still controlled by that side of the brain; if not we would repeat the experiment up the right carotid to prove the speech centre had shifted to the right.' I couldn't argue with his logic, and in fact it was a procedure sometimes used before neurosurgery to help localise key brain functions. But, perhaps not surprisingly, when Dahl suggested his 'nifty little test' to Pat she replied with 'two words I would not like to repeat.'

This separation of different language functions between the left and right side of the brain leads to some fascinating neurological syndromes, with bizarre consequences. Not long ago I saw one such patient whose problems would certainly have appealed to Dahl.

It is a busy clinic, and I am mildly irritated to be bleeped again by switchboard, when they know I am not on call. 'Sorry to bother you again, Dr Solomon. I have a Dr Johnson on the phone for you, and she wondered if she could have a quick word. She thought you wouldn't mind her being put through.'

'Tom, I'm really sorry to bother you. I've got this patient with me, he's a businessman, forty-two; we rarely see him. Says he woke up this morning feeling a bit odd and then found he couldn't read the newspaper. Drove himself down here, no problem. Everything else is fine. Examination is normal. Eyes are fine. But he still says he can't read anything I put in front of him. It's very odd. I was going to put it all down to stress – there's a big takeover at work – and tell him to have a few days off, but we so rarely see him ... I don't know ... Could it be an unusual migraine?'

'Is he there now?'

'Yes he's just waiting outside.'

'Bring him back in, and give him a pen ...' I waited a few moments.

'OK, he's here now.'

'Ask him to write something down, anything ...' I held on whilst the instruction was passed over.

'OK, he's just done it, no problem.'

'Now ask him to read it back to you ...' I could hear him in the background, struggling.

'He says he can't. He knows what it says, because he just wrote it – *I had cornflakes for breakfast* – but he says he can't actually make sense of the letters. It's just a series of lines, and squiggles.'

'Yes,' I declare, 'thought so! *Alexia without agraphia.* You'd better send him in. But don't let him drive.' And sure enough, his MRI scan, which we arrange the next day, shows a small stroke in the corpus callosum, the bundle of neurons that connect the two halves of the brain. This means he can write normally, which is motor control of the hand. He can also see the words he has just created, because the neural pathways from the eyes to the visual cortex at the back of his head are intact. However, his right visual cortex cannot send this information to the language areas on the left side of the brain, because of the damaged corpus collosum, and so the lines and squiggles cannot be interpreted and 'read'. Thankfully this patient improved over a few days.

It is cases like this that make neurology such a satisfying medical art: the ability, based on a few words of history from the patient, to diagnose the condition and pinpoint exactly where the lesion is, and what has caused it. Sometimes you don't even need the history. Just watching how a patient walks, or their posture, or face can be enough. A famous neurologist in London used to get through dozens more patients in clinic than his colleagues, because he didn't waste time on the *niceties*. If he could make the diagnosis, he would just crack on, barely pausing even to say hello. He was once gazing out of the window, and saw a stooped patient shuffling slowly across the hospital car park towards his clinic. Making the diagnosis immediately, he called out to them through the open window, 'Are you coming to see Dr H——? Don't bother – no need. I'll write to your doctor. Bye-bye!'

Roses

By 1967, Patricia Neal's walking had improved considerably, although she still had a mild limp. Dahl's limp, from his war injuries and operations, became more noticeable as the years went on. Farrell describes how when they walked together with Pat on Dahl's left their shoulders bumped every other step; if Pat was on his right they came apart at the top like callipers. Pat's greatest anxiety after the stroke was its effect on her ability to remember names and lines, whilst Dahl's concerns were over her judgement and morale. They were both agreed, though, that the stroke had not affected her abilities of empathy and expression, which were key to her acting. Indeed, Dahl thought the stroke added to her range of life experiences, just as Theo's accident and Olivia's death had done; these gave a depth to her acting, which younger, less experienced performers could not match.

When *The Subject was Roses* was released in 1968, the reviewers appeared to agree. She received great critical acclaim. The performance would have been 'worth waiting a decade for', said *Time* magazine, 'she no longer indicates suffering, she defines it.'

Pat won another Oscar nomination for the film. Dahl was keen to ensure her career did not stall. He wrote the screenplay and arranged financing for *The Night Digger*, in which Pat had a starring role. It was based on the novel *Nest in a Falling*

Tree, in which a recovered stroke victim falls in love with a maniac. You can see why Dahl felt it would work for Pat. She received many honours, including the 1968 Heart of the Year award from American President Lyndon B. Johnson, and she even had a rose named after her. The same honour would be accorded to Dahl in 2016, as part of the hundredth-anniversary celebrations of his birth.

Dahl wrote a television documentary in 1970, *Stroke Counter Stroke*, to help educate brain-injured people and their families about rehabilitation; Pat and Val were sent off to Hollywood to make it. Over the next few years, she was invited to all sorts of conferences and meetings on both sides of the Atlantic to talk about her stroke and recovery. In America the intensive approach to stroke rehabilitation initiated by Dahl was introduced through the Patricia Neal Therapy Extension Programme. The Patricia Neal Rehabilitation Centre opened in Knoxville Tennessee in 1978 and thrives to this day. Pat visited it every year until her death in 2010, aged eighty-four. She remained forever grateful for Dahl's initiative after her stroke. As she wrote in *As I Am*, 'Roald the slave driver, Roald the bastard, Roald the Rotten' had thrown her back into the deep water, where she belonged.

Shattered Vows

'We liked to think that she had recovered one hundred per cent, you know,' Dahl told me with a wry smile, 'but she hadn't. She changed ... That was the problem. She got her speech back, and her walking, and her Hollywood career. She could act, all right. But she had changed as a person.'

At his London Club Pat would disturb nearby diners, asking whether they were enjoying their food, before choosing her own. Meeting new people, she would ask them embarrassing questions – were they a virgin? Had they ever had an abortion? It had always preyed on her mind, since having her own, and it was one of a few big regrets in her life. Indeed, during her most morose moments she wondered if all the troubles she and her family suffered were a punishment for this.

Others were aware of a change in Pat's personality after the brain injury. Susan Denson, one of their nannies, noticed she had become vindictive particularly towards their longstanding housekeeper, who soon handed in her notice. Pat's nephew thought she was no longer so openly demonstrative and affectionate, but more obsessive.

The journalist Farrell noted that after Pat's stroke she was certainly approachable, if not effusive; he felt she was terribly frank and direct, giving answers to questions that one did not dare even ask. These disinhibited behaviours were clearly a sign of frontal lobe damage, more striking than the subtle changes that Dahl perhaps suffered following his plane crash.

Pat noticed some personality changes in herself: 'Nothing makes me nervous,' she observed before collecting the award from President Johnson. 'It's not right.' Even when she was on a plane that was in difficulties and the passengers and crew feared a crash landing, she laughed and joked, asking for Martinis so they could toast all the people they would leave behind. During her rehabilitation she noticed that she did not have any abstract ideas, at one stage complaining that she had not had any dreams since the stroke.

'Not *one dream*. I guess I just don't have a brain left to dream with.' Farrell, who was eating with the family, noted that she laughed briefly to herself. 'What can you do to make yourself dream?' She went on, 'It's sad not to dream. I would sincerely like to have some dreams again.' The journalist noticed that Dahl was uncorking a fresh bottle of Beaujolais, and appeared not to be listening. But one cannot help wondering whether as he heard Pat's complaint and fiddled with the bottle an idea didn't begin to form.

> *'If you is really wanting to know what I am doing in your village,' the BFG said, 'I is blowing a dream into the bedroom of those children.'*
>
> *'Blowing a dream?' Sophie said. 'What do you mean?'*
>
> *'I is a dream-blowing giant,' the BFG said. '... I is scuddling away to other places to blow dreams into the bedrooms of sleeping children. Nice dreams. Lovely golden dreams. Dreams that is giving the dreamers a happy time.'*
>
> *'Now hang on a minute,' Sophie said. 'Where do you get these dreams?'*
>
> *'I collect them,' the BFG said, waving an arm towards all the rows and rows of bottles on the shelves. 'I has billions of them.'*

Dahl remained married to Pat for nearly twenty years after her stroke, but the relationship had changed, and they were divorced in 1983. He'd grown increasingly close to Felicity 'Liccy' Crosland, a family friend with three daughters of her own, and married her later that year. She was more than twenty years his junior, and the 'love of his life'. He told me, with tears in his eyes 'how wonderful marriage can be' and implored me not to marry too young.

Liccy herself came from a medical family. 'My grandfather was a doctor; my uncle was a doctor; my father was a doctor and the Dean, and my mother was a nurse. And then I married a writer who wanted to be a doctor.'

Liccy's mother was a descendant of one of the ladies-in-waiting to Elizabeth I, who had married Sir Walter Raleigh. Her father was Professor

Alphonsus Ligouri D'Abreu, CBE, a cardiac surgeon and Dean of the Faculty of Medicine at Birmingham University. D'Abreu's family hailed from Mangalore in India, which had been under Portugese and then British rule. This mixture of Asian and English ancestry, perhaps with some Portugese blood too, might perhaps explain Liccy's striking beauty and vaguely oriental features, with olive skin, almond eyes and black hair. Whenever she came into Dahl's hospital room, he would immediately perk up. The warmth that radiated between them was almost palpable. This was more than fifteen years after they first met, but at times I felt as though I was with a couple of teenagers newly in love, and would look away with embarrassment.

I noticed Dahl had nodded off to sleep with a gentle smile on his face. Even talking about Liccy was a comfort for him. We had been chatting for hours, and I was very tired myself. It was nearly six in the morning and a few birds had started chirping. It would be getting light soon. I tidied a few items on his bedside table, and moved his book and reading glasses into reach, in case he woke again. Then I went for some rest.

As I dozed, I pondered what Dahl had been saying about Patricia and her stroke, the hints he had dropped. Back then I'd had no idea how much of it was true. Like his comments about the valve for hydrocephalus, it all seemed so fantastical, the work of a great raconteur, surely. It is only today, having investigated more fully, that I realise he was not exaggerating at all. Just as he had with the Wade-Dahl-Till valve, Dahl had once again catalysed events that would have a major impact on treatment for a neurological disease around the world. Again, his instinctive feeling that there must be *something* he could do had driven him on. The great storyteller's desire to write the narrative even before the plot unfolded, to predict Pat's recovery even as she lay critically ill, to envision her return to the screen even as she struggled to speak, had become self-fulfilling. The force of his belief had made it happen.

And again, even though as a schoolboy, and through his writing, Dahl had fantasised about changing the world, about being the great inventor, the magnificent benefactor who helped thousands across the planet, when all this happened, he did not recognise it in himself.

Apparently Dahl could be proud, boastful, arrogant and argumentative when discussing his writing. But when talking about these major medical breakthroughs he was happy to minimise his role, modestly downplaying his critical part, and giving the credit to others. In the invention and production of the groundbreaking Wade-Dahl-Till valve he described himself merely as a go-between, just a middle-man who carried messages between the engineer and the neurosurgeon, when we have seen how, really, this valve would never have come about without his inventiveness and determination.

For the revolutionary approach to stroke recovery he was happy to give all the credit to Valerie Eaton Griffith. He ignored the fact that without him none of this medical marvel would have happened: it was Dahl who pushed Pat to try and speak when others thought he was being cruel; it was Dahl who instigated the intensive treatment, the roster of amateur teachers, when others thought he was overdoing it; it was Dahl who pushed and pushed and pushed Pat until she was back where she belonged on the silver screen; it was Dahl who first outlined this new rehabilitation approach in his letter sent to thousands of patients. And it was Dahl who encouraged Valerie, a modest retired shop manager, to capture it all in her book, and pursue the vision to develop such stroke services across the world.

In *Boy: Tales from Childhood*, Dahl teasingly notes:

When writing about oneself, one must strive to be truthful. Truth is more important than modesty. I must tell you, therefore, that it was I and I alone who had the idea for the great and daring Mouse Plot. We all have our moments of brilliance and glory, and this was mine.

Yet when it came to his medical interventions, Dahl allowed modesty to all but hide the truth about his moments of brilliance and glory. Not only was Roald Dahl's medicine marvellous, it was also marvellously modest.

'Never do anything by halves if you want to get away with it. Be outrageous. Go the whole hog.'

– Matilda

PART FIVE

NO BOOK EVER ENDS

Chapter 15

Rusting to Pieces

Over the decades Dahl's productivity grew and grew, like the giant peach that had started it all. For him there was no magic powder, just the regular couple of hours every morning and afternoon spent in his hut. Whilst the 1970s saw a balance of adult short stories and children's books, by the 1980s Dahl was writing almost exclusively for children, producing some of his best-loved work, including *The Twits, George's Marvellous Medicine, The BFG, The Witches* and *Matilda*.

'In my little work hut I enter a dreamlike state,' he explained to me, 'sinking back into childhood. I really have a six- or seven-year-old's mind in this ancient body.' He grimaced as he tried to get comfortable on the pillows. 'I have ideas swirling around in my head throughout the day, in the bath, out in the garden, everywhere. The only time I am not dreaming is when I go up to my club in London to gamble – blackjack. You have to concentrate then. That's why I go; takes my mind off the work. I can't manage more than two hours writing at a time. I don't think you can focus, and anyway my back couldn't stand it.'

Although Dahl had suffered severe facial and head wounds in the plane crash, it was the back injuries that caused him lifelong problems. 'An irregular, short-long, short-long limping gait which reminded one somehow of the swing of a maladjusted pendulum ...' Dahl could have been writing about himself, when he described a fictional RAF pilot in his adult novel *Some Time Never: A Fable for Supermen*, published in 1948. This futuristic book was notable for being the first ever novel about nuclear war, and included some extraordinary descriptions of biological warfare. However, it was not well-received by the critics and Dahl rarely spoke about it.

By 1944, four years after the crash, Dahl was 'hobbling ... like an old man' and had the first of many back operations. He was living in America at the time and his wealthy friend Charles Marsh paid for the removal of an intervertebral disc.

Things did not go well in the pre-operative investigations. This was before magnetic resonance imaging, and the only way to examine the spine was with a myelogram: 'I had a ruddy great needle stuck into my back, and that dreadful lipiodol stuff squirted in.' Lipiodol was an oily contrast medium used to outline the spinal cord and vertebral discs on X-rays. However, as Dahl discovered, it can occasionally irritate the meningeal membranes causing a painful meningitis with 'great headaches and pains all over the body, especially in the neck'. The medical team eventually managed to extract the oil under general anaesthetic, and Dahl began to feel better.

Some Sort of Dead Matter

Dahl continued to need back procedures in the years ahead. These included an emergency removal of another intervertebral disc in Oxford in 1978, following which he developed a painful lumbar abscess. His favourite nurse from the Chiltern Clinic, Rosemary Higgs, visited Gipsy House regularly to change the dressing. She became a great friend, and remembers Dahl bringing her some 'fantastic wine' one Christmas, with the strict instruction that it was for her and the family only, and should not be shared with any guests. In a circularity that Dahl would have loved, Rosemary's grandson Jack Costello was the aspiring young actor who played the first ever Charlie Bucket, when the musical *Charlie and the Chocolate Factory* opened in the West End in 2013.

1978 saw yet another cerebral insult to a member of the extended Dahl family: Liccy's daughter Charlotte was involved in a terrible car accident in Scotland, being thrown through the window and sustaining a skull fracture. Liccy went straight away to Glasgow, where Charlotte was under Samuel Galbraith, the leading neurosurgeon who later became an MP. When Dahl was visiting during her convalescence, he expressed to Galbraith his concerns that Charlotte had not moved her bowels for two weeks.

'Well, I shouldn't worry,' the rather pompous surgeon told Dahl condescendingly. 'The Guinness World Record is forty-two days.'

'Is that so?' Dahl retorted. 'I am glad I wasn't there when it manifested.'

Charlotte eventually made a good recovery, and went on to become an award-winning interior designer.

Despite Rosemary Higgs's ministrations, the wound in Dahl's back would not heal. As he recorded in a detailed note headed: 'Patient Roald Dahl, Male, 70 years', a sinogram was arranged by a microbiologist at Northwick Park Hospital to investigate further. The radio-opaque dye was injected deep into the abscess and the X-rays revealed a 'long, branching sinus travelling down past the spine ... into the pelvic region just short of the top of the bowel'. Dahl was treated with intravenous antibiotics for a month, but was worried this would not be enough, feeling sure there must be a 'foreign body or some sort of dead matter' providing the focus of infection.

He was right.

A procedure by 'the finest orthopaedic surgeon around' found an area of spinal necrosis within which there was indeed a foreign body, a small piece of loose bone containing a cavity that was presumed to be the source of the persistent infections. Things still did not settle, and Dahl was back on 'the old mixture of antibiotics' to treat the *Actinomyces israelii* bacteria they had earlier isolated.

Again Dahl felt better for a while, but as he wrote to the microbiologist, 'I am unwilling to go on like this for the remaining years of my life and I'm prepared to try drastic new measures to clear up the situation.' Dahl's proposal was to attack the sinus by syringing the antibiotic mixture down its whole length, using radio-opaque fluid so they could check on progress. 'I recognise this would be on an experimental basis. I would agree to do it on that basis. I have had lots of experiments done to me before.' Once the job was done, Dahl suggested they might syringe in a sclerosant like that used for varicose veins to seal up the sinus. 'If you finally succeeded you will be able to write another paper on the treatment of a six inch long congenital sinus. I would gladly write an appreciation at the end of it for you,' Dahl concluded, 'so what do you say?'

All these procedures required a lot of hanging around in hospital. One morning Dahl was told he would need to wait a couple of hours for his next investigation. He looked out of the window and noticed a primary school nearby. He changed from his hospital gown into his 'raincoat, flowerpot hat, and shoes, and shuffled off to knock on the door'. The school secretary opened it to see what looked like a giant tramp on the doorstep.

'Can I help?' she asked in a snooty voice.

'Is your headmistress in?' came the reply. 'Please tell her that Roald Dahl is here.'

Once the secretary and headmistress had got over their shock, Dahl spent 'a wonderful couple of hours' going round all the classrooms telling the children his latest stories.

In addition to exploring all the conventional therapeutic approaches, Dahl was also happy to experiment with alternative medicines, such as a sugar solution to be rubbed on the wound to help healing. In 1980 he sent a sample of hair to be assessed by a proponent of Radionics that he was told 'lies outside the field of orthodox medicine [and seeks] to find the underlying cause of diseases and disharmony and not simply the cause'. Dahl was told that his problems were the 'result of accumulation of poisons and toxins in the body. You should stop taking ordinary salt replacing it with brine salt and using cider vinegar for salad dressings instead of ordinary vinegar'.

According to Ophelia, he was always interested in unorthodox approaches, 'but I don't think he took them too seriously'. Radionics was invented in the early 1900s by an American doctor, Albert Adams, who claimed to be able to diagnose any condition using his Dynomizer instruments, which he leased out at a hefty price. Treatment could be administered using the Oscilloclast. It all sounds like fantastical nonsense from one of Dahl's stories, but it certainly worked wonders for Adams, who became a millionaire.

'Eleven altogether!' Dahl told me proudly one evening, 'I've had eleven major operations. The big facial job in the war; three total hip replacements, that's including one revision, of course; the bowel; and six laminectomies from the back injuries.'

I discovered years later that he had collected macabre mementos from some of the procedures in his famous writing hut. Liccy had invited me, Rachel and our four girls to visit Gipsy House one summer. The hut had been preserved shrine-like, exactly as Dahl had left it when he'd made his last visit to the John Radcliffe Hospital in 1990. Even cigarette ash and the shavings from his pencil lay unswept on the floor. It was quite eerie, as if Dahl had just popped out to check on his onions, and would be back in a minute. The large winged armchair where he sat and wrote had a hole cut in the centre of its back cushion to ease the pressure on his spine. In front of the chair lay Dahl's old travelling trunk – he would prop his feet up on it to try to get comfortable.

On the adjacent table lay all sorts of curios and souvenirs from his life. There was a jar with shavings from one of his intervertebral discs, a testament to all the procedures he had undergone. The head of one of his femurs lay next to it: 'the biggest hip bone the surgeon had ever seen', according to Dahl. An artificial steel hip, which had replaced the original before itself being removed, was wedged into the drawer handle of a filing cabinet, making it easier to open. Ironically the table also had a model Hurricane fighter plane, a reminder of how he got the injuries in the first place, as well as a 'star of the desert' stone, picked up in the Libyan Desert. There was also the large silver ball made of foil wrappers from the two-penny chocolate bars Dahl used to eat every day whilst working at Shell – a nod to the lifelong fascination with chocolate that led to the classic *Charlie and the Chocolate Factory*. I was horrified when Eva, our littlest, grabbed it to see how heavy it was.

'No, don't worry,' said Liccy, encouraging us all to feel its weight, and examined the other curios, before gently replacing each back in its spot.

All these artefacts, along with the entire contents of the hut, are now carefully protected behind glass at the Roald Dahl Museum and Story Centre.

Country of the Blind

Despite his many ailments – the aches and pains and back trouble resulting from his plane crash, and the bowel problems, which were perhaps a result of tropical infections – it was not until he was in his mid seventies that Dahl's aging body finally began to fall apart.

'My body may be rusting to pieces,' he wrote, 'but my mind is something absolutely separate and is as young as ever.'

In the summer of 1989 he developed blurred vision in his left eye, and was found to have a branch retinal vein occlusion, a blockage of one of the blood vessels at the back of the eye.

'In the country of the blind the one-eyed man is king,' Dahl wrote to his ophthalmologist in August, 'but England is not that country. So what do I do about my left eye? It is uncomfortable walking about, and reading and writing with one eye, I have to focus. It is also mentally disturbing ... what shall I do ... ? I am a bit in the dark ...'

Although such thrombosis can sometimes be a harbinger of more severe disease, like diabetes or hypertension, or even a hidden malignancy, Dahl's blood tests were normal and no cause could be found. There was no established treatment for the condition, but Dahl was keen to embark on an experimental therapy that was being used in London. Some doctors believed that in retinal vein occlusion there was not a complete obstruction but a partial blockage, with reduced flow of blood. People with very viscous, thick blood are more likely to get occlusion, and so it was postulated that reducing the blood's thickness might help the flow through the vessels. Since the red blood cells are one of the main contributors to blood viscosity, the experimental treatment involved replacing a pint or two of blood with saline solution to reduce the number of red blood cells in circulation.

Dahl 'was whistled off to Saint Thomas's' for the treatment. His haematocrit, the percentage of red cells in the blood, was reduced from 44 to 34. But Dahl found this too much of a drop. He was now anaemic, and feeling generally lousy. They experimented over the next couple of months, with Dahl, as always, taking charge of his care.

'We have established that I can tolerate a count of 38 and that's what we wanted to know,' he reported in December. 'There is now beginning to be a very slight improvement in the left eye. I can actually find my way around the house and garden with the good eye closed. Things are of course blurry but as I said there is a definite improvement. I must continue with your treatment.'

'You are aware bloodletting is one of the oldest treatments known to medicine,' I teased Dahl. 'This was hardly a revolutionary therapy.'

'Well, it seemed to be working, whatever it was.'

Venesection was practised by the ancient Egyptians from about 1000 BC, and then spread to the Romans and Greeks. The Louvre in Paris has a famous vase from the fifth century BC depicting the Greek physician Iatros – the healer – bleeding a patient. Today we use the term iatrogenic – literally, 'caused by the healer' – to describe illnesses due to medical interventions. '*Primum non nocere*,' instructed Hippocrates – first do no harm – and every other medical practitioner has been taught this since then.

When bloodletting was first used, disease was thought to be the result of an imbalance of the four humours – blood, phlegm, black bile and yellow bile – which were related to the four Greek classical elements of air, water, earth and fire. To balance the humours physicians would remove excess blood, induce vomiting with an emetic, or use a diuretic to induce urination. Hippocrates thought menstruation purged women of bad humours, and so bleeding a patient through bloodletting would achieve the same effect. Diseases were thought to be caused by blood stagnating in the limbs; this was nearly two millennia before English physician William Harvey showed that blood circulates through the body. By the Middle Ages the theories of the four humours had been abandoned, but bloodletting itself was still thought to be useful. The treatment would be recommended by physicians, and the barber surgeons would perform it; the red-and-white pole outside the barbers persists to this day as a reminder of the blood that flowed and the bandages needed afterwards. Venesection is also still used today for just a few conditions where there is a good rationale and evidence of benefit. In retinal vein thrombosis it was experimental treatment and ultimately has not been taken up widely, but for other conditions including polycythaemia and haemochromatosis it is a well-established therapy.

Jamaica Inn

With his vision apparently improving and his blood count held steady by regular venesection, Dahl took Ophelia, Liccy and her youngest daughter, Lorina, on holiday to Jamaica in January 1990. Like her mother, twenty-six-year-old Lorina had a strong artistic bent. 'Loopy', as she was known in the family, was a fashion editor at *Harper's* magazine, and had 'her own, very original avant-garde style'.

The family stayed at Dahl's old haunt the Jamaica Inn, which had been founded by Charles Marsh nearly fifty years previously. Dahl basked in the sunshine, making up fanciful stories about the other hotel guests, and teasing Lorina about her stylish clothes and unique outlook. Ever the individual, Lorina loved monkeys, and had kept one in her tall, narrow London house, inspiring Dahl to write *The Giraffe, The Pelly and Me*.

Although Dahl felt his health was bearing up, Lorina was troubled by headaches and buzzing in her ear. A local doctor in Jamaica thought her symptoms were due to an ear infection. When things still had not settled on their return to London, another diagnosed labyrinthitis, an inflammation of the inner ear usually cause by a virus. She had already had a skull X-ray, which was normal. An osteopath even tried to treat the headaches, but with no success.

Lorina was not one to make a fuss; Dahl sometimes called her 'the Burmese Cat' because of her calm inscrutable demeanour. She headed off to South Africa to supervise a photo shoot for her magazine, with a suitcase full of painkillers. Apartheid was just ending, and it was an exciting time to be visiting. Dahl meanwhile had looked up everything on labyrinthitis to see what might be done, and had discovered that cranberry juice was meant to be helpful. The photoshoot over, Lorina was on her way home to London. At the airport in Johannesburg, where she and the *Harper's* team had stopped over, she began to feel a lot worse. Several of the team had upset stomachs and, thinking they must all have food poisoning, no one was too alarmed when Lorina started vomiting. They were more concerned when she needed to lie down. Once she became unresponsive she was rushed to hospital.

At Gipsy House, Ophelia was home from university with Dahl and Liccy, and expecting to hear from Lorina the next day.

'Loopy's back tomorrow,' said Liccy just as the telephone rang late that evening. Ophelia answered to an unfamiliar voice, a work colleague of Lorina who was phoning from South Africa and wanted to talk to her father. She gave him the phone.

'You'd better talk to her ...' Dahl said into the receiver, realising it was some news about Lorina and wanting to pass the phone to Liccy. Then suddenly he stopped.

'I watched my father's face as he held the phone,' Ophelia recalled. 'He said nothing. His mouth opened and he raised his scared eyes to me.' Both she and Liccy knew immediately something dreadful had happened. Dahl listened carefully.

'Thank you. Goodbye.' He finally put the phone down, and turned to his wife 'Lic, Lorina's dead.' She had died that same evening at the hospital.

'I sometimes have moments of wondering about all these calamities striking the brain,' Dahl said to me quietly. 'Theo, Olivia, Pat, now poor Lorina. But I can't really believe that there is any doom, or curse on the family … I think it is just a terrible series of coincidences, don't you?'

I thought about all the tragedies. Although some would see a great mystical significance to it all, I had to agree with Dahl that it was just bad luck; each disaster had its own explanation – a pram being smashed … measles attacking the brain … a weakened blood-vessel wall … an abnormal cell growing to form a tumour – there was nothing supernatural linking them all together.

'As a child, you avoid the cracks in the pavement, the black lines on a carpet,' Dahl continued, 'but you realise it makes no difference.'

'I suppose it depends how you look at things. In Mozambique I was talking to a woman whose child had died of malaria. She was convinced it was due to a curse on her family. I tried to explain: "It's not a curse; it's the mosquito that bit your child and injected the malaria parasite."'

'"Yes –" she gripped my arm – "but what made the mosquito bite *my* child?"'

With Lorina's death the family was once again thrown into turmoil. For Liccy the loss of her daughter was almost unbearable. Dahl had been through it, and so perhaps understood the grief, but somehow he seemed unable to console her, and adopted a practical, pragmatic manner. Lorina was buried at St Peter and St Paul's Church in Great Missenden, her gravestone adorned with the carving of a monkey Quentin Blake had drawn.

When Liccy said she wanted to be buried next to her daughter in Great Missenden, Dahl bought the next six plots for all the family. Although the church in Little Missenden, where Olivia was buried, might have seemed the obvious choice for the family graves, it had been out of favour for years, since the vicar decided to build a splendid new vicarage that took up half the graveyard. Dahl had tried to fight it, creating a petition with the villagers, and contacting lawyers, but he discovered that in matters such as this, the Church of England is a law unto itself.

His youngest daughter, Lucy, felt he had an 'inability to be able to withstand the pain of Lorina's death'. After Olivia's death, her father had 'made an unconscious decision not to open his heart … Olivia was the one thing he never spoke about – ever'. Lorina's death seemed to bring to the surface all these haunting memories that had been buried for decades.

When Olivia died in 1962, Dahl initially gave up the will to live, as his bereaved father had a generation earlier. But after a few terrible weeks, he packaged his grief away, and since then had battled on, fighting every challenge, including Theo's hydrocephalus, Pat's devastating stroke and his own ill health.

But to the family it seemed that the tragic and sudden death of Lorina had been the final straw. Dahl could keep going no more.

I have clung for so long now that I cannot hold on much longer. Soon I will have to let go. It is like hanging over the edge of a cliff, that's what it is like; and I've been hanging on too long now, holding on to the top of the cliff with my fingers, not being able to pull myself back up, with my fingers getting more and more tired, beginning to hurt and to ache, so that I know that sooner or later I will have to let go

– *'Death of an Old Old Man'*

These words of Charlie the fighter pilot facing death in World War II, written by Dahl many years earlier, perhaps best reflect how he was feeling.

When Dahl first told me about Lorina, late one night in Oxford, something puzzled me. Cancer, especially in the brain, almost never causes sudden death in someone who has not already been diagnosed. There is something poignantly tragic about dying so far from home, so suddenly, and I thought perhaps Dahl was just conveying the essence of a quick and unexpected death. He could see I was thinking it over, and he seemed about to say more, then hesitated and changed the subject.

'Dahl was angry with the doctors about the misdiagnosis,' Liccy told me later, 'and angry with himself.' Somehow he felt that despite his medical acumen she had slipped through his care. 'But we don't think it would have made any difference,' she added quietly.

Back in the 1990s the prognosis for malignant brain tumours was terrible, and it is not that much better today. But over the years, the more patients with brain tumours I have seen, the more Lorina's death has nagged away at me; it just didn't make sense. Without wishing to pry too much I mentioned my anxiety to Ophelia. She promised to try to help.

'I saw this patient yesterday afternoon, 25 March 1990, approximately 45 minutes after she collapsed ...' So began a rather chilling letter sent to Dahl by the neurosurgeon in Johannesburg who had been involved in Lorina's care. Ophelia had just found it among a box of correspondence and emailed it straight to me.

'The patient was taken for a scan and whilst this was happening the patient collapsed ... the patient was brain dead by the time I saw her.'

The letter confirmed that Lorina had undergone some imaging that had indeed shown a tumour in her head. However, it was not a malignant cancer at all – it was a large ependymoma. Compared with malignant tumours, these are more benign, and the surgeons usually try to remove them. The scan had shown the five-centimetre mass was reducing the normal flow of spinal fluid, thus causing obstructive hydrocephalus similar to Theo's. This was the cause of Lorina's headaches. Eventually, like a ping-pong ball blocking a sink, the tumour had completely stopped flow through the third ventricle, causing the brain to rapidly swell. When this occurs, the vital centres in the brainstem that control breathing and the heart rate become crushed, and death follows very suddenly. An ependymoma is a thus a rare but well-recognised cause of a sudden and unexpected death.

The letter from the neurosurgeon ended: 'According to all the clinical cryteria [sic] the patient was brain dead and all further measures were stopped. Yours truly …'

This was such a cold clinical account I felt a shiver go down my spine. I was staggered that any doctor could write a letter like this; not to mention Lorina's name, or express any sympathy or sorrow seemed callous beyond belief. At the top of the letter there was faint handwriting that I recognised, and as I slowly deciphered the words I was overcome by sorrow: *growing for 18 months non-malignant slow growing operable always.* It was clear that Dahl had completely appreciated the significance of the scan.

It seemed cruelly ironic that Dahl, who had worked hard for imaging machines to be made widely available across the country, had not pushed for Lorina to be scanned. The doctors had said it was labyrinthitis and he had no reason to believe otherwise. Of course even with surgery there is no guarantee of the outcome. Patients can be left in a devastating condition, and sometimes a sudden death can seem like a mercy; this at least provided some comfort to Liccy. But I don't think Dahl saw it like that. I remembered his sad, heavy smile as he told me about 'Loopy', and his hesitancy about saying more. I could understand at last why he had been so heartbroken.

A Bit Off-colour

By April 1990, Dahl was growing increasingly weak, and it was clear that his own health was failing. He had been bled regularly for months to keep his red blood cell count low; now the count remained low without any bleeds. He was developing anaemia. Dahl's GP, Dr Streule, admitted him to a local private hospital for a top up blood transfusion, whilst investigations were underway to look for a cause. Streule recalled that he had set up the drip and planned to come back in six hours when it would be completed: blood has to be infused slowly or there can be dangerous reactions. He was therefore very surprised to be called back two hours later because the transfusion was finished; the nurses were completely perplexed trying to understand what had gone wrong.

'You speeded it up yourself, didn't you?' Streule challenged Dahl quietly as he removed the drip.

'Of course I did,' replied Dahl with a chuckle. 'And it's not done me any harm, has it?'

Although Streule could treat the anaemia with transfusions, he told Dahl he did not have a clue as to what was causing it. Dahl appreciated his honesty. The general physician at the local hospital also seemed to be struggling to find the cause, and so Streule referred Dahl to one of the country's leading haematologists – Professor Sir David Weatherall in Oxford. Weatherall had trained in medicine at the University of Liverpool, and did a haematology research fellowship at Johns Hopkins, Baltimore, before becoming Chair of the Nuffield Department of Medicine in Oxford in 1974. He was one of the first to realise the potential of modern molecular genetic approaches to improve clinical medicine, founding the Institute of Molecular Medicine and inspiring generations of clinical scientists to pursue this vision. As one of the most distinguished clinicians in the country, knighted in 1987, he was about to be appointed Regius Professor of Medicine.

'I've been a bit off-colour these last few months,' Dahl wrote in a summer newsletter for his young fans, published by Puffin, 'feeling sleepy when I shouldn't have been and without that lovely old bubbly energy that drives one to write books and drink gin and chase after girls. I could actually feel the ancient body beginning to creak a bit here and there whenever I went too fast round a corner. So I consulted the quacks … who came up with the news that I was suffering from some sort of a blood disorder known as anaemia.'

Dahl went on to explain about the bone-marrow factory that manufactures the red corpuscles in the blood, and how his had partly gone on strike. He described the blood transfusions to treat it, and how 'the quacks' could go on topping him up like this 'more or less for ever, anyway for quite a few more years. So don't put me into the grave quite yet. I usually manage to climb out again. I've done it many times before.'

The bone-marrow biopsy showed Dahl had sideroblastic anaemia caused by a myelodysplastic syndrome. There was no curative treatment for myelodysplastic syndrome, but, in addition to the regular blood transfusions, Weatherall gave Dahl some corticosteroids, which seemed to work wonders.

'Dear Professor Wolfgang Amadeus,' Dahl wrote in July to Weatherall, a great lover of Mozart, 'I have been through a few physical bad times in my life, but never have I experienced such a rapid and miraculous transition from acute unbearable pain to normality as I did last week. It was like a renaissance blooming into a state of wild euphoria. The nearest mental experience to it that I've ever had was my feelings immediately after landing in one piece at the end of the battle of Athens in 1941. Chapter 11 in *Going Solo*, which I think I gave you. Have a look at it.'

Having previously needed steel braces to support his wrists, Dahl found he could now hit golf balls from the orchard, landing 'smack into the middle of our lawn between the annex and work hut, a dicey business at the best of times ... Your genius,' he went on, 'is in discovering ways of helping patients to survive.' Dahl included with the letter a rare first edition of *James and the Giant Peach*, by way of thanks.

'The book was marvellous,' Weatherall replied in August, 'and after reading the first two paragraphs I read it from cover to cover. Presumably in every obese middle-aged male there is a young child trying to get out.' Dahl responded by promising a new book every week. He had met a great many medical people over the years, but admired Weatherall more than any, for his combination of great clinical skill and enormous academic prowess, combined with humility and modesty unusual for someone so accomplished.

The two enjoyed each other's company, and Weatherall would sometimes visit the ward at the end of the day to discuss their shared interests in literature and music: *which violin concerto was more sublime? Beethoven's in D or Mozart's 3rd*? As a birthday present, Dahl arranged for Weatherall's car to be surreptitiously removed from the hospital car park, fitted with the latest high-tech CD player, which could be pre-loaded with six discs, and returned the same day. When Weatherall drove home that evening, he couldn't understand how his car was playing such wonderful music, until he realised there was Dahl magic involved.

Dahl had experienced both private and National Health Service treatments through his many ailments. His last adult short story, 'The Surgeon', published towards the end of his life, reflected the high esteem in which he held those working for the NHS: Robert Sandy, a surgeon at the Radcliffe Infirmary in Oxford, has saved the life of a Saudi Arabian prince injured in a road traffic accident. The following day the Saudi ambassador wants to move him to a far more luxurious private hospital where he will be cared for by all manner of celebrated Harley Street surgeons. But the prince refuses to move:

> 'He says he wants only you to look after him,' the ambassador said to Robert Sandy ... 'He says you have saved his life and he has absolute faith in you.'

After his recovery, the prince tries to pay Sandy for his efforts.

'I suppose you still refuse to take a fee?' he said.

'I've never taken one yet and I don't propose to change my ways at this time of life,' Robert Sandy told him pleasantly. 'I work entirely for the National Health Service and they pay me a very fair salary ...'

'But dash it all, you saved my life,' the prince said, tapping the palms of his hands on the desk.

'I did no more than any other competent surgeon would have done,' Robert Sandy said.

Sandy refuses payment, but agrees to accept a gift from the prince's father, thinking it might be a dozen bottles of wine. When this turns out to be a large pure white diamond, Sandy is in quite a pickle. The story includes a description of an operation in theatre, as usual thoroughly researched, with some banter over the operating table, which Dahl doubtlessly borrowed from a medical guest to Gipsy House.

'He loved to have medical friends dine with us at home,' Ophelia recalled, 'and he would always be quizzing them about something: "What would happen if you swallowed an object?" he once asked Brian Higgs. "A large diamond, for example; how far would it get before it became stuck?"'

You can read 'The Surgeon' for yourself to discover the answer.

Chapter 16

The Patient

'Polycythaemia ... rubra ... vera ...' Dahl let the term roll around his mouth, as if he were savouring a good claret. 'Yes, I like that. Polycythaemia – busy, grave, important, serious; and yet rubra ... vera – a touch of colour ... lightness ... hope ...'

'Surely characters from a story,' I countered. 'Poly Cythaemia, a nasty ugly aunt with awful breath and crooked teeth; Ruby and Vera, her younger sisters, more pleasant and amenable, who try to make up for Polly's terrible ways.'

It was late one evening, and Dahl and I were discussing some of the various maladies that one encounters on the haematology ward. I'd had a good day; my malaria review, the article with Rodney Phillips, had just been accepted by the *Lancet* and would be published soon.

'The term *polycythaemia rubra vera* is actually a bit of a hybrid,' I explained to Dahl. It combines the Greek words: 'polys', too many; 'kytos', cells; 'haema', in the blood; and the Latin 'ruber' meaning red, and 'verus' meaning true, so the direct translation is *truly too many red cells in the blood*. 'Truly' because sometimes the red cell count can falsely appear to be elevated due to a reduction of the plasma fluid in the blood. The disease is also known as Osler Vaquez disease, after the French physician Louis Henri Vaquez, who first reported it towards the end of the nineteenth century, and Sir William Osler, who subsequently described its full features.

Osler, the great Victorian physician, was a hero of mine, and Dahl wanted to know more. He was born in Canada, and with others founded the famous Johns Hopkins Hospital in Baltimore before coming to Oxford as the Regius Professor of Medicine. This position was created by King Henry VIII around 1546; Osler was appointed to the post in 1904, and Sir David Weatherall was made Regius eighty-eight years later. Dahl liked the sense of continuity. Osler had many other conditions named after him, including Osler's nodes on the hand, and Osler Rendu Weber syndrome, in which there are blood-vessel abnormalities and a tendency to bleeding. But there was so much more to him than that. He essentially defined medicine the way we are still practising it today; he was the 'father of modern medicine' as many would have it. He emphasised the importance of learning at the bedside rather than in lecture theatres, and of carefully observing patients and their diseases right through to autopsy if required, rather than simply coming up with fanciful theories. He was also widely read, a prolific author and tremendous practical joker.

Egerton Y. Davis

Despite being a great physician and scientist, Osler did not take himself or anything else too seriously, and tried to see the funny side if he could. Dahl could see why I liked the fellow, and was warming to him as well.

He poured himself a small whisky. Paused. Produced a second glass from his locker, looked at me uncertainly and then placed it gently on the bedside table. Although the scotch smelt glorious I resisted the temptation.

'Osler had this alter ego,' I continued, 'Dr Egerton Y. Davis, a retired US Army surgeon, and through him came up with all sorts of mischief.'

As E. Y. Davis, Osler would write humorous or scurrilous reports for medical journals, and would sign himself into medical conferences using the pseudonym to give credence to the existence of this slightly eccentric physician. His most famous prank was in response to a publication by a colleague in the *Philadelphia Medical News* in 1884 on vaginismus; Dr Theophilus Parvin wrote about this spasmodic contraction of the vagina, which occurs in response to physical contact, especially during intercourse. Three weeks later the same journal published a report from Dr Egerton Y. Davis that described in lurid detail a case of *penis captivus*; Davis reported he had been called to the house of a gentleman who had surprised his coachman and maid by catching them *in flagrante delicto*.

> *She screamed, he struggled, and they rolled out of bed together and made frantic efforts to get apart, but without success ... When I arrived I found the man standing up and supporting the woman in his arms, and it was quite evident that his penis was tightly locked in her vagina, and any attempt to dislodge it was accompanied by much pain on the part of both. It was, indeed, a case of 'De cohesione in coitu'. I applied water, and then ice, but ineffectually, and at last sent for chloroform, a few whiffs of which sent the woman to sleep, relaxed the spasm, and released the captive penis, which was swollen, livid, and in a state of semi erection, which did not go down for several hours, and for days the organ was extremely sore.*

Osler's spoof article on *penis captivus* added confusion to the longstanding controversy about whether or not the condition really exists.

'So does it exist?' Dahl asked.

'Apparently there are a few well documented cases in the medical literature.' Dahl leaned forward to hear more. 'Of course some gentlemen have a bigger ... risk than others.' I tried not to smirk.

The article was quoted as if it were real nearly a hundred years later, in no less a publication than the *British Medical Journal*. Nowadays a very dim view is taken of such misbehaviour, and anyone attempting it risks a severe reprimand from the General Medical Council. However, a senior colleague of mine, who was rather fed up with the number of people he'd had to acknowledge at the end of a *Lancet* publication did slip in a thanks to U. T. Cobley, and got away with it.

Dahl thought Osler's spoof article was a hoot. I could see a light dancing in his eyes as he considered how he might put this delightful tale with its sexual twist to good use.

Much of Dahl's adult writing explored relationships between men and women. Initially he was intrigued by the tensions between couples who have known each a long time: in *The Way Up to Heaven* Mrs Foster has a pathological fear of being late, and her husband takes great delight in causing delays to deliberately torment her; William likes to control every aspect of his wife Mary's life in 'William and Mary', even after he has died; in 'Nunc Dimitis', a wealthy bachelor Lionel considers himself adored by his friends, especially a young lady on whom he has been doting, only to discover she has been describing him as a crashing bore. Each of these tense skirmishes ends with an unexpected twist.

Some critics, pointing to these and other Dahl short stories, accused him of being misogynistic in his writing. For example, in 'Mrs Bixby and the Colonel's Coat', he describes America as the 'land of opportunities for women': divorced or cuckolded men sit in huddles in bars bemoaning their lot and comforting each with stories; 'the wife is cunning, deceitful, and lecherous, and she is invariably up to some sort of jiggery pokery with the dirty dog'. In 'Georgy Porgy', a rather innocent vicar envies men who display 'astonishing aplomb in their dealings with the fairer sex'; the 'incredibly lascivious, stop at nothing' spinsters of the parish have their eye on him, but he cannot bear any physical contact with them.

Whilst poor Georgy is terrified of being eaten alive by these local ladies, in Dahl's next short story, 'The Visitor' published in *Playboy* in 1965, we meet for the first time Oswald Hendryks Corenlius, who was quite the opposite, described later as 'without much doubt the greatest fornicator of all time'. Oswald's life and travels are chronicled, we are told, in twenty-eight volumes of diaries. We learn of his exploits in 'The Visitor' and 'Bitch' before he gets a complete novel of his own, *My Uncle Oswald*.

> *Wherever he went, he left an endless trail of females in his wake, females ruffled and ravished beyond words, but purring like cats ... Casanova's* Memoirs *read like a Parish Magazine in comparison.*

There was quite a bit of Dahl himself in Oswald Hendryks Corenlius. Described as 'drop dead gorgeous' by his old friend Antoinette Haskell, Dahl had numerous liaisons during his bachelor days in America, keeping a 'whole stable' of women who tended to his every need.

Dahl describes Oswald as tall, well spoken and having a 'first rate intellect, an abundance of charm, and a reputation for excessive promiscuity'. Like Dahl, he has strong interests. Dahl was a collector of antique furniture and paintings, and an expert on chocolate and wine. Oswald is an expert on nineteenth-century Italian opera, an international authority on Chinese porcelain and a collector of walking sticks (from the famous and infamous) as well as spiders; his collection of *Arachnida* is 'as comprehensive as any outside a museum'. Oswald delights his women visitors by describing their mating habits:

> *... the female spider is so savage in her lovemaking that the male is very lucky indeed if he escapes with his life at the end of it all. Only if he is exceedingly agile and marvellously ingenious will he get away in one piece.*

Like Dahl himself, Oswald felt it was important to be an enthusiast in life:

> *... if you are interested in something, no matter what it is, go at it at full speed ahead. Embrace it with both arms, hug it, love it and above all become passionate about it. Lukewarm is no good. Hot is no good either. White hot and passionate is the only thing to be.*

Nobody ever found it dull to be in Oswald's company, wrote Dahl, 'and perhaps that, more than anything else, was the reason for his success'.

But it was not just Oswald's great intellect, charming wit and enchanting blue eyes that fascinated women; when he was aroused 'something odd would begin to happen around the edges of his nostrils, a tightening of the rims, a visible flaring which enlarged the nostril holes and revealed whole areas of the bright red skin inside'. This 'queer, wild, animalistic impression', inspired surely by a bull smelling a cow in season, had an 'electric' effect upon the ladies.

'The Visitor' continues with descriptions of several of Oswald's conquests, including a rather surreal liaison in the Sinai desert where he got rather more than he bargained for. The attraction between the sexes was at the core of several subsequent tales, including 'The Last Act', in which a bereaved woman reunites with her childhood sweetheart, and 'The Great Switcheroo', a crazy plan hatched by a married man who lusts after the wife of his best friend and neighbour. These stories are more about the sentiment of passion than the science behind it, but soon afterwards Dahl began to explore the physiology of attraction.

Marvellous

In 'Bitch', Uncle Oswald meets a Belgian chemist, named Henri Biotte, who has devoted his life to the study of olfaction. He reminds Oswald about the smell of a bitch on heat that drives a dog wild with sexual drive. 'All self control disappears. He has only one thought in his head, which is to fornicate on the spot.' The same applied to primitive man, Biotte explains, before civilisation and evolution suppressed man's ability to be stimulated sexually by smell. He outlines an ingenious plan to set back the sex habits of civilised man by half a million years.

'What I intend to do,' he continues, 'is to produce a perfume which will have the same electrifying effect upon a man as the scent of a bitch in heat has upon a dog! One whiff and that'll be it! The man will lose all control. He'll rip off his pants and ravish the lady on the spot!'

Biotte then describes how smell works, the receptors on the end of the nasal olfactory nerve filaments acting as receivers for odorous molecules. The explanation is as thorough and accessible as you will read in any popular science book. He discusses the theory of seven pure primary odours – camphoraceous, pungent, musky, ethereal, floral, pepperminty, and putrid – explaining that he has found an eighth, 'the sexual stimulant that caused primitive man to behave like a dog thousands of years ago'. And so Biotte and Oswald embark on a scheme to create a perfume containing this stimulant, and their adventures begin.

Five years after 'Bitch' was published in 1974, Oswald was at it again with a potent pheromone to drive men mad with passion. In *My Uncle Oswald*, the aphrodisiac was not created chemically, but was produced from the Sudanese blister beetle. With the scientific know-how of Cambridge chemistry tutor Professor A. R. Woresley, and the assistance of the lovely Yasmin Howcomely, Oswald uses the potion to trick the world's most brilliant, rich and famous men into unwittingly donating semen for a sperm bank. He plans to then sell this produce to rich women around the world who want to have the most gifted offspring. This plan predated the formation of the so called 'Nobel Prize Sperm Bank', which recruited the semen of geniuses, mostly bright student and lecturers on college campuses, but also including three Nobel laureates.

Where did Dahl get the ideas for these stories? Even back in 1944 when Dahl was working in Washington for the British Ambassador Lord Halifax, he would write spoof letters, ostensibly from Lord Halifax, describing his unusually vigorous sex life, and offering to communicate the secrets of his success with the young. Papers in the Dahl archive hint at how some of the other concepts may have evolved over the years. In the 1960s there are notes about a doctor, President of the Indian Atomic Energy Commission, suggesting contraceptives be added to staples such as salt to help with population control. But who would be willing to take such contraceptives? If an aphrodisiac were added, that might make contraceptives more palatable. In one of his notebooks Dahl jotted down, 'The man who invented a perfume which literally drove man crazy.'

Although in later years his focus shifted to children's books, Dahl remained interested in the attraction between the sexes, and did some light-hearted research around the subject. In preparation for a prize-giving speech at Dr Challoner's boys' school, he sent a questionnaire to the headmistress of a famous girls' school to ask the girls, aged between fifteen and eighteen, such key questions as:

Would you rather your boyfriend was intelligent or that he was good looking?

Would you rather your boyfriend was short, medium, or tall?

When you see a boy walking down the street, which part of him do you find the most sexy?

What would you like a boy to do on your first date?

How long before you would like a boy to try to kiss you?

The most common answer to the last question, as reported to the boys' school, was three weeks. But curiously, when Dahl gave the same speech to the girls at Beaminster School sometime after, he told them the most common answer was one week.

Whilst the hormonal drives underlying sexual behaviour clearly fascinated Dahl, he was also intrigued by other chemically driven biological processes.

In the adult story 'Royal Jelly', he considers how the glandular secretion of bees, for which the story is named, mystically transforms larvae into queen bees. The protagonist in the story, an expert bee keeper, is fretting over his newborn daughter's poor feeding and weight loss when he begins to have an idea: 'royal jelly must be a substance of tremendous nourishing power, for on this diet alone, the honey-bee larva increases in weight fifteen hundred times in five days …' What if he put some royal jelly in the baby's milk? His daughter certainly puts on weight with his clever new diet, but what other changes are induced?

The concepts of growth and shrinking came through in many of Dahl's stories. There was the peach that grew and grew; the tortoise in *Esio Trot* that *appeared* to grow and grow; Mrs Twit, who seemed to have 'the shrinks' and then finally did. There were giants in *The BFG*; the tiny Minpins; and in *Charlie and the Chocolate Factory* the Oompa-Loompas.

The Oompa-Loompas were black pygmies from deepest, darkest Africa in the original 1964 book, but became 'dwarfish hippies' with long 'golden-brown hair' and 'rosy-white skin' in the 1972 revision, reflecting changing political sensitivities.

'You're growing too fast,' George's 'grizzly old grunion of a grandma' tells him in *George's Marvellous Medicine*. 'Growing's a nasty childish habit,' she continues, 'never grow up, always grow down.'

How George hates the horrible old witchy woman with her 'pale-brown teeth and a small puckered-up mouth like a dog's bottom'. The brown medicine she takes doesn't seem to do her any good – she is just as horrid after taking it as before – so George decides to concoct a potion of his own, containing pretty much every liquid or powder that he can find in the bathroom, bedroom, kitchen and shed. This includes some 'Brillident for Cleaning False Teeth', 'Nevermore Ponking Deodorant Spray' and a medicine for 'Chickens with Foul Pest'. That will shake the old woman up a bit. He cooks the concoction on the stove and then feeds a spoonful to Grandma. The effect is instantaneous.

Grandma yelled "Oweeeee!" and her whole body shot up whoosh *in the air.*

Smoke comes out of her mouth and nostrils, and after George has put the fire out Grandma begins to grow and grow until her head is poking out of the roof. George feeds the medicine to a hen, which grows into a giant bird. 'It's fantastic!' shouts George's dad, once he has got over the shock. 'It's a miracle … for years and years I have been trying to breed bigger and bigger animals.'

They use up the medicine on all the farm animals, and decide to make more the next day. George's father plans to build a Marvellous Medicine Factory and sell the concoction to farmers all over the world.

'We will become rich and you will become famous ... Nobody will ever go hungry again.'

The problem is George cannot remember quite what he put in his recipe, and despite a series of experiments is unable to produce the same mixture again, with disastrous result for Grandma, who grabs some thinking it is tea.

Dahl dedicated the book to doctors everywhere.

Labels

'What type of man was Dahl?' I have been asked many times in recent years. 'Wasn't he racist or a misogynist or anti-Semitic?'

The question varies a bit, but is usually followed by some isolated quote or fact about *Charlie and the Chocolate Factory*, or *The Witches*, or something he said about Israel.

Dahl was a complex man, but I don't think he was any of these things. Yes, in *Charlie and the Chocolate Factory* the Oompa-Lumpas were originally black pygmies, who were later changed, but in the first drafts the hero, Charlie, was a little black boy – hardly the choice of a racist. It is true that in *The Witches*, and some of his short stories, women were portrayed as evil and conniving, but in others they were the complete opposite – think of Grandma in *The Witches*, or Miss Honey in *Matilda*. And men fared pretty badly in some Dahl stories too, such as the terrifying giants in *The BFG*, or the hapless Boggis, Bunce and Bean in *Fantastic Mr Fox*. I don't think Dahl was bothered about the gender of his characters, or how this might be interpreted; he cared about what would make them compelling, and part of a great story, which would keep his readers captivated, and have them gasp and laugh in equal measure. The staggering 120 million Dahl books now sold worldwide attest to the fact that he knew what he was doing.

With Israel, things are not so straightforward: having initially been impressed by the determination and resolution of the early settlers he met near Haifa during the war, he clearly became very unhappy with what happened in the country subsequently. But Dahl sometimes made the mistake of confusing the Israeli government with the Jewish people, and was sloppy with the words he used. However, when challenged on this, rather than admit he had not quite said what he meant and apologise, Dahl dug in, and came up with even more outrageous comments. This was characteristic of him. He would rarely own up to being wrong, or change his mind. Indeed he would often say something provocative just to get a reaction out of people, and the more upset they became the further he would push his argument, adopting even more extreme views. Perhaps this was the frontal lobe damage exerting itself, or perhaps it was just him. Despite his utterings on Israel, he had several good Jewish friends, such as Tom Maschler, head of Jonathon Cape; Peter Mayer, Chief Executive of Penguin Books; and the philosopher Isaiah Berlin.

'I thought he might say anything,' commented Berlin. 'Could have been pro-Arab or pro-Jew. There was no consistent line. He was a man who followed whims, which meant he would blow up in one direction, so to speak.'

Certainly when I met Dahl on the wards in Oxford, he was not at all bothered that I was Jewish or that my friend Anwar was Muslim and he had no issues with the women doctors. Dahl just took people at face value. He was interested in who you were, not any labels that might be attached to you.

Rings of Iron

During the autumn Dahl was in and out of the John Radcliffe Hospital, and by November he was spending more time in than out. Although he was increasingly frail, his spirits remained high. I bumped into him one morning as I was taking a shortcut through the back of the radiology department. He was sitting in a wheelchair, with a blanket over his knees, reading *The Times*.

'Hello, Roald, what are you doing here?' It wasn't an area in which you normally saw patients.

'Waiting for a scan. I think the porters are trying to keep me out of harm's way.' He was cheery and pleased to see me. 'There's some delay with the machine, so they popped me here, rather than the waiting room.'

I knew that if Dahl needed a test doing, the hospital porters would aim to bring him down at the last moment, get him through the investigation, then straight back up to the ward with no hanging about. Reporters from the seedier end of the tabloid market were creeping around the hospital by this stage, pretending to be patients' relatives, trying to gather titbits of information. The world-famous author Roald Dahl was ill in hospital. Because this was the 1990s, and he was an artist, there were even newspaper headlines saying he had AIDS. I decided to wait with Dahl rather than leave him on his own in this back room. We got to talking about his illness. He had undergone a repeat bone-marrow examination a few days earlier, and I had been looking at it with the registrar. By this stage we knew he had a myelodysplastic syndrome, but it wasn't clear why he was feeling so lousy, and was in such pain. Despite repeated blood transfusions, he remained very weak. Dahl quizzed me about his illness. If only he could understand the disease properly, perhaps he could find a way through it.

'Do you think the bone-marrow failure is anything to do with the terrible trauma my bones suffered in the plane crash all those years ago?'

I could at least reassure him on that. Myelodysplastic syndromes have nothing to do with trauma. Normally the marrow is a hive of activity with a constant turnover of pluripotent stem cells; these are precursor cells, baby cells if you like, which are ready to grow into a whole array of different types – the red cells, the platelets and the varied specialist white cells. In a bone-marrow biopsy, we suck out tissue with a large needle to examine the cells as they are maturing into the final products that will enter the blood. In the myelodysplastic syndrome, named from the Greek for marrow, *myelo*, and abnormality, *dysplasia*, there are abnormalities in the production line.

We now recognise several different types of myelodysplastic disease depending on where the problem lies. In Dahl's case, it was production of the red cells, or *red corpuscles* as he preferred to call them (he liked to use medical rather than lay terms, probably to sound more like a medical professional). Iron is a crucial component of the haemoglobin inside red cells, but instead of seeing healthy erythroblasts, which are the precursors to red blood cells, in Dahl's marrow we saw ring sideroblasts, abnormal cells with clumps of iron accumulated around the cell's nucleus. Using Prussian blue stain, they actually look quite pretty, but they spell trouble. The peripheral blood film is also highly abnormal. Instead of a uniform army of identical red cells, carrying oxygen to the tissues, you see a rag bag of shapes and size, with all sorts of oddities. Some red cells are too large, some too small; some have dots around their edges – *basophil stippling*; others have clumps of iron inside – *Pappenheimer bodies*; others, called target cells, look like a bull's eye.

Back then this was as much as we knew about sideroblastic anaemia. Quite why Dahl's bone marrow should suddenly start misbehaving in this way after seventy-four years of good service was not known. We could only talk in general terms about the presumed genetic mutations that lead to blood and bone marrow cancers. Twenty-five years later, we now know that some cases of sideroblastic anaemia and indeed other bone marrow disorders are associated with alterations in an enzyme called JAK2. A single change in one letter of the genetic code, on the ninth chromosome, leads to a swap of one amino acid building block among the one thousand or so that make up the protein JAK2. This mutation seems to make the stems cells in the bone marrow more sensitive to natural growth factors such as erythropoietin. EPO as it is more commonly known is the substance athletes take illicitly to boost their performance: it stimulates the bone marrow to make more red blood cells, so that more oxygen is delivered to the muscles. The presence of such a mutation would make the bone marrow too sensitive to the EPO, which is produced naturally, so the bone marrow burns itself out.

Today many more therapies are available than the blood transfusions and steroids we gave Dahl. These include new drugs targeted specifically against the deviant JAK2 mutation, and other genetic abnormalities that underlie these diseases. So Dahl was right: if you can just understand the disease a bit better, you can work out a way to climb out of the hole. Unfortunately, though, this type of progress takes years if not decades, rather than the short time that Dahl had left.

There was a steady stream of visitors to Dahl's side room at the end of the ward. The adjacent day room had become something of a camp for the extended family. For Dahl the arrival of his daughter Lucy flying over from America with her new baby was an especially ominous sign. Later the same day his sisters came.

'I didn't particularly want to,' he confided in me that evening, 'but I did my duty in seeing them.' In case the significance of their visit was lost on him, one of them spelled it out. 'My dear sweet sister very gently told me that I was going to die,' he informed me, with laughter accompanied by tears.

The Alchemist

In the middle of November, Dahl was driven home after a few days in hospital, but by the time he arrived he felt so terrible that Liccy brought him straight back. We admitted him on to the ward, the single room down by the day room, and found he had a chest infection and was septicaemic, with bacteria in his blood; patients with myelodysplastic bone marrow fail to make properly functioning white cells and so are at risk of infection. However, he was more ill than he should have been and Weatherall suspected his myelodysplastic syndrome was turning into something more sinister.

'I remember you taking the bloods at night,' Ophelia told me later, 'sending them down to the lab to see if he was becoming leukemic ... You tried so hard, with antibiotics for the chest,' she continued, 'then antifungals as a last ditch effort. I think you even put a central line in ...'

She was right. It was frightening to see this giant of a man, who had looked like he should live forever, weakening before our eyes.

'We did what we could, but he was still deteriorating … We think he was probably transforming to acute myeloid leukaemia.'

Such transformation signifies a critical change in the bone marrow, perhaps due to another genetic mutation, causing one of the white cell lines to go into massive over-production. Leukaemia, literally *white blood*, means there are too many white cells and they are mostly immature 'blast' forms, which do not function normally.

At the handover that evening, my friend Anwar updated me on Dahl's condition during the day. The blood infection had been confirmed, and because of Dahl's generally frail state he had deteriorated into septic shock, when the blood pressure falls dangerously low. Weatherall had seen him, and after some antibiotics and fluid Dahl had rallied somewhat.

'But he is still in dangerous territory,' Anwar continued, 'and I wouldn't hesitate to call intensive care if I were you.'

He could see the look of surprise on my face. To put a frail man in his seventies on to the intensive care unit when he had a condition that was ultimately terminal was questionable to say the least.

'That's Roald Dahl, the author,' Anwar explained as a justification.

'No,' I replied. 'That's Roald Dahl, the patient.'

I was busy elsewhere in the hospital that evening and by the time I got to ward 5E it was quite late. I knocked gently on Dahl's door, not wanting to disturb him if he were asleep. He looked tired and frail, and somehow smaller, as if he were shrinking into the bed. His face brightened when he saw me.

He gestured to the chair. 'Come and sit down.'

'How are you feeling now?' I had one eye on the monitor by his bed.

'He's an alchemist. That's what he is – a fucking alchemist!'

'Who?' I feigned puzzlement, although I knew full well.

'Prof Weatherall. He mixed the potions – juggled with them, and here I still am!' Dahl grinned meekly. 'I think I almost bought it, you know.' It was as if George had been in the room mixing his marvellous medicine, and somehow it had worked. I had seen Weatherall do it before, when someone was deteriorating, and the junior staff were getting panicky. Weatherall would come along and gently examine the patient with his slightly podgy hands. Offer an encouraging word or two. Suggest a minor change in the medication. And everything would get better. For Dahl, he had just changed the antibiotics, modified the pain relief and increased the fluid, but it was enough.

Sadly, though, this was only buying a bit of extra time.

Although acute leukaemia is often curable if it is a new diagnosis in a young person, when it occurs as part of a myelodysplastic syndrome it is untreatable.

The end was approaching. Dahl was quiet for a few minutes, his mind clearly miles away. Then he turned to me, slightly agitated.

'Most great artists are bastards, half mad or homosexuals ...' He was searching my face earnestly. 'I don't think I'm mad; I know I am not homosexual; I really hope I am not a bastard.'

What could I say? 'Well, I don't think you are ...'

'I'm not afraid of dying, you know.' Dahl's voice was frail. 'I watched my daughter die, Olivia. *That's easy*, I thought. There's nothing to be frightened of.'

Dahl had seen more than his fair share of death, especially during the war. In his first book, *Over to You*, seven of the ten short stories involved violent deaths. Initially, flying in the Royal Air Force had seemed like one great adventure, but as the conflict progressed, and so many of his peers died, Dahl's anxiety grew, as expressed in 'Death of an Old Old Man'. Alone in the cockpit, RAF pilot Charlie admits to himself that he is terrified of dying:

> *It touches you gently on the shoulder and whispers to you that you are young, that you have a million things to do and a million things to say, that if you are not careful you will buy it, that you are almost certain to buy it sooner or later, and that when you do you will not be anything any longer; you will just be a charred corpse.*

Some of his stories portrayed death as a gentle transition to another world. In 'Katina', a young girl murdered by the Luftwaffe appears mystically unharmed through a haze of flames. An RAF pilot, Fin, has a near death experience in 'They Shall Not Grow Old'. He emerges from a thick white cloud surrounded by blueness, in a trance-like state, and finds he is being pulled inexorably towards a line of aircraft, pilots and aircrews who had been killed in battle:

> *I never once during that time felt either hot or cold or hungry or thirsty; I felt none of those things. I felt no fear, because I knew nothing of which to be afraid. I felt no worry, because I could remember nothing or think of nothing about which to be worried. I felt no desire to do anything that I was not doing or to have anything that I did not have, because there was nothing that I wished to do and there was nothing that I wished to have. I felt only pleasure at being where I was, at seeing the wonderful light and the beautiful colour around me.*

Fin survives this experience only to be fatally shot down shortly afterwards. As his plane dived towards the sea Fin's voice was heard over the radio: 'I'm a lucky bastard,' he was saying. 'A lucky, lucky bastard.'

Nearly forty-five years later, as Dahl's health was failing, he wrote what would prove to be his last book, *The Minpins*. Donald Sturrock, Dahl's biographer, believes he may have had his own end in mind as he wrote some of the final passages. Little Billy, who has been enjoying his adventures on Swan's back, takes his last flight, a journey through the sky, to a peaceful place joining those who have already gone:

> *Suddenly there was a brightness like sunlight below them, and Little Billy could see a vast lake of water, gloriously blue, and on the surface of the lake thousands of swans were swimming slowly about. The pure white of the swans against the blue of the water was very beautiful.*

'No one can know what the dead know,' Dahl once said to Pat years earlier. 'We have no reason to believe that death comes with any theatrical side effects...'

'So if you die, you just die, and then you're dead,' Pat said reproachfully. 'You don't see ... anything.'

'I don't know, Pat,' said Dahl, 'you have to die to find that out.'

Darwin's Elephants

'Why is it,' Dahl asked me suddenly as he wiped away a tear, 'that men are meant to cry? Why do the lacrimal glands give out tears?'

Remarkably, we then discussed crying in humans and animals in a quite remote and detached way. We could have been dining on high table in college, or deliberating in a tutorial. At the time it did not seem strange. I think Dahl found the distraction a relief. Even at this late stage, he would rather do some intellectual jousting than dwell on his own discomfort.

'I don't think anyone knows for sure why we cry,' I pondered. The basic function of the tears is to keep the cornea, the sensitive front of the eye, moist and clean. Tears are produced by the lacrimal gland, which sits just behind the eyelid; they get washed across the eye when you blink, and drain away through a small duct into your nose. Hence the rather unattractive runny nose when we cry. If we get emotionally upset, we produce more tears than the system can drain, and out they spill. We know how it happens – overstimulation of the glands by the nerves that come from the limbic system, the emotional centres of the brain; but, as to why, that is still an open question. It is clearly a form of communication, possibly a vestige from when we are babies, and the only way we can convey that we are hungry, or tired, or unhappy is to bawl our little hearts out. Though even for a baby, the noise on its own would probably do the trick, without the tears.

'Maybe there are evolutionary advantages for adults crying,' I suggested. 'It is all regulated by the autonomic nervous system – we cannot control it directly. So maybe the point is to convey messages of sadness or anger, even if we are trying to hide it. You can see there might be survival benefits of that.'

For many years there has been debate about whether humans are the only animals to shed emotional tears. Dogs and other animals will whimper and vocalise to express pain or distress, but do any cry? I remembered reading Darwin's notes that captured elephants 'lay motionless on the ground, with no other indication of suffering than the tears which suffused their eyes and flowed incessantly'.

'Is this just a physiological response, or are they actually feeling anything?' Dahl wondered.

In humans we can now observe the brain's physiological changes during emotional encounters using functional magnetic resonance imaging. Brain MRIs have also been performed on elephants, primarily to try and understand their phenomenal memories, rather than emotional responses. But for chimpanzees electroencephalograms, measuring electrical activity or 'brain waves', have been used to assess responses to emotional stimuli, such as pictures of happy or angry chimps. Intriguingly the patterns seen are similar to those in humans, suggesting they may be feeling similar things.

'I am certain dogs understand human emotions,' Dahl continued. 'When one of the children was hurt or upset, they would go to comfort them, rest their head on their lap, that kind of thing.' Dahl was missing his dogs. He knew they were not allowed on the wards and at one stage wanted to winch them up in a basket outside his window, *Esio Trot*-like. I don't think he realised quite how high up we were. 'I never cried during the war, you know. Despite being shot down, and having to crawl out of the wreckage, and get back to camp. I was very close to death. But no tears at all. I don't even remember being scared.'

A few tears rolled down his cheek and my eyes welled up too.

Dahl was sorry to see the effect he was having: 'Don't mind me, I'm just a silly old fool.'

Chapter 17

The Last Night

'When he stopped smoking and drinking in hospital,' Ophelia recalled, 'that was a clear indication to me the end was near.' She and Dahl's other children felt he was suffering too much as the days dragged on, but Liccy couldn't bear to let go. Ophelia felt her father was fighting on just for Liccy.

> *'I would never want to live longer than you ... I couldn't stand being looked after by anybody else ... I'll be a very old mouse and you'll be a very old grandmother and soon after that we'll both die together.'*
> *'That would be perfect.'*
>
> – The Witches

It had been another awful day for Dahl: his blood pressure had been low, his temperature up and down, and his bones aching terribly despite the analgesics. When I came on the ward in the early evening, he was more comfortable, and by midnight everything seemed settled. Dahl was asleep, and Liccy and Ophelia were with him, so I decided to go and get some rest, but at one in the morning I was woken by a bleep from the nurses.

Could I come down? Roald was in distress.

I examined him, and talked with Liccy and Ophelia. Dahl was in pain, especially when he was turning. I altered his medication, upping the doses of his painkillers. He relaxed again, and after twenty minutes was sleeping.

But an hour later I was called back. The discomfort had returned. I adjusted the drugs once more, adding oral opiates, the strongest painkillers short of morphine.

Again he settled. Liccy and Ophelia had been upset by his distress, but were also calmer now. It was four in the morning. I thought we were through the worst of it. Once the sun came up things would be brighter. We could talk with Weatherall to see if we should move onto a morphine drip. I offered to stay but Liccy said I should rest; they would be fine now.

However, I was called again about half an hour later.

Even as I entered the ward I could hear Dahl's distress echoing down the corridor: a low-pitched howling sob, loud at the start, and then becoming fainter. It spoke of pain, anxiety, sorrow and disappointment. It was terrible, like the noise that came from the large beech tree in 'The Sound Machine' as it was axed:

a harsh, noteless, enormous noise, a growling, low-pitched, screaming sound ... drawn out like a sob lasting fully for a minute ... fading gradually fainter and fainter until it was gone.

I examined him once more, to see if I could pinpoint the source of the pain. My tears dripped on to the page as I was trying to write my notes. Liccy, Ophelia and I were equally upset and agreed it was not acceptable for Roald to be in this much pain. I called Professor Weatherall at home.

Policy Statement

Professor Sir David Weatherall is not often phoned in the middle of the night. In theory I should have contacted the registrar on call, and indeed this is what hospital etiquette demands. But Weatherall had said months ago, when we first started looking after Dahl, that I should call him any time of the day or night if worried. In fairness to the prof, this would apply to any patient, and not just this world-famous author.

At first Weatherall can not understand why I have called him:

'What is it, Tom? What's happened?' I think he was expecting that something dramatic has occurred, like a cardiac arrest.

'He's in too much pain,' I say. 'I think it's got to the point of ensuring relief from pain as a top priority.'

'Tom, what do you mean? You've not phoned me at 5 a.m. to give me a policy statement – what has happened?'

I am too tired and upset to explain myself clearly, and am talking in riddles.

'Sorry, Prof, I think you just need to come in.'

I wait nervously on the ward. We do what we can to ease Roald's pain, then I sit anxiously at the nurses' station. Twenty minutes later Weatherall arrives. As soon as he steps on to the ward, and can hear Dahl's unbearable howling, I see his expression change. He understands exactly why I called him.

'You are right, Tom. He needs a morphine infusion. Thank you for calling me.'

I apologise that I have not called the registrar, but it would have just delayed things, and I knew only Weatherall could make the decision.

Liccy and Ophelia leave us whilst we examine Roald together. Weatherall asks him if he wants us to stop the pain.

'Yes,' says Roald, 'please do.'

And that is it.

My hand is shaking as I write up the morphine on the drug card. I have asked the nurses to get everything ready in advance so there will be no delay.

'Ow, fuck!' Roald exclaims as the needle goes into his skin. Within a few moments the syringe driver is working, and the pain is easing. Dahl relaxes into his pillow, and you can almost feel the whole world relaxing around us.

How nice it is not to struggle. There is no point in struggling. I was a fool to have struggled so much and for so long ... Nothing will worry me any more now, nothing nothing nothing

– 'Death of an Old Old Man'

As he lies dying, and his brain slips into unconsciousness, I wonder at the thoughts and memories travelling down those neural pathways one last time ... The ground is hurtling up at seventy miles an hour, and frontal lobes are smashed against the inside of the cranium; an eye floats in a basin above a brain, the pupil dilating in fury as cigarette smoke is blown on to it; the brain of a hydrocephalic baby is compressed tight within the skull, awaiting the relief of a new valve; a young girl peers round a curtain at an enormous shadow coming down the street; a mass of neural tissue inflamed with measles virus is turning dark and necrotic; wires are connected, circuits joined and distant sounds become sharply focused; a blood vessel leaks then bursts, haemorrhaging dark, hot fluid and words jumble into disarray; a tumour is slowly enlarging, insidious and ominous, until it is too late; the pain of consciousness eases as morphine gently takes its hold.

I make some toast for Prof Weatherall in the ward kitchen, and then pack him off to his office to do some work. There is no point in him going home at this time. Liccy is enormously relieved that Roald's distress is easing, and gives me a big, emotional hug. She seems unwilling to let go. Ophelia hugs me too, but is more tentative.

By now it is time to get ready for the day's work. I shower, put on clean clothes and go down to the acute medical unit. It is just beginning to get light outside, and the birds are singing. To them, just another day, but for Roald Dahl it will be his last.

At lunchtime I visit Roald's room to see how things are. By this stage all the drips and paraphernalia of medical intervention have been removed. Roald is lying there peacefully, but has the erratic Cheyne-Stokes breathing of someone who is close to death. Liccy, Ophelia and other family members surround the bed, holding his hand, caressing his arm. I recognise the music coming at high volume from the tape player in the corner, Tchaikovsky's Violin Concerto in E. It is an inspiring piece I have loved since childhood, and always play at key moments – preparing for exams, heading off to interviews, driving from my wedding. It seems fitting; wonderful music to which to die.

As I watch the scene I can almost see Dahl rise from the death bed, spirit-like, and take a position in the corner; eyes half closed like his character Mr Bottibol, he is conducting both the imaginary orchestra and those acting out the scene before him. He likes to be in control, and this is to be his last creative piece. Dahl's raging is over, and he is gently slipping away.

What Ifs?

By two in the afternoon, it was all over. I bumped into Liccy in the hospital foyer by the lifts, and she hugged me with relief. I had work to finish off upstairs. However sad you are about one patient, there is always another who needs your help. By 5 p.m., though, I was exhausted and ready to go home, but Professor Weatherall had sent a message: he wanted to see me. I headed across to his research labs, the Institute of Molecular Medicine, with mild trepidation.

I should not have been anxious. All he wanted to do was make me a coffee, which he did himself, and see that I was okay – such a simple gesture that spoke volumes. My respect and admiration for him grew even more, and we have remained good friends to this day. I have often turned to him in times of difficulty, such as when my brother was dying of cancer, or when making the big decisions, like applying for my chair, and the directorship of the new research institute in Liverpool.

I arrived at my digs in East Oxford just in time for the six o'clock news. For some reason it shocked me to hear that the author Roald Dahl had died at a hospital in Oxford; he was seventy-four. That is when the enormity of it all hit me: he was not just Roald Dahl, the patient. I sobbed. I couldn't help feeling that if we had just managed to get through the night, and not called in Weatherall, we would somehow have got away without the morphine, and he would have pulled through, and still be alive. This was nonsense, of course. Yes, he might have managed another twelve or twenty-four hours in terrible pain, but it was inevitable that he would need morphine sooner rather than later. And, once a patient is on intravenous morphine, if the pain keeps increasing they will need more and more until eventually the breathing stops. After nearly thirty years in hospital medicine, I still sometimes struggle with the 'what ifs'.

Sir William Osler used to call pneumonia the old man's friend, because it would gently and painlessly carry you across into the next world. To our generation, intravenous morphine seems to have the same role. Or at least it did until the Manchester GP Harold Shipman used it to ease his patients into the next world whether they were in pain or not.

'In thirty years of clinical practice I cannot remember ever being so moved or privileged in caring for a patient,' Weatherall wrote to Liccy soon after Dahl died. 'Roald was quite unique. I have never seen anyone have such an effect on the medical and nursing staff – the sense of loss at every level was quite extraordinary. You all must be very proud of him. I was so glad he retained his extraordinary intellect to the end and that he died with the calm and dignity which was so important to him.'

Dahl's funeral was six days later at the Church of St Peter and St Paul in Great Missenden. It was a splendid affair, and like all the best funerals a mixture of great sadness and celebration, combined with relief that the suffering is over. There was an enormous crowd of which Dahl would have been justifiably proud. He didn't want a 'rotsome memorial service', so this was burial, memorial and celebration all rolled into one. The music came from Mozart's Coronation Mass, and Fauré's Requiem, more of my favourites, and there was a proper choir, which made the whole thing spine-tinglingly spiritual.

Peter Mayer, Dahl's publisher, gave a brilliant tribute and the readings included Dylan Thomas's 'Do Not Go Gentle into that Good Night', and a quote from Dahl's *The Giraffe and the Pelly and Me*:

> *We have tears in our eyes*
> *As we wave our goodbyes,*
> *We so loved being with you, we three.*
> *So do please now and then*
> *Come and see us again,*
> *The Giraffe and the Pelly and me.*
>
> *All you do is to look*
> *At a page in this book*
> *Because that's where we always will be.*
> *No book ever ends*
> *When it's full of your friends*
> *The Giraffe and the Pelly and me.*

After Dahl was buried in the churchyard, we all walked back to Gipsy House, where a great marquee had been set up in the garden. Somehow it incorporated flowerbeds, and trellises, and there were tantalising glimpses beyond the flapping windows and walls: is that bright yellow door the entrance to the writing hut of which Dahl spoke to me with such warmth? Do I see Danny's gipsy caravan behind that hedge? Was that large tree up the road the inspiration for *Fantastic Mr Fox*?

Gipsy House

A few weeks later these questions are answered when Liccy and Ophelia invite me for dinner at Gipsy House. As I ring the doorbell, I am nervous, and maybe even a bit embarrassed. I do not know quite what to expect. Last time I was alone with them there had been such raw emotion that I wonder how the evening will go. A maid answers the door, and asks me to wait in the lounge. I recognise the large open fireplace with an armchair beside it. This is where Dahl had sat as he introduced each of his *Tales of the Unexpected* on television in the 1970s. I can hear faint echoes of the theme tune, and his booming voice ...

'Tom, hello, lovely to see you.' It is Liccy, bringing me out of my reverie. We hug, get through a difficult moment when we both well up and then move on. Ophelia soon appears with her brother, Theo. It is wonderful to meet him for the first time after hearing so much about him. He is tall, and charming, just like his father. But beyond this I can see a pale baby struggling for life as the doctors argue about what to do; the anguished parents rushing him back to hospital each time he relapses; the toymaker, surgeon and author poring over sketches for a new device.

We sit at a large pine table in the extended kitchen, Liccy at the head, where Dahl should be. His presence is everywhere. It is as though he was just too big a personality not to be in this house, at this table, even though he was buried some weeks earlier. We talk about him and the family stories, and my family, and our stories. After dinner, I choose a chocolate from the red Tupperware that Dahl would always pass round the table. Chopper the Jack Russell Terrier, sits on Liccy's knee, just as he used to sit on Dahl's, and is offered some Smarties. His crumpled tail-end is winking at me, like the mean small puckered up mouth of the disgusting grandma in *George's Marvellous Medicine*.

Then Ophelia shows me around the house. I am to call her 'Min', a sign that I have made the transition to friend.

'I don't know where the name came from,' she laughs. 'I think it was because Theo couldn't say *Ophelia* when I was born. He must have chosen something to do with a Mini car, I guess.'

'Ha, my brothers couldn't say Thomas when I was born,' I explain, 'so they called me *Momus* ever after.'

Min also delights in my sisters' nicknames, *Pel* and *Mag*, for Penelope and Madeline. She tells me her dad had all sorts of variations on hers: 'Min, Don Minni, Minipin, Minpin.' His last book was named for her.

In the lounge, next to the fireside armchair, Dahl had installed a small control knob.

'What is it for?' I ask.

'To adjust the volume of the music being piped through from the study, quite advanced for its time.'

'Ah, the ever-inventive Roald Dahl!' We laugh.

Here on the landing the wallpaper has been stripped back to reveal caveman-like carvings in the plaster. Dahl was surprised when none of the children believed they were authentic, and accused him of doing it with a chisel. Here is the bedroom window where, when Min and Lucy had friends to stay, Dahl would climb up an outside ladder, and *The BFG* would appear with his dream trumpet.

An upstairs study has floor-to-ceiling bookcases, containing all of Dahl's works in every language imaginable. Min gives me copies of the autobiographical *Boy: Tales of Childhood* and *Going Solo.*

'Thank you.' I take them carefully. 'I will treasure these.'

Theo has been following us around the house, busying himself with this and that, not wanting to interfere, but ready to step in. I don't think he is concerned with me and Min. I think he is protecting his father's estate, his memory, his presence.

We play snooker on Dahl's table. He used to play most Sunday evenings with the surgeon Brian Higgs, and other friends from the village. Min beats me convincingly. Later, we head out to the annex where there are a couple of guest bedrooms for us. But we are not ready to sleep and stay up late into the night, chatting. The moon lights up the orchard and owls are hooting in the distance, and in this atmosphere there are echoes of my night-time discussions with her father. Dahl was at the end of his life, but this feels different: Min and I are at the start of ours, kindred spirits, with shared interests and passions. Years later, working on the Ebola outbreak, we discover we have arrived at similar destinations, but by different routes.

'Wow, I love it,' says Min at breakfast the next morning, indicating my Morris Minor, which is sitting outside on the gravel. 'We used to have one, not convertible. I learned to drive in it.'

'Yes,' adds Liccy wryly, 'and didn't you use to drive it around Buckinghamshire underage?'

Min laughs at the memory. 'Dad caught me once,' she confides. 'The car had broken down, but he wasn't angry at all, just said I needed to learn how to fix it if I was going to drive it.'

She shows me around the garden.

Here is the writing hut, though it is still too soon, too raw, for anyone to go in.

Here is the gipsy caravan that became the home for Danny, Champion of the World.

Just up the track from Gipsy House is the enormous old beech, 'the witches' tree', as the family call it; underneath is a hole in which, according to the stories Dahl told them, 'lived Mr Fox and Mrs Fox and their four Small Foxes'. Behind that, at the top of the field, is the Minpin Forest ...

We stop side by side, looking beyond it, lost in our own thoughts. I feel tired, numb and gut-wrenchingly sad at the loss of this great man, but suddenly, in the distance we see a swan soaring high above the trees, and my heart lifts.

Min laughs again, and it is an echo to me of Dahl's own booming laughter.

I know that she has also been transported instantly into the world of the Minpins where Little Billy's swan carries him off to new adventures and friendships.

It is a bittersweet reminder that whilst the storyteller himself is gone, his wonderful stories and marvellous medicine will be with us for a very, very long time.

*'Giants is never dying ... mostly us giants is simply
going on and on like whiffsy time-twiddlers.'*

– The BFG

Acknowledgements

For nearly twenty years I said nothing about my patient Roald Dahl. The confidentiality a patient can expect of their doctor does not end when they die. However in 2009 I was asked to talk about Dahl in a BBC Radio Four programme *Archive on Four* that his grand-daughter Sophie was making. Although wary at first, I was reassured by the fact that it was being produced by an old friend of mine, Anna Horsbrugh-Porter, who has also been a great support for this book.

The programme went well, and afterwards Dahl's wife Liccy allowed me to share some more private moments, initially in a BBC Radio Four *Great Lives* Programme with Matthew Parris, and now here. As we are all advancing in years, I think there is a feeling that if we don't capture these poignant memories for posterity they will be lost for ever. I am incredibly grateful to Liccy. I know it has not always been easy revisiting many sad times. Dahl's daughter Ophelia has also been an enormous source of help and encouragement, as has his grandson Luke Kelly, and others at the Dahl Literary Estate, especially Dominic Gregory, John Collins, and Bernie Hall. The literary agent Sally Holloway provided some helpful suggestions and encouragement early on, as did Ffinlo Dyde, Gideon Rochman, Alice Taylor, Nick McNulty, John Scotland, and Claire Rainford. Donald Sturrock has been a great source of support, information and general encouragement.

Anthony Cond, at Liverpool University Press, was key in helping me understand exactly what type of book I was trying to write. He has been amazingly patient, understanding and flexible, as the day job kept meaning deadlines were pushed back. At the press Katherine Pulman, Heather Gallagher and Whitney Linder have worked hard on the marketing and public relations. I am grateful to Justin Somper for his advice and assistance with this too. Samantha Stanton Stewart was masterful in her editing, and worked incredibly hard, along with Sue Barnes and Lucy Frontani, to help me meet the final deadlines and ensure the book was ready for launch on the 100th anniversary of Roald Dahl's birth.

It has been fun revisiting memories with the various friends and colleagues involved in Dahl's care, including Anwar Hussein, David Weatherall, Michael Streule and Rosemary Higgs. I am grateful to them and also to other patients whose experiences are shared in this book; for some the details have been changed to preserve anonymity.

Ava Easton of the Encephalitis Society has been a constant source of encouragement. I'd like to thank her, and Phillippa Chapman along with supporters from the other partner charities: Sarah Reilly and Sophie Dziwinski of Roald Dahl's Marvellous Children's Charity; Dominic Brand and Jane Cryer of the Stroke Association; Debra Chand and Joan Pheasant at Shine; and Helen Hunt and Chris Harrop of the Walton Centre.

I am grateful to the following who provided expert review to ensure that whilst presenting science to the lay reader I remained factually accurate: general surgeon, Gill Tierney, haematologist Cheng Hock Toh, vascular neurologist Hedley Emsley, immunologist Lance Turtle, neurosurgeon Conor Mallucci, and neuropsychologist Barbara Wilson. Any errors or oversights are, of course, my own.

I spent many happy hours lost in the archive at the Roald Dahl Museum and Story Centre, and could have spent many more. I'd like to thank the archivist Rachel White, her assistant Florence Ravenscroft, and Director Steve Gardam for their assistance. Hans Treffers kindly gave access to previously unseen footage of Dahl campaigning on polio elimination, and Jan Baldwin generously provided the cover photograph, which has never been published previously. I'm grateful to the artist Lucy Freegard and designer Lucy Frontani for sharing ideas about the front cover.

Anka Taylor and her lovely family provided a home-from-home whilst I was working in Great Missenden, and Reverend John Simpson gave access to St John the Baptist Church Little Missenden, at an unseemly hour.

I'd like to thank colleagues at the Institute of Infection and Global Health in Liverpool for helping ensure the Institute continued to achieve its mission of delivering world-leading research impact, whilst I have been slightly distracted with the book; particularly my assistant Angela Cucchi, the Institute Management Team, the team supporting the National Institute for Health Research Health Protection Research Unit in Emerging and Zoonotic Infections, and the Liverpool Brain Infections Group. In addition I am grateful to colleagues at the Walton Centre NHS Foundation Trust and the Royal Liverpool University Hospital NHS Trust.

I'm grateful to Jenny and Jim Morris, Bruce Solomon, Penelope Rochman, Madeline Rushefsky, Renee McCulloch, Billy Ashley, Tony and Isobel Wagstaff, and many local friends in Crosby too numerous to name for their general encouragement and support. Michael and Juniper Solomon gave help with some family history. Finally I would like to thank five rather special women – Eva, Rosie, Daisy, Leah, and Rachel – for sharing ideas on the contents of the book, the cover, helping with its delivery, and tolerating a dad/husband who was hidden away for weeks in the attic, when he should have been doing other things.

Bibliography

Short Stories and Collections

Stories are listed by year of original publication [the first collection in which each story appeared is shown in brackets]

'Shot Down Over Libya', in *Saturday Evening Post*, August 1942[1]

'The Sword', *Atlantic* magazine, August 1943

'Katina', *Ladies Home Journal*, March 1944; [*Over To You*, 1946]

'Only This', *Ladies Home Journal*, September 1944 [*Over to You*, 1946]

'Beware of the Dog', *Harper's* magazine, October 1944 [*Over to You*, 1946]

'Missing: Believed Killed', *Tomorrow* magazine, November 1944[1]

'They Shall Not Grow Old', *Ladies Home Journal*, September 1945 [*Over to You*, 1946]

'Madame Rosette', *Harper's* magazine, August 1945 [*Over to You*, 1946]

'Death of an Old Old Man', *Ladies Home Journal*, September 1945 [*Over to You*, 1946]

'Someone Like You', *Town & Country Magazine*, November 1945 [*Over to You*, 1946]

'An African Story', *Over to You*, 1946

'A Piece of Cake', *Over to You*, 1946[1]

'Yesterday was Beautiful', *Over to You*, 1946

---

1 'Shot Down Over Libya' and 'Missing: Believed Killed' were combined, modified and republished as 'A Piece of Cake'.

'Collector's Item' (later renamed 'Man from the South'), *Collier's* magazine, September 1948 [*Someone Like You*, 1953]

'The Sound Machine', *The New Yorker* magazine, September 1949 [*Someone Like You*, 1953]

'Poison', *Collier's* magazine, June 1950 [*Someone Like You*, 1953]

'Girl Without a Name', *Today's Woman* magazine, November 1951

'Taste', *Ladies Home Journal*, March 1945 [*Someone Like You*, 1953]

'Dip in the Pool', *The New Yorker* magazine, January 1952 [*Someone Like You*, 1953]

'A Picture for Drioli' (renamed 'Skin'), *The New Yorker* magazine, May 1952 [*Someone Like You*, 1953]

'My Lady Love, My Dove', *The New Yorker* magazine, June 1952 [*Someone Like You*, 1953]

'Mr. Feasey', *The New Yorker* magazine, August 1953 [*Someone Like You*, 1953]

'Lamb to the Slaughter', *Harper's* magazine, September 1953 [*Someone Like You*, 1953]

'The Devious Bachelor' (renamed 'Nunc Dimittis'), *Collier's* magazine, September 1953, [*Someone Like You*, 1953]

'Edward the Conqueror', *The New Yorker* magazine, October 1953 [*Kiss Kiss*, 1960]

'Galloping Foxley', *Town & Country* magazine, November 1953, [*Someone Like You*, 1953]

'The Soldier', *Someone Like You*, 1953

'The Wish', *Someone Like You*, 1953

'Neck', *Someone Like You*, 1953

'The Great Automatic Grammatizator', *Someone Like You*, 1953

'The Ratcatcher', *Someone Like You*, 1953

'Rummins', *Someone Like You*, 1953

'Mr. Hoddy', *Someone Like You*, 1953

'The Way Up to Heaven', *The New Yorker* magazine, February 1954 [*Kiss Kiss*, 1960]

'Parson's Pleasure', *Esquire* magazine, April 1958, [*Kiss Kiss*, 1960]

'The Champion of the World', *The New Yorker* magazine, January 1959 [*Kiss Kiss*, 1960]

'The Landlady', *The New Yorker* magazine, November 1959 [*Kiss Kiss*, 1960]

'Mrs. Bixby and the Colonel's Coat', *Nugget* magazine, December 1959 [*Kiss Kiss*, 1960]

'A Fine Son' (renamed 'Genesis and Catastrophe'), *Playboy* magazine, December 1959 [*Kiss Kiss*, 1960]

'William and Mary', *Kiss Kiss*, 1960

'Royal Jelly', *Kiss Kiss*, 1960

'Georgy Porgy', *Kiss Kiss*, 1960

'Pig', *Kiss Kiss*, 1960

'In the Ruins', World Book Fair Program, June 1964

'The Visitor', *Playboy* magazine, May 1965, [*Switch Bitch*, 1974]

'The Last Act', *Playboy* magazine, January 1966 [*Switch Bitch*, 1974]

'The Great Switcheroo', *Playboy* magazine, April 1974 [*Switch Bitch*, 1974]

'The Butler Did It', (renamed 'The Butler') May 1974, *Travel and Leisure* magazine, May 1974 [*More Tales of the Unexpected*, 1980]

'Bitch', *Playboy* magazine, July 1974 [*Switch Bitch*, 1974]

'Ah, Sweet Mystery of Life', *The Daily Telegraph* newspaper 1974 [*Ah, Sweet Mystery of Life*, 1989]

'The Hitch-Hiker', *Atlantic Monthly* magazine, July 1977 [*The Wonderful Story of Henry Sugar and Six More*, 1977]

'The Boy Who Talked with Animals', *The Wonderful Story of Henry Sugar and Six More*, 1977

'The Mildenhall Treasure', *The Wonderful Story of Henry Sugar and Six More*, 1977

'The Swan', *The Wonderful Story of Henry Sugar and Six More*, 1977

'The Wonderful Story of Henry Sugar', *The Wonderful Story of Henry Sugar and Six More*, 1977

'Lucky Break', *The Wonderful Story of Henry Sugar and Six More*, 1977

'The Umbrella Man', *More Tales of the Unexpected*, 1980

'Mr. Botibol', *More Tales of the Unexpected*, 1980

'Vengeance is Mine Inc.', *More Tales of the Unexpected*, 1980

'Princess and the Poacher', *Two Fables*, 1986

'Princess Mammalia', *Two Fables*, 1986

'The Bookseller', *Playboy* magazine, January 1987 [*The Complete Short Stories Volume Two*, 2013]

'The Surgeon', *Playboy* magazine, January 1988 [*The Complete Short Stories Volume Two*, 2013]

'Death in the Square: A Christmas Mystery in Four Parts' [First part by Dahl], *Telegraph* Weekend Magazine, December 1988

Short Story Collections

Listed by year of original publication

Over To You, New York: Reynall & Hiychcock, 1946

Someone Like You, New York: Alfred A. Knopf, 1953

Kiss Kiss, New York: Alfred A. Knopf, 1960

Twenty-Nine Kisses from Roald Dahl, London: Michael Joseph, 1969

Switch Bitch, New York: Alfred A. Knopf, 1974

The Wonderful Story of Henry Sugar and Six More, London: Jonathan Cape, 1977

The Best of Roald Dahl, New York: Vintage Books, 1978

Tales of the Unexpected, London: Michael Joseph, 1979

More Tales of the Unexpected, London: Michael Joseph, 1980

A Roald Dahl Selection: Nine Short Stories, London: Longmans, 1980

Two Fables, London: Viking Press, 1986

Ah, Sweet Mystery of Life: The Country Stories of Roald Dahl, London: Michael Joseph, 1989

The Roald Dahl Treasury, London: Jonathan Cape, 1997

The Great Automatic Grammatizator and Other Stories, London: Puffin, 2001

Skin and Other Stories, New York: Puffin, 2002

The Complete Short Stories Volume One, 1944–53, London: Penguin Books, 2013

The Complete Short Stories Volume Two, 1954–88, London: Penguin Books, 2013

Books

The Gremlins, New York: Walt Disney/Random House, 1943

Sometime Never: A Fable for Supermen, New York: Charles Scribner's Sons, 1948

James and the Giant Peach, New York: Alfred A. Knopf, 1961

Charlie and the Chocolate Factory, New York: Alfred A. Knopf, 1964

The Magic Finger, New York: Harper & Row, 1966

Fantastic Mr Fox, New York: Alfred A. Knopf, 1970

Charlie and the Great Glass Elevator, New York: Alfred A. Knopf, 1972

Danny, the Champion of the World, New York: Alfred A. Knopf, 1975

The Enormous Crocodile, New York: Alfred A. Knopf, 1978

My Uncle Oswald, London: Michael Joseph, 1979

The Twits, London: Jonathan Cape, 1980

George's Marvellous Medicine, London: Jonathan Cape, 1981

Roald Dahl's Revolting Rhymes, London: Jonathan Cape, 1982

The BFG, New York: Farrar, Straus and Giroux, 1982

Dirty Beasts, London: Jonathan Cape, 1983

The Witches, New York: Farrar, Straus and Giroux, 1983

Boy: Tales of Childhood, London: Jonathan Cape, 1984

The Giraffe and the Pelly and Me, New York: Farrar, Straus and Giroux, 1985

Going Solo, London: Jonathan Cape, 1986

Matilda, New York: Viking Kestrel, 1988

Esio Trot, London: Jonathan Cape, 1989

Rhyme Stew, London: Jonathan Cape, 1989

The Vicar of Nibbleswicke, London: Century, 1991

The Minpins, London: Jonathan Cape, 1991

Roald Dahl's Guide to Railway Safety, British Railways Board, 1991

Memories with Food at Gipsy House (with Felicity Dahl; later renamed *The Roald Dahl Cookbook*), London: Viking, 1991

The Roald Dahl Diary (later renamed *My Year*), London: Jonathan Cape, 1991

The Roald Dahl Treasury, London: Jonathan Cape, 1997

More About Boy, Puffin Books, 2008

Journalism (Selected)

'The Amazing Eyes of Kuda Box', *Argosy* magazine, July 1952

'My Wife: Patricia Neal', *Ladies Home Journal*, May 1949

'What I told Ophelia and Lucy about God', *Redbook* magazine, July 1952

'MEASLES: A Dangerous Illness', Sandwell Health Authority, 1988 (first published as a letter in 1986)

Other Sources (Selected)

Barry Farrell, 'The Gallant Fight of Pat Neal', *Life* magazine, October 1965

Barry Farrell, *Pat and Roald* (London: Hutchinson & Co, 1970)

Valerie Eaton Griffith, *A Stroke in the Family* (London: Penguin, 1970). Note this out of print book is available to order, or download from the East Kent Stroke Association website. http://s475526256.websitehome.co.uk/ekshome/family_stroke/index.html

Patricia Neal, *As I Am* (New York: Simon and Schuster, 1988)

Jeremy Treglown, *Roald Dahl, A Biography* (London: Faber and Faber, 1994)

Jennet Conant, *The Irregulars: Roald Dahl and the British Spy Ring in Wartime Washington* (New York: Simon and Schuster, 2008)

Donald Sturrock, *Storyteller: The Life of Roald Dahl* (London: HarperPress, 2010)

Anna Ritchie, *Stroke Association: History Perspective 1898–2012 Parts 1 & 2*. The Stroke Association, 2011. https://www.stroke.org.uk/what-we-do/who-we-are/our-history

Inside Roald Dahl's Writing Hut (Roald Dahl Museum and Story Centre, 2012)

Lucy Mangan, *Inside Charlie's Chocolate Factory* (London: Penguin Books, 2014)

Susan Rennie (Ed.), *Oxford Roald Dahl Dictionary* (Oxford: Oxford University Press, 2016)

Donald Sturrock (Ed.), *Love from Boy* (London: John Murray, 2016)

Notes

In the citations below, RDMSC is The Roald Dahl Museum and Story Centre. [The year of first publication is shown in square brackets].

Chapter 1: The Witching Hour

p.8   *The witching hour* ... Roald Dahl, *The BFG* (London: Puffin Books, 1984 [1982]), p.10.

p.9   *Somebody ran to fetch* ... Roald Dahl, *Boy* (London, Jonathan Cape, 1984), p.13.

p.10   As you may surmise ... P. Blomstedt, 'Orthopedic Surgery in Ancient Egypt', *Acta Orthopaedica* 85 (2014), pp.670–6.

p.10   Some scientists believe ... Patricia C. Rice and Norah Moloney, *Biological Anthropology and Prehistory: Exploring our Human Ancestry* (New York: Pearson Education, 1985), pp.178–9.

p.11   *... we stood there spellbound* ... Roald Dahl, *Boy*, p.87.

p.11   *'Toothbrush bristles* ... Ibid., p.88.

p.11   'they got it just in time ... Roald Dahl, letter to Sofie Magdalene, 18 April 1945, cited in Donald Sturrock (ed.), *Love From Boy: Roald Dahl's Letters to His Mother* (London: John Murray, 2016), p.272.

p.12   Darwin proposed this small ... Charles Darwin, 'Jim's Jesus' in *The Descent of Man, and Selection in Relation to Sex* (London: John Murray, 1871).

p.12   In recent years ... Rob Dun, 'Your Appendix Could Save Your Life', *Scientific American* online, 2 January 2012, http://blogs.scientificamerican.com/guest-blog/your-appendix-could-save-your-life/

p.12   Bacteria play a key role ... Ibid.

p.12   A study published in 2011 ... G. Y. Im, R. J. Modayil, C. T. Lin, S. J. Geier, D. S. Katz, M. Feuerman, J. H. Grendell, 'The appendix may protect against

Clostridium difficile recurrence', *Clinical Gastroenterology and Hepatology* 9 (2011), pp.1072–7.

p.12 Why not replace the bacteria ... William Kremer, 'The brave new world of DIY faecal transplant', *BBC World Service* online, 27 May 2014, http://www.bbc.co.uk/news/magazine-27503660

p.13 'Thanks awfully for the ... Roald Dahl, letter to Sofie Magdalene, 3 June 1934, cited in Donald Sturrock, *Love From Boy*, p.85.

p.13 'acted on me like ... Roald Dahl, letter to Sofie Magdalene, 7 November 1932, cited in Donald Sturrock, *Love From Boy*, p.67.

p.13 These included *Superdophilus* ... *Superdophilus* product insert, RDMSC, RD16/1/5.

p.14 'You writers should know ... Roald Dahl. Speech given at 'Beaminster', RDMSC, RD/6/1/1.

p.14 In *Boy*, Dahl described ... Roald Dahl, *Boy*, p.116.

p.15 It was at Repton ... Ibid., p.134.

p.15 'I have no doubt at all,' ... Ibid., p.135.

p.16 the Bristol Stool Chart ... S. J. Lewis, K. W. Heato, 'Stool form scale as a useful guide to intestinal transit time', *Scand J Gastroenterol* 32 (1997), pp.920–4.

p.16 An unscheduled visit ... Roald Dahl, 'The Wonderful Story of Henry Sugar' in *The Wonderful Story of Henry Sugar* (London: Penguin Books, 1988 [1977]), p.193.

p.16 At Repton one of ... Roald Dahl, *Boy*, p.145.

p.16 *Culture of the Abdomen* ... F. A. Hornibrook, 'The Culture of the Abdomen: Obesity and Reducing in Britain, circa 1900–1939', *Zweiniger–Bargielowska Journal of British Studies* 44:2 (April 2005), pp.239–73.

p.17 Ophelia thought that perhaps ... Ophelia Dahl, conversation with the author, 18 January 2016.

Chapter 2: Prodding and Poking

p.18 However, following *The Great Mouse Plot* ... Roald Dahl, *Boy* (London, Jonathan Cape, 1984), pp.35–7.

p.18 *I lay on the* ... Ibid., p.89.

p.19 In the 1950s, Richard Asher ... R. Asher, 'Munchausen's syndrome', *The Lancet* (1951), pp.339–41.

p.19 Asher named the syndrome ... Rudolf Erich Raspe, *The Surprising Adventures of Baron Munchausen* (Lulu Press, 2013 [1785]).

p.19 'Asher thought there was ... Asher, 'Munchausen's syndrome', pp.339–41.

p.21 *Astri was far and ... .* Roald Dahl, *Boy*, p.21.

p.21 Mr Wormwood, her brutish ... Roald Dahl, *Matilda* (London: Puffin 2013 [1988]), p.16.

p.24 *'Open your mouth,' ...* Roald Dahl, *Boy*, p.65.

p.25 *Still crouching low ...* Ibid., p.113.

p.26 He didn't agree ... Ibid., p.22.

p.26 The indignation Dahl felt ... Roald Dahl, 'Galloping Foxley', in *Completely Unexpected Tales* (London: Penguin Books, 1986 [1953]), pp.72–86.

p.26 His academic record at ... Donald Sturrock, *Storyteller: The Life of Roald Dahl* (London: HarperPress, 2010), p.91.

Chapter 3: Into Africa

p.28 Now he would have ... Roald Dahl, *Boy* (London: Jonathon Cape, 1984), p.152.

p.29 *What the snake did ...* Roald Dahl, *Going Solo* (London: Jonathon Cape, 1986), p.56.

p.29 *Wham! Salimu struck first. ...* Ibid., p.37.

p.29 In 'The Wish', a boy ... Roald Dahl, 'The Wish', in *The Complete Short Stories, Volume One, 1944–1953* (London: Penguin Books, 2013 [1953]), pp.471–5.

p.29 *'I was reading,' ...* Roald Dahl, 'Poison', in *Completely Unexpected Tales* (London: Penguin Books, 1986 [1950]), p.288.

p.30 'If a black mamba ... Roald Dahl, *Boy*, p.159.

p.31 A lot of this is ... D. A. Warrell, 'Snake bite', *The Lancet* 375 (2010), pp.77–88.

p.31 In South Asia, ... F. Chappuis, S. K. Sharma, N. Jha, L. Loutan, P. A. Bovier, 'Protection against snake bites by sleeping under a bed net in southeastern Nepal', *American Journal of Tropical Medicine and Hygiene* 77 (2007), pp.197–9.

p.32 Newer molecular approaches ... D. A. Warrell, J. M. Gutierrez, J. J. Calvete, D. Williams, 'New approaches and technologies of venomics to meet the challenge of human envenoming by snakebites in India', *Indian Journal of Medical Research* 138 (2013), pp.38–59.

p.33 This blood-pressure treatment ... J. M. Crow, 'Venomous drugs: the cancer-killing scorpion', *New Scientist* online, 2 May 2012, https://www.newscientist.com/article/mg21428632-000-venomous-drugs-the-cancer-killing scorpion/

p.34 Dr Michael Streule ... Michael Streule, conversation with the author, 19 June 2016.

p.34 Dahl wanted to know ... Ibid.

p.34 'They wanted to take ... Roald Dahl, letter to Sofie Magdalene, 18 February 1961, cited in Donald Sturrock (ed.), *Love From Boy: Roald Dahl's Letters to His Mother* (London: John Murray, 2016), p.286.

p.36 Dahl proudly wrote ... Roald Dahl, letter to Sofie Magdalene, 15/16 April 1939, cited in Donald Sturrock, *Love From Boy*, p.122.

p.36 Years later when ... Ophelia Dahl, conversation with the author, 27 April 2016.

p.37 'Last week I finally ... Roald Dahl, letter to Sofie Magdalene, undated June/July 1939, cited in Donald Sturrock, *Love From Boy*, p.129.

p.39 Marsh was more than ... Donald Sturrock, *Storyteller: The Life of Roald Dahl* (London: HarperPress, 2010), p.210.

p.41 Together we studied hundreds ... M. Mallewa, P. Vallely, B. Faragher, D. Banda, P. Klapper, M. Mukaka, H. Khofi, P. Pensulo, T. Taylor, M. Molyneux, T. Solomon, 'Viral central nervous system infections in children from a malaria-endemic area of Malawi: a prospective cohort study', *Lancet Global Health* online 1 (2013), pp.e153–e60.

Chapter 4: Crash

p.45 Here there were ... Roald Dahl, letter to Sofie Magdalene, 8 May 1940, cited in Donald Sturrock (ed.), *Love From Boy: Roald Dahl's Letters to His Mother* (London: John Murray, 2016), p.174.

p.46 'My injuries in that ... Roald Dahl, *Going Solo* (London: Jonathon Cape, 1986), p.104.

p.46 *I think there was something* ... Roald Dahl, 'A Piece of Cake', in *The Wonderful Story of Henry Sugar, and Six More* (London: Penguin Books, 1988 [1946]), p.227.

p.46 *'I'm a wreck!' groaned* ... Roald Dahl, *James and the Giant Peach* (London: Puffin Books, 2001), p.114.

p.46 'My face hurt ... Roald Dahl, 'Shot Down Over Libya', in *Saturday Evening Post* (August 1942), p.38.

p.47 *'Where's your blasted nose* ... Ibid., p.39.

p.47 '... blindness, not to mention ... Roald Dahl, *Going Solo*, p.112.

p.47 *'What is it called* ... Ibid., p.110.

p.49 *'We can't have you* ... Ibid., p.113.

p.49 *It seemed to me* ... Ibid., p.112.

p.49 'She had a lovely ... Ibid., p.115.

p.51 'Hepatticus' described the musings ... 'Hepatticus', *Oxford Medical School Gazette* (1989–1992).

p.51 For Dahl, 'Dippy Dud' ... Roald Dahl, 'Whips and Scorpions', in *The Shell Magazine* (September 1937), p.434.

p.51 It was later moved ... 'Sir Hepatticus', *BMA News Review* (October 1992 – September 1998).

Chapter 5: A Lucky Piece of Cake

p.55 *This was a magnificent* ... Roald Dahl, 'Lucky Break', in *The Wonderful Story of Henry Sugar, and Six More* (London: Penguin Books, 1988 [1977]), p.216.

p.55 Good heavens, *I thought* ... Roald Dahl, *Going Solo* (London: Jonathon Cape, 1986), p.139.

p.55 Landing at a remote ... Ibid., p.193.

p.56 *I got them only* ... Ibid., p.200.

p.56 After a year ... Jennet Conant, *The Irregulars: Roald Dahl and the British Spy Ring in Wartime Washington* (New York: Simon and Schuster, 2008), p.30.

p.56 They agreed to go ... Roald Dahl, 'Lucky Break', p.213.

p.56 *'Wouldn't that be easier* ... Ibid., p.214.

p.57 *'Hell's bells,* ... Roald Dahl, 'Shot Down Over Libya', in *Saturday Evening Post* (1 August 1942), p.38.

p.58 'I don't remember ... Roald Dahl, 'A Piece of Cake', in *The Wonderful Story of Henry Sugar, and Six More* (London: Penguin Books, 1988 [1946]), p.226.

p.58 *... there is an aspect* ... Roald Dahl, *Going Solo*, p.101.

p.58 In *Going Solo*... Donald Sturrock, *Storyteller: The Life of Roald Dahl* (London: HarperPress, 2010), p.133.

p.60 'I don't lie,' Dahl wrote ... Roald Dahl, Ideas Book No. 1 (c.1945–8), RDMSC, RD/11/1.

p.60 'had woven around himself ... Donald Sturrock, *Storyteller: the Life of Roald Dahl*, p.429 .

p.62 'hair like a fuzzie-wuzzie' ... Donald Sturrock, *Storyteller: The Life of Roald Dahl*, p.75.

p.62 Dahl's official biographer ... Roald Dahl, cited in Donald Sturrock (Ed.),

Love From Boy: Roald Dahl's Letters to His Mother (London: John Murray, 2016), p.37.

p.62   This was more than ... Roald Dahl, *The BFG* (London: Puffin Books, 1984 [1982]), p.10.

p.63   After leaving school ... Donald Sturrock, *Storyteller: The Life of Roald Dahl*, p.100.

p.64   Or a sexually repressed ... Roald Dahl, 'Georgy Porgy', in *Completely Unexpected Tales* (London: Penguin Books, 1986 [1960]), pp.312–35.

p.64   Dahl's stories for children ... Roald Dahl, *James and the Giant Peach* (London: Puffin Books, 2001 [1961]; *Charlie and the Chocolate Factory* (London: Puffin Books, 1985 [1964]); *The Twits* (London: Puffin Books, 2001 [1980]).

p.65   But one of the ... Anwar Hussein, conversation with the author, 9 December 2015.

p.65   Later, in one of ... Roald Dahl, Notebook of Limericks, RDMSC, Archive RD/7/4.

p.65   'The filthy old fizzwiggler!' ... Roald Dahl, *The BFG*, p.39.

Chapter 6: Tales

p.67   For Dahl to write ... Donald Sturrock (dir.) 'An Awfully Big Adventure: Roald Dahl', in the BBC TV Omnibus series *The Making of Modern Children's Literature* (1 January 1998), transcript RDMSC, AC/1.

p.68   Sometimes, when I'm trying ... Roald Dahl, Speech about Roald Dahl's Fascination with Medicine, RDMSC, RD/6/1/1/7.

p.68   Dahl was a great ... Roald Dahl, *Matilda* (London: Puffin, 2013 [1988]), p.180, includes a quote by Miss Honey of Dylan Thomas's *In Country Sleep*; 'Fern Hill' by Dylan Thomas was included in Dahl's list for BBC Radio 4, *Desert Island Discs*, 2 November 1979. http://www.bbc.co.uk/programmes/p009mwxz/segments

p.68   Dahl had a set ... Roald Dahl, Notes in preparation for a Speech Given to the Speech Rehabilitation Institute, April 1971, RDMSC, RD/6/1/16.

p.69   At the party to welcome ... Roald Dahl, letter to Sofie Magdalene, 27 November 1942, cited in Donald Sturrock (Ed.), *Love From Boy: Roald Dahl's Letters to His Mother* (London: John Murray, 2016), p.233.

p.69   'It was called *The Gremlins* ... Roald Dahl, 'Lucky Break', in *The Wonderful Story of Henry Sugar, and Six More* (London: Penguin Books, 1988 [1977]), p.216.

p.70 'I'm so busy these … Roald Dahl, letter to Sofie Magdalene, 7 January 1943, cited in Sturrock, *Love From Boy*, p.237.

p.70 *He glanced down again* … Roald Dahl, 'Beware of the Dog', in *The Complete Short Stories, Volume One, 1944–1953* (London: Penguin Books, 2013 [1944]), p.44.

p.70 They were first introduced … Patricia Neal, *As I Am* (New York: Simon and Schuster, 1988), p.155.

p.71 'I behaved badly, … Barry Farrell, *Pat and Roald* (London: Hutchinson & Co, 1970), pp.123–4.

p.71 To Pat 'there seemed … Patricia Neal, *As I Am*, p.156.

p.71 'My God, you make … Ibid., p.160.

p.71 *'Up the scale* … Roald Dahl, 'The Sound Machine', in *Completely Unexpected Tales* (London: Penguin Books, 1986 [1949]), p.300.

p.72 Twenty years earlier as … Roald Dahl, *The Kumbak II*, 1926, RDMSC, RD/5/4.

p.73 *Sometimes, on a very* … Roald Dahl, *The BFG* (London: Puffin Books, 1984 [1982]), p.44.

p.73 *'An absolutely clean child* … Roald Dahl, *The Witches* (London: Jonathan Cape, 2010 [1983]), p.33.

p.73 Dahl was fascinated … Roald Dahl, 'Kuda Bux', *Argosy* magazine 335 (1952), pp.16–19, 99–95.

p.74 *Even the doctors who* … Roald Dahl, 'The Wonderful Story of Henry Sugar', *The Wonderful Story of Henry Sugar* (London: Penguin Books, 1988 [1977]), p.144.

p.74 'Everyone thought he had … Jeremy Treglown, *Roald Dahl, A Biography* (London: Faber and Faber, 1994), p.97.

p.75 Douglas Bisgood was a … Ibid., p.62.

p.75 She was treated with … Patricia Neal, *As I Am* (New York: Simon and Schuster, 1988), p.183.

p.75 Its name was changed … Patricia Neal, *As I Am*, p.219.

p.76 He had just published … E. N. Goodman, I. A. Ginsberg, M. A. Robinson, 'An improved apparatus for measuring the electrogastrogram', *Science* 113 (1951), pp.682–3.

p.76 Dahl's gastrointestinal rumblings … E. N. Goodman, H. Colcher, G. M. Katz, C. L. Dangler, 'The clinical significance of the electrogastrogram', *Gastroenterology* 29 (1955), pp.598–608.

p.76 *'I should immediately* … Roald Dahl, 'William and Mary', in *Completely Unexpected Tales* (London: Penguin Books, 1986 [1960]), p.162.

Chapter 7: Threats and Dangers

p.80 *It was a crisp ...* Patricia Neal, *As I Am* (New York: Simon and Schuster, 1988), p.215.

p.80 *Theo was in the ...* Roald Dahl, A Note on Theo's Accident, RDMSC, RD/11/2.

p.81 *First she strapped ...* Ibid.

p.81 'His general attitude ... Ibid.

p.81 *You may or may ...* Roald Dahl, 'William and Mary', in *Completely Unexpected Tales* (London: Penguin Books, 1986 [1960]), p.164.

p.82 By Christmas 1960, ... Patricia Neal, *As I Am*, p.218.

p.82 Luckily Ransohoff, whose initial ... J. Ransohoff, R. B. Hiatt, 'Ventriculo-peritoneal anastomosis in the treatment of hydrocephalus; utilization of the suprahepatic space', *Transactions of the American Neurological Association* 56 (1952), pp.147–51.

p.83 'It is a long ... Roald Dahl, 'My Wife Patricia Neal', in *Ladies Home Journal* September 1965.

p.84 The shunt 'had a ... Patricia Neal, *As I Am*, p.219.

p.84 'Very distressing, the whole ... Roald Dahl, letter to Sofie Magdalene Dahl, 16 February 1961, RDMSC, RD/14/5/10/1.

p.84 Cary Grant's wife, for ... Roald Dahl, A Note on Theo's Accident, RDMSC, RD/11/2.

p.85 *I don't think much ...* Roald Dahl, letter to Sofie Magdalene, 18 February 1961, RDMSC, RD/14/5/10/10, cited in Donald Sturrock, *Storyteller: The Life of Roald Dahl* (London: HarperPress, 2010), p.373.

p.85 Till later described... Kenneth Till in conversation with Jeremy Treglown, cited in Jeremy Treglown *Roald Dahl, A Biography* (London: Faber and Faber, 1994), p.131.

p.85 Till found 'he had ... Ibid., p.132.

p.85 He could be obsessional ... H. Brown, 'Kenneth Till', *The Lancet* 372 (2008), p.1216.

p.86 For example, when they ... Roald Dahl, 'Simple method for testing flow from two liquid filled areas with pressure differential of 40 mm', RDMSC, RD/16/1/4.

p.86 Another shows Stanley Wade's ... Roald Dahl, Stanley Wade, 'Sketches for the development of the valve', RDMSC, RD/16/1/4.

p.87 'A Valve for the ... Kenneth Till, 'A Valve for the Treatment of Hydrocephalus', *The Lancet* 1 (1964), p.202.

p.87   'The basis of many ... Roald Dahl, 'Draft article for *The Lancet*',
       RD/6/2/1/1.

p.87   'I think the end ... Kenneth Till, letter to Roald Dahl, 11 September 1963,
       RDMSC, RD/16/1/4.

p.87   Perhaps surprisingly, the Americans ... A. L. Sandler, D. Sturrock,
       J. Branfield, R. Abbott, J. T. Goodrich, A. Biswas, L. B. Daniels III,
       E. S. Flamm, 'Marvelous Medicine: the untold story of the Wade-Dahl-Till
       valve', *Journal of Neurosurgical Pediatrics* 9 (2012), pp.482–90.

p.88   He moved, soon after ... Kenneth Shulman, letter to Roald Dahl, 1964,
       cited in ibid.

p.88   'I am still worried ... Roald Dahl, letter to Kenneth Till, October 1968,
       RDMSC, RD/16/1/4.

p.88   America is America ... Roald Dahl, letter to Kenneth Till, 30 September
       1968, RDMSC, RD/16/1/4.

p.89   'I would like to ... Roald Dahl, handwritten note to Stanley Wade, 28
       October 1965, RDMSC, RD/16/1/4.

p.89   'We were not instructed ... Ian Wilson, letter to Roald Dahl, 28 July 1965,
       RDMSC, RD/16/1/4.

p.89   This group was one ... ASBAH (Association for Spina Bifida and
       Hydrocephalus), WebHealth online, http://webhealth.co.uk/support-groups/
       asbah-association-for-spina-bifida-and-hydrocephalus

p.89   This was renamed as ... 'Shine's Golden Anniversary', Shine (Spina Bifida,
       Hydrocephalus, Information, Networking, Equality) Charity online, http://
       www.shinecharity.org.uk/goldenanniversary

p.89   the archive reveals ... Roald Dahl, typescript of the first draft of *Matilda*,
       RDMSC, RD/2/27/2, pp.45–6.

p.90   However, English Professor Damian Walford Davies ... Roald Dahl,
       Matilda (London: Puffin, 2013 [1988]) p.171; and Damian Walford Davies,
       'Dahl and Dylan: *Matilda*, "In Country Sleep" and Twentieth-century
       Topographies of Fear', in Damian Walford Davies (Ed.), *Roald Dahl, Wales
       of the Unexpected* (Cardiff: University of Wales Press, 2016), p.93.

p.90   'He was not cruel or nasty ... Ophelia Dahl, conversation with the author,
       6 June 2016.

p.91   Indeed, Liccy had to restrain ... Liccy Dahl, conversation with the author,
       14 November 2014.

Chapter 8: 'It'll Be Good for Them'

p.95 Although the Dahl family ... Ophelia Dahl, conversation with the author, January 2016.

p.96 By this stage its ... Lucy Mangan, *Inside Charlie's Chocolate Factory* (London: Penguin Books, 2014), p.32.

p.96 However, the Dahls had ... Patricia Neal, *As I Am* (New York: Simon and Schuster, 1988), p.230.

p.96 "This was the same" ... Roald Dahl, *Boy* (London: Jonathon Cape, 1984), p.116.

p.97 *I was sitting on her* ... Roald Dahl, 'Measles, a Dangerous Illness', 1986, RDMSC, RD/17/1/1.

p.98 'Olivia's body was still ... Patricia Neal, *As I Am*, p.231.

p.98 To Pat this seemed ... Ibid.

p.99 *He said I'm afraid* ... Roald Dahl, *Olivia*, RDMSC, RD/7/2.

p.100 Long before we could ... Robert R. Jarrett, 'Numbered Diseases of Childhood: Rashes', *Pediatric Housecalls* online, 2 March 2014, http://pediatric-house-calls.djmed.net/numbered-skin-rash-diseases-childhood

p.100 The numbering reflects ... C. Bialecki, H. M. Feder, Jr., J. M. Grant-Kels, 'The six classic childhood exanthems: a review and update', *Journal of the American Academy of Dermatology* 21 (1989), pp.891–903.

p.101 However the virus... David Shultz, 'What does measles actually do?' *Science* online, 30 January 2015, http://www.sciencemag.org/news/2015/01/what-does-measles-actually-do

Chapter 9: A Clue Here

p.106 'There must be some ... Roald Dahl, letter to John Adams, 7 September 1966, RDMSC, RD/16/1/5.

p.106 In 1972 Adams sent ... J. M. Adams, 'Measles and vaccinia antibodies in multiple sclerosis', *Journal of the American Medical Association* 240 (1978), p.637.

p.106 Dahl thanked Adams for ... Roald Dahl, letter to John Adams, 25 August 1952, RDMSC, RD/17/1/1.

p.106 Butler's reply describes ... Neville Butler, letter to Roald Dahl, 20 March 1982, RDMSC, RD/17/1/1.

p.107 Casanova and his team ... S. Y. Zhang, E. Jouanguy, S. Ugolini, A. Smahi, G. Elain, P. Romero, D. Segal, V. Sancho-Shimizu, L. Lorenzo, A. Puel, C. Picard, A. Chapgier, S. Plancoulaine, M. Titeux, C. Cognet,

H. von Bernuth, C. L. Ku, A. Casrouge, X. X. Zhang, L. Barreiro, J. Leonard, C. Hamilton, P. Lebon, B. Heron, L. Vallee, L. Quintana-Murci, A. Hovnanian, F. Rozenberg, E. Vivier, F. Geissmann, M. Tardieu, L. Abel, J. L. Casanova, 'TLR3 deficiency in patients with herpes simplex encephalitis', *Science* 317 (2007), pp.1522–7.

p.108 The sequencing of the ... Robbie Gonzalez, 'Breakthrough: now we can sequence a human genome for just $1,000', *io9* online, 15 January 2014, http://io9.gizmodo.com/breakthrough-now-we-can-sequence-a-human-genome-for-ju-1502081435

p.109 According to Pat, Dahl ... Patricia Neal, *As I Am* (New York: Simon and Schuster, 1988), p.238.

p.109 *The emptiness when...* Roald Dahl, 'Only This', in *The Complete Short Stories, Volume One, 1944–1953* (London: Penguin Books, 2013 [1944]), p.38.

p.109 *The old man looked* ... Roald Dahl, 'Yesterday Was Beautiful', in *The Complete Short Stories, Volume One, 1944–1953* (London: Penguin Books, 2013 [1946]), p.81.

p.110 During his most sombre ... Donald Sturrock, *Storyteller: The Life of Roald Dahl* (London: HarperPress, 2010), p.390.

p.110 Liccy recalled that ... Liccy Dahl, conversation with the author, 14 November 2014.

p.110 Pat felt the Dahl family ... Patricia Neal, *As I Am*, p.235.

p.110 'How long are you ... Barry Farrell, *Pat and Roald* (London: Hutchinson & Co, 1970), p.83.

p.111 For Tessa, her father's ... Tessa Dahl, cited in Donald Sturrock, *Storyteller: The Life of Roald Dahl*, p.389.

p.111 *Thanks for your letter...* Roald Dahl, *Boy* (London, Jonathon Cape, 1984), pp.83–5.

p.112 'It happened so swiftly ... Barry Farrell, *Pat and Roald*, p.135.

p.112 Pat was able to ... Donald Sturrock, *Storyteller: The Life of Roald Dahl*, p.392.

p.112 Pat's 'mystical self' found ... Patricia Neal, *As I Am*, p.238.

p.112 Mormor often amazed ... Ibid., p.234.

p.112 Many years later she ... Roald Dahl, *The Witches* (London: Jonathan Cape, 2010 [1983]), p.18.

p.112 He needed to be ... Donald Sturrock, *Storyteller: The Life of Roald Dahl*, p.390.

p.112 'I would love to ... Roald Dahl, *The Weekend Guardian*, 1989.

p.113 Although he no longer... Barry Farrell, *Pat and Roald*, p.210.

p.113 *'Commune! I didn't know* ... Ibid.

Chapter 10: A Shot in the Arm

p.118 The polio vaccine developed ... J. L. Melnick, 'Current status of poliovirus infections', *Clinical Microbiology Reviews* 9 (1996), pp.293–300.

p.119 Dahl had offered ... Department of Health and Social Security, letter to Roald Dahl, 20 December 1985, RDMSC, RD/17/1/1.

p.119 His first letter ... Liccy Dahl, conversation with the author, 14 November 2014.

p.119 He discussed the importance ... Barry Smith, 'A Tale of the Unexpected'. (Unknown West Midlands hospital journal), RDMSC, RD/17/1/1.

p.119 Dahl was surprisingly reluctant ... Roald Dahl, letter to Barry Smith, 24 March 1986, RDMSC, RD/17/1/1.

p.119 'A pop star has ... Julie Porter, 'Olivia: A Tale of Tragedy', *Chiltern Newspapers*, 11 August 1986.

p.120 His open letter to ... Roald Dahl, 'Measles: a Dangerous Illness,' RDMSC, RD/17/1/1.

p.120 He appealed directly to ... Ibid.

p.120 'Do correct me if ... Roald Dahl, letter to Barry Smith, 24 February 1986, RDMSC, RD/17/1/1.

p.121 still quoted in British ... Tom Solomon, 'It shouldn't take the death of a child from measles for people to realise the importance of vaccines', *The Independent* online, 9 February 2015. http://www.independent.co.uk/voices/comment/it-shouldnt-take-the-death-of-a-child-for-people-to-realise-the-importance-of-vaccines-10034647.html

p.121 a legacy he 'would ... Liccy Dahl, conversation with the author, 10 June 2016.

p.121 The introduction of the ... 'Swansea measles: Ex-health minster Edwina Currie backs mandatory jabs', *BBC News* online, 21 April 2013, http://www.bbc.co.uk/news/uk-wales-22238818

p.121 'Dad would have been ... Ophelia Dahl, conversation with the author, 27 April 2016.

p.122 A rather curious film ... Hans Treffers (director), *Europe for Children*, Henk Van Mierlo Kreative Kommunikatie BV, 1988, personal collection of Hans Treffers.

p.122 'I have been invited ... Ibid.

p.122 Appealing to these industrialists ... Ibid.

p.122 The idea of eliminating ... Roald Dahl, speech for 'Europe for Children: Talk in Brussels for Europe for Children campaign', 24 March 1988, RDMSC, RD/6/1/2/25.

p.123 The Europe for Children ... Hans Treffers, conversation with the author, 25 January 2016.

p.123 The ninety-nine per cent ... M. Morales, R. H. Tangermann, S. G. F. Wassilak, 'Progress Toward Polio Eradication — Worldwide, 2015–2016, *Morbidity and Mortality Weekly Report* 65 (2016), pp.470–3.

p.123 Around the time Olivia ... Mario Borrelli and Anthony Thorne, *A Street Lamp and the Stars* (London: Peter Davies, 1963).

p.123 Dahl wrote in 'The Last Act' ... Roald Dahl, 'The Last Act', in *The Complete Short Stories, Volume Two, 1954–1988* (London: Penguin Books, 2013 [1966]), p.337.

p.124 Ophelia remembers a childless ... Ophelia Dahl, conversation with the author, 27 April 2016.

p.124 Ever since he was a young man ... Donald Sturrock, *Storyteller: The Life of Roald Dahl* (London: HarperPress, 2010), p.311.

p.124 'I myself have seen ... Roald Dahl, letter to Harold Oppenheimer, 25 April 1974, RDMSC, RD/17/1/1.

p.124 'He would pack me ... Ophelia Dahl, conversation with the author, 27 April 2016.

p.125 'Now I have a ... Roald Dahl, letter to Neville Butler, 1 June 1982, RDMSC, RD/16/1/5.

p.125 He studied children over ... Harvey Goldstein, 'Neville Butler – Paediatrician at the forefront of research into children's growth', *The Guardian* online, 15 March 2007, http://www.theguardian.com/society/2007/mar/15/health.guardianobituaries

p.125 'This one has got ... Roald Dahl, letter to Neville Butler, 1 June 1982, RDMSC, RD/16/1/5.

p.125 'As an author, the written ... Roald Dahl, 'British Dyslexia Association Awareness Campaign', 23 January 1990, RDMSC, RD/17/1/1.

p.125 This is about a reverend ... Roald Dahl, *The Vicar of Nibbleswike* (London: Penguin, 1992 [1991]).

p.125 In 1991 the charity appointed ... 'Anne's Story', The Land of remarkable People online http://www.remarkablepeople.org.uk/annes-story-first-ever-roald-dahl-nurse-specialist-creates-sense-community-epilepsy-patients

p.126 In 2010 the charity became ... Roald Dahl's Marvellous Children's Charity http://www.roalddahl.com/charity/about-the-charity/history-of-the-charity

p.126 'Liccy has done a ... Donald Sturrock, conversation with the author, 16 June 2016.

p.126 An old coaching inn and yard ... Ibid.

p.126 There are now aspirations ... Declan Butler, 'Measles by the numbers: A race to eradication', in *Nature* online, 11 February 2015, http://www.nature.com/news/measles-by-the-numbers-a-race-to-eradication-1.16897

p.127 'What I want to ... Roald Dahl, 'A Christmas Message to Children', RDMSC, RD/14/6/71.

p.127 Dahl later recorded... Roald Dahl, 'What I told Ophelia and Lucy about God', in *Redbook* magazine, December 1971.

Chapter 11: A Bubble Bursts

p.132 *Dr Carton examined her ...* Roald Dahl, letter to Sofie Magdalene, 28 Feburary 1965, RDMSC, RD/14/5/11/1.

p.133 *Whilst I was there ...* Ibid.

p.137 *'Her condition is very ...* Barry Farrell, *Pat and Roald* (London: Hutchinson & Co, 1970), p.11.

p.138 'No doctor likes ... Roald Dahl, typed notes for a speech about his fascination with medicine; audience unknown, RDMSC, RD/6/1/1/7.

p.139 'Reports of my death ... Patricia Neal, *As I Am* (New York: Simon and Schuster, 1988), pp.224–5.

p.140 'It was wonderful to ... Roald Dahl, 'My Wife Patricia Neal', in *Ladies Home Journal*, September 1965.

p.140 'The squeezes were good ... Ibid.

p.140 'She's going to live ... Barry Farrell, *Pat and Roald*, p.21.

p.140 'It was one of ... Roald Dahl, 'My Wife Patricia Neal', p.121.

Chapter 12: The Mysterious Joy of Language

p.144 Dr Nancy Helm-Estabrooks ... Bridget Murray Law, 'Getting in Tune With Clients With Aphasia', *American Speech-Language-Hearing Association (ASHA)* online, 17 (2012), pp.12–13. http://leader.pubs.asha.org/article.aspx?articleid=2280522

p.144 More recent functional ... A. Zumbansen, I. Peretz, S. Hebert, 'Melodic intonation therapy: back to basics for future research', *Frontiers in Neurology* 5 (2014), p.7.

p.146 *After a stroke...* Patricia Neal, *As I Am* (New York: Simon and Schuster, 1988), p.261.

p.146 *Her speech is coming* ... Roald Dahl, 'My Wife Patricia Neal', in *Ladies Home Journal*, September 1965.

p.147 One friend who visited ... Patricia Neal, *As I Am*, p.236.

p.147 In constraint-induced ... E. Taub, G. Uswatte, R. Pidikiti, 'Constraint-Induced Movement Therapy: A new family of techniques with broad application to physical rehabilitation – a clinical review', *Journal of Rehabilitation Research and Development* 36 (1999), pp.237–51.

p.147 'I want a ... Roald Dahl, 'My Wife Patricia Neal'.

p.148 *Just because I is* ... Roald Dahl, *The BFG* (London: Puffin Books, 1984 [1982]), p.53.

p.148 *'Us giants is making* ... Ibid., p.67.

p.149 *The BFG* had many more ... J. Cheetham, 'Dahl's Neologisms', *Children's Literature in Education* online 47 (2015), pp.1–17, http://link.springer.com/article/10.1007/s10583-015-9254-2

p.149 From his very earliest ... Roald Dahl, *The Gremlins* (New York: Walt Disney/Random House, 1943).

p.149 In *Charlie and the Chocolate Factory*, the snozzberry ... Roald Dahl, *Charlie and the Chocolate Factory* (London: Puffin Books, 1985 [1964]), p.113.

p.149 *'How did you manage* ... Roald Dahl, *My Uncle Oswald* (London: Penguin Books, 1980 [1979]), p.234.

p.150 Then, as Cheetham's analysis ... J. Cheetham, 'Dahl's Neologisms'.

p.150 Also for the first time in... Roald Dahl, *Charlie and the Great Glass Elevator* (London: Puffin Books, 1986 [1973]).

p.151 *'There never was any* ... Roald Dahl, *The BFG*, p.50.

p.151 *'... you must simply try* ... Ibid., p.53.

p.152 'No, he was not ... Liccy Dahl, conversation with the author, 10 June 2016.

p.152 Some experts have ... J. Culley, 'Roald Dahl – "It's about children and it's for children" – but is it suitable?', *Children's Literature in Education* 1 (1991), pp.59–73.

p.152 *The BFG* regularly features ... Christine Hall and Martin Coles, *Children's Reading Choices* (London: Routledge, 1999).

p.152 Twenty-five years after ... Kat Brown, 'Survey reveals 50 books that every child should read by 16', *The Telegraph* online, 2 March 2015, http://www.telegraph.co.uk/culture/books/booknews/11444349/Survey-reveals-50-books-that-every-child-should-read-by-16.html

Chapter 13: The Cabbage and the Giant

p.153 'Once in a while … Patricia Neal, *As I Am* (New York: Simon and Schuster, 1988), p.264.

p.154 *She had no self-pity,* … Roald Dahl, 'My Wife Patricia Neal', in *Ladies Home Journal*, September 1965.

p.155 'The prediction is … Patricia Neal, *As I Am*, p.268.

p.155 'Jolly good,' said Dahl … Ibid., p.270.

p.155 Constant stimulation was … Ibid., p.268.

p.156 As he later wrote … Roald Dahl, 'Foreword', in Valerie Eaton Griffith, *A Stroke in the Family* (London: Wildwood House 1975 [1970]), p.9.

p.156 Pat had difficulty counting … Patricia Neal, *As I Am*, p.280.

p.157 Dahl took over the … Donald Sturrock, *Storyteller: The Life of Roald Dahl* (London: HarperPress, 2010), p.422.

p.157 'How many sleeping pills … Barry Farrell, *Pat and Roald* (London: Hutchinson & Co, 1970), p.98.

p.157 Whilst Pat rested … Ibid., p.109.

p.158 Dahl stood behind … Ibid., p.111.

p.158 'It never for a … Valerie Eaton Griffith, *A Stroke in the Family* (London: Wildwood House 1975 [1970]), p.18.

p.158 *When I walked into* … Patricia Neal, *As I Am*, p.283.

p.159 On some days they … Ibid., p.285.

p.159 At one stage Tessa … Valerie Eaton Griffith, *A Stroke in the Family*, p.18.

p.159 However, when the 'omnipresent … Barry Farrell, *Pat and Roald*, p.156.

p.159 His sister Else looked … Ibid., p.156.

p.160 'Slowly, insidiously, and quite … Roadl Dahl, 'Foreword', in Valerie Eaton Griffith, *A Stroke in the Family*, p.10.

p.160 'A stroke patient… Roald Dahl, open letter to stroke patients and their families, 1966, cited in Barry Farrell, *Pat and Roald*, p.147.

p.161 Dahl would back them … Ibid.

p.162 In his introduction Dahl … Roald Dahl, 'Foreword', in Valerie Eaton Griffith, *A Stroke in the Family*, p.11.

p.162 *'How are you, Alan?'* … Valerie Eaton Griffith, *A Stroke in the Family*, p.22.

p.163 Forty years after … East Kent Stroke Association. Accessed at http:// eastkentstrokes.org/ 15 January 2016. With the reorganisation of the website to https://www.stroke.org.uk/finding-support/east-kent-strokes the relevent webpage is not currently available, but the book can be ordered online at: http:// www.cpibookdelivery.com/book/9780956512604/A_Stroke_in_the_Family

p.163 In the preface… Tony Rudd, 'Preface', Valerie Eaton Griffith, *A Stroke in the Family* (East Kent Strokes, 2010 [1970]).

Chapter 14: Thousands across the Country

p.164 they were also key … Anna Ritchie, *Stroke Association: History Perspective 1898–2012 Part 1*, p.29. The Stroke Association online, https://www.stroke.org.uk/sites/default/files/history_of_sa_web_p1.pdf

p.164 The programme was judged … V. E. Griffith, 'Volunteer scheme for dysphasia and allied problems in stroke patients', *British Medical Journal* 3 (1975), pp.633–5.

p.165 As noted in Dr Anne … Anna Ritchie, *Stroke Association: History Perspective 1898–2012 Part 1*, p.31.

p.165 Following Pat's death in 2010 … Mo Wilkinson, 'The Stroke Association Tribute to Patricia Neal 1926–2010, Honorary Vice President', in Anna Ritchie, *Stroke Association: History Perspective 1898–2012 Part 2*. The Stroke Association, p.81. https://www.stroke.org.uk/sites/default/files/history_of_sa_web_p2.pdf

p.166 'You'd better get … Patricia Neal, *As I Am* (New York: Simon and Schuster, 1988), p.292.

p.166 'The old pro … Roald Dahl, 'Foreword', in Valerie Eaton Griffith, *A Stroke in the Family* (London: Wildwood House 1975 [1970]), p.12.

p.167 From footage of the … Oscars YouTube Channel, 'Patricia Neal presenting Best Foreign Language Film Oscar® to *A Man and a Woman*'. https://www.youtube.com/watch?v=zQXXvjEJG_w

p.167 Dahl joined them … Barry Farrell, *Pat and Roald* (London: Hutchinson & Co, 1970), p.235.

p.169 Farrell describes how … Ibid., p.125.

p.169 Pat won another Oscar … Patricia Neal, *As I Am*, p.313.

p.169 It was based on … Shane Pitkin 'Plot Summary', *The Road Builder*, Internet Movie Database (IMDb) online, http://www.imdb.com/title/tt0067486/plotsummary?ref_=tt_ov_pl

p.170 The same honour… Olivia Parker, Chelsea Flower Show 2016: the debut of the Roald Dahl Rose, *Daily Telegraph* online, 22 May 2016, http://www.telegraph.co.uk/gardening/chelsea-flower-show/chelsea-flower-show-2016-the-debut-of-the-roald-dahl-rose/

p.170 Dahl wrote a television… Roald Dahl (screenplay), Allen Hooshire (director) Stroke Counter Stroke 1971.

p.170 Over the next few … Patricia Neal, *As I Am*, p.314.

p.170 The Patricia Neal Rehabilitation ... The Patricia Neal Rehabilitation Centre, http://www.patneal.org/

p.170 Susan Denson, one of their nannies ... Donald Sturrock, *Storyteller: The Life of Roald Dahl* (London: HarperPress, 2010), p.426.

p.171 Pat noticed some personality ... Barry Farrell, *Pat and Roald*, p.221.

p.171 'Not *one dream* ... Barry Farrell, *Pat and Roald*, p.157.

p.171 '*If you is really* ... Roald Dahl, *The BFG* (London: Puffin Books, 1984 [1982]), p.41.

p.171 She was more than ... Ophelia Dahl, conversation with the author, 27 April 2016.

p.171 'My grandfather was... Liccy Dahl, conversation with the author, 14 November 2014.

p.171 Liccy's mother was a descendant ... Donald Sturrock, *Storyteller: The Life of Roald Dahl*, p.453.

p.171 Her father was Professor ... Alphonsus Ligouri D'Abreu, (Dr.), *Geni* online https://www.geni.com/people/Alphonsus-D-Abreu/6000000001344929396

p.173 *When writing about oneself* ... Roald Dahl, *Boy* (London: Jonathan Cape, 1984), p.35.

Chapter 15: Rusting to Pieces

p.177 Dahl could have been ... Roald Dahl, *Sometime Never: A Fable for Supermen* (New York: Scribner's, 1948), p.129.

p.177 descriptions of biological warfare ... Ibid., p.209.

p.177 By 1944, four years ... Roald Dahl, letter to Sofie Magdalene, 9 August 1944, RDMSC, RD/14/5/3/17 cited in Donald Sturrock, *Storyteller: The Life of Roald Dahl* (London: HarperPress, 2010), p.238.

p.177 This was before magnetic ... J. R. Hesselink, 'Spine imaging: history, achievements, remaining frontiers', *American Journal of Roentgenology* 150 (1988), pp.1223–9, http://www.ajronline.org/doi/pdf/10.2214/ajr.150.6.1223

p.178 However, as Dahl discovered ... Roald Dahl, letter to Sofie Magdalene, 24 October 1944, RDMSC, RD/14/5/3/26 cited in Donald Sturrock, *Storyteller: The Life of Roald Dahl*, p.238.

p.178 She became a great ... Rosemary Higgs, conversation with the author, 14 June 2016.

p.178 Liccy's daughter Charlotte was involved ... Liccy Dahl, conversation with the author, 14 November 2014.

p.178 'Well, I shouldn't worry,' ... Ibid.

p.178 Charlotte eventally made ... Jake Fitzjones, 'One Hundred Leading Interior Deisgners – Charlotte Crosland', *House and Garden* online, http://www.houseandgarden.co.uk/top100/charlotte-crosland/

p.178 'Patient Roald Dahl, Male ... Roald Dahl, 'Patient Roald Dahl', RDMSC, RD/16/1/5.

p.179 'I am unwilling ... Roald Dahl, letter to David Seal, 11 December 1986, RDMSC, RD/16/1/5.

p.179 He changed from his ... Liccy Dahl, conversation with the author, 10 June 2016.

p.180 You should stop taking ... Astri Stuart, letter to Roald Dahl, 4 October 1980, RDMSC, RD/16/1/5.

p.180 Radionics was invented ... Mark Pilkington, 'A Vibe for Radionics', *The Guardian* online, 15 April 2004, https://www.theguardian.com/science/2004/apr/15/farout

p.180 The head of one ... Roald Dahl, *My Year* (London: Jonathan Cape 1993 [First published as *The Dahl Diary* 1992]), p.7.

p.181 'My body may be ... Donald Sturrock, *Storyteller: The Life of Roald Dahl*, p.552.

p.181 'In the country of ... Roald Dahl, letter to Hung Chen, 25 August 1989, RDMSC, RD/16/1/5.

p.181 Some doctors believed ... H. C. Chen, J. Wiek, A. Gupta, A. Luckie, E. M. Kohner, 'Effect of isovolaemic haemodilution on visual outcome in branch retinal vein occlusion', *British Journal of Ophthalmology*, 82 (1998), pp.162–7.

p.181 Dahl 'was whistled off ... Roald Dahl, letter to Hung Chen, 7 September 1989, RDMSC, RD/16/1/5.

p.181 'We have established ... Roald Dahl, letter to Michael Sanders, 5 December 1989, RDMSC, RD/16/1/5.

p.182 Like her mother ... Ophelia Dahl, conversation with the author, 6 July 2016.

p.183 Lorina loved monkeys... Liccy Dahl, email correspondence with the author, 15 June 2016.

p.183 She had already... Liccy Dahl, conversation with the author, 10 June 2016.

p.183 Lorina was not one ... Donald Sturrock, *Storyteller: The Life of Roald Dahl*, p.549.

p.183 Dahl meanwhile had looked ... Liccy Dahl, conversation with the author, 10 June 2016.

p.183 'Loopy's back tomorrow,' ... Ophelia Dahl, conversation with the author, 6 July 2016.

p.183 'You'd better talk to ... Liccy Dahl, conversation with the author, 10 June 2016.

p.184 His youngest daughter, Lucy ... Lucy Dahl, conversation with Donald Sturrock, cited in Donald Sturrock, *Storyteller: The Life of Roald Dahl*, p.551.

p.185 *I have clung for* ... Roald Dahl, 'Death of an Old Old Man', *Over to You* (London: Hamish Hamilton, 1946 [1945]), p.151.

p.185 'Dahl was angry ... Liccy Dahl, conversation with the author, 10 June 2016.

p.185 'I saw this patient ... Dr T—— B—— to Mr Crossland [*sic*], 26 March 1990, Dahl Family, private collection.

p.186 Streule recalled that he ... Michael Streule, conversation with the author, 19 June 2016.

p.187 'Of course I did ... Ibid.

p.187 'I've been a bit off ... Roald Dahl, Newsletter for Puffin Books, August 1990, RDMSC, AC/56.

p.187 'Dear Professor Wolfgang ... Roald Dahl to David Weatherall, 9 March 2015, RDMSC, RD/16/1/5.

p.188 'The book was marvellous ... David Weatherall, letter to Roald Dahl, August 1990, RDMSC, RD/16/1/5.

p.188 His last adult short ... Roald Dahl, 'The Surgeon', in *The Complete Short Stories, Volume Two, 1954–1988* (London: Penguin Books, 2013 [1988]), pp.767–802.

p.189 *'He says he wants* ... Ibid., p.678.

Chapter 16: The Patient

p.191 *She screamed, he struggled* ... Egerton Y. Davis, 'Penis Captivus', *Philidelphia Medical News*, 13 December 1884.

p.192 in *The Way Up to Heaven* ... Roald Dahl, 'The Way Up To Heaven', in *Completely Unexpected Tales* (London: Penguin Books, 1986 [1954]), pp.181–94.

p.192 William likes to control ... Roald Dahl, 'William and Mary', in *Completely Unexpected Tales* (London: Penguin Books, 1986 [1960]), pp.154–80.

p.192 in 'Nunc Dimitis', ... Roald Dahl, 'Nunc Dimitis, in *Completely Unexpected Tales* (London: Penguin Books, 1986 [1953]), pp.122–43.

p.192 For example, in 'Mrs Bixby ... Roald Dahl, 'Mrs Bixby and the Colonel's Coat', in *Completely Unexpected Tales* (London: Penguin Books, 1986 [1959]), p.220.

p.192 In 'Georgy Porgy', a ... Roald Dahl, 'Georgy Porgy', in *Completely Unexpected Tales* (London: Penguin Books, 1986 [1960]), p.313.

p.192 'The Visitor' published in ... Roald Dahl, 'The Visitor', *The Complete Short Stories, Volume Two, 1954–1988* (London: Penguin Books, 2013 [1965]); Dahl's memorable description as the *world's greatest fornicator* is in Roald Dahl, *My Uncle Oswald* (London: Penguin Books, 2011 [1979]), p.1.

p.193 We learn of his exploits ... Roald Dahl, 'Bitch', in *The Complete Short Stories, Volume Two, 1954–1988* (London: Penguin Books, 2013 [1974]), and Roald Dahl, *My Uncle Oswald*.

p.193 *Wherever he went,* ... Roald Dahl, 'The Visitor', p.276.

p.193 Described as 'drop dead ... Antoinette Haskell to Donald Sturrock, 14 January 1998, cited in Donald Sturrock, *Storyteller: The Life of Roald Dahl* (London: HarperPress, 2010), p.230.

p.193 Oswald is an expert ... Roald Dahl, 'The Visitor', p.280.

p.193 *the female spider* ... Ibid., p.281.

p.193 *if you are interested* ... Roald Dahl, *My Uncle Oswald*, p.41.

p.193 Nobody ever found it ... Roald Dahl, 'The Visitor', p.283.

p.193 This 'queer, wild, animalistic ... Roald Dahl, 'The Visitor', p.279.

p.194 The attraction between ... Roald Dahl, 'The Last Act' and 'The Great Switcheroo', in *The Complete Short Stories, Volume Two, 1954–1988*, (London: Penguin Books, 2013 [1966] and [1974]), pp.337–77, and pp.378–412.

p.194 He reminds Oswald... Roald Dahl, 'Bitch', in *The Complete Short Stories, Volume Two, 1954–1988*, p.442.

p.194 In *My Uncle Oswald*, the ... Roald Dahl, *My Uncle Oswald*, p.6.

p.195 This plan predated... Paul Olding, 'The Genius Sperm Bank', *BBC Magazine* online, 15 June 2006, http://news.bbc.co.uk/1/hi/magazine/5078800.stm

p.195 Even back in 1944 ... Jeremy Treglown, *Roald Dahl, A Biography* (London: Faber and Faber, 1994), p.4.

p.195 In the 1960s there ... T. J. Gordon, 'Interaction of Technology and Values': a typewritten lecture presented to the University of Pittsburgh, September 1966, RDMSC, RD/16/1/5.

p.195 *Would you rather your* ... Roald Dahl, speech given at Dr Challoner's school prize-giving, RDMSC, RD/6/1/1/3.

p.196 In the adult story ... Roald Dahl, 'Royal Jelly', in *Completely Unexpected Tales* (London: Penguin Books, 1986 [1960]), pp.237–64.

p.196 'You're growing too fast ... Roald Dahl, *George's Marvellous Medicine* (London: Puffin Books, 1984 [1981]), p.10.

p.196 *Grandma yelled "Oweeeee!"* ... Ibid., p.46.

p.197 *'We will become rich* ... Ibid., p.82.

p.198 'I thought he might ... Jeremy Treglown, *Roald Dahl, A Biography*, pp.255–6.

p.202 *It touches you gently* ... Roald Dahl, 'Death of an Old Old Man', *Over to You* (London: Hamish Hamilton, 1946 [1945]), p.150.

p.202 Some of his stories... Roald Dahl, 'Katina', *Over to You* (London: Hamish Hamilton, 1946 [1944]), pp.76–105.

p.202 *I never once during* ... Roald Dahl, 'They Shall Not Grow Old', *Over to You* (London: Hamish Hamilton, 1946 [1945]), p.126.

p.203 Donald Sturrock, Dahl's biographer ... Donald Sturrock, *Storyteller: The Life of Roald Dahl*, p.554.

p.203 *Suddenly there was a brightness...* Roald Dahl, *The Minpins*, (London: Puffin Books, 2008 [1991]), p.43.

p.203 'No one can know what ... Barry Farrell, *Pat and Roald* (London: Hutchinson & Co, 1970), p.82.

p.204 I remembered reading Darwin's ... Charles Darwin, *Expression of Emotions in Man and Animals* (London: John Murray 1872), p.167.

Chapter 17: The Last Night

p.205 When he stopped smoking ... Ophelia Dahl, conversation with the author, 27 April 2016.

p.205 *'I would never want to* ... Roald Dahl, *The Witches* (London: Jonathan Cape, 2010 [1983]), p.234.

p.206 *a harsh, noteless, enormous* ... Roald Dahl, 'The Sound Machine', in *Completely Unexpected Tales* (London: Penguin Books, 1986 [1949]), p.306.

p.207 *How nice it is* ... Roald Dahl, 'Death of an Old Old Man', *Over to You* (London: Hamish Hamilton, 1946 [1945]), p.161.

p.208 As I watch the ... Roald Dahl, 'Mr Botibol', in *Completely Unexpected Tales* (London: Penguin Books, 1986 [1980]), p.362.

p.209 He didn't want a ... Peter Meyer, Tribute at Roald Dahl's Funeral 29 November 1990, the author's personal collection.

p.209 *We have tears in* ... Roald Dahl, *The Giraffe and The Pelly and Me* (London: Puffin Books, 2016 [1985], p.34.

Photo Credits

The War Years

Gloster Gladiator. Courtesy of The Roald Dahl Museum and Story Centre (RDMSC).

Crashed Vichy French plane. © Roald Dahl Nominee Ltd (RDNL), Courtesy of RDMSC.

Dahl in safari gear, 1938. © RDNL, Courtesy of RDMSC.

Dahl in full RAF uniform. © RDNL, Courtesy of RDMSC.

Theo

Theo sleeping. © RDNL, Courtesy of RDMSC.

Theo with his mother. © RDNL, Courtesy of RDMSC.

The taxi which collided with Theo's pram. Photo by Arthur Pomerantz, © NYP Holdings Inc./Getty Images.

Theo enjoying his pipe, early 1970s. © RDNL, Courtesy of RDMSC.

The WDT Valve

Dahl and Stanley Wade. Photos by Leonard McCombe/Time & Life Pictures/Getty Images.

Dahl's original draft, 1963. © RDNL. Courtesy of RDMSC.

The Lancet Publication, 1964 © The Lancet. Reproduced by permission of the Lancet.

The Wade-Dahl-Till valve, kept in Dahl's hut, 2007. Photo by Tom Solomon.

In the background, Dahl's notes. © RDNL. Courtesy of RDMSC.

Olivia

Olivia in school uniform, c.1962. © RDNL. Courtesy of RDMSC.

Dahl restoring the statue, c.1963. © RDNL. Courtesy of RDMSC.

The statue in the Church, 2016. Photograph by the author.

Dahl at Olivia's rock garden grave. Photo by Leonard McCombe/The LIFE Picture Collection/Getty Images.

Olivia's grave today, 2016. Photo by Tom Solomon.

Charity

Dahl signing books, 1986. © RDNL, Courtesy of RDMSC.

Dahl meeting the mayor, 1986. © RDNL, Courtesy of RDMSC.

Measles letter, Courtesy of RDMSC.

Dahl visiting a child in hospital. © RDNL, Courtesy of RDMSC.

Dahl handing over a cheque, 1986. © RDNL, Courtesy of RDMSC.

Pat's Stroke

Patricia Neal recovering after her stroke at Gipsy House, 1965. Photo by George Stroud/Express/Getty Images.

Dahl with Pat and Valeria Eaton Griffith. © RDNL, Courtesy of RDMSC.

Physiotherapy at RAF Halton. Photo by Leonard McCombe/The LIFE Picture Collection/Getty Images.

Dahl, Pat, and baby Lucy, 1965. Photo by Leonard Mccombe/The LIFE Picture Collection/Getty Images.

Pat's words. © RDNL, Courtesy of RDMSC.

Gobblefunk. © RDNL, Courtesy of RDMSC.

The Writer

Dahl writing in his hut. Photo REXMAILPICS.

Dahl's table of artefacts, 2007. Photo by Tom Solomon.

Dippy Dudd, 1987, Courtesy of Shell Company.

Hepatticus, 1992, BMA News Review, Courtesy of British Medical Association.

The author with his first delivery, 1989. © Tom Solomon.

Dahl with Liccy at his 70th birthday party, 1986. © RDNL, Courtesy of RDMSC.

The Final Years

Dahl and Liccy's wedding, 1983. © RDNL, Courtesy of RDMSC.

Dahl outside his hut. Photo by Ian Cook/The LIFE Images Collection/Getty Images.

Liccy and the author's children, 2007. Photo by Tom Solomon.

Dahl in bed with Chopper, 1990. Photo by Jan Baldwin. © Jan Baldwin.

Cover

Dahl in his writing hut © Stephen Umpleby, Outside Studios/Roald Dahl Nominee Limited (RDNL). Courtesy of The Roald Dahl Museum and Story Centre (RDMSC).

Index

Oscar for performance in *Hud* 124, 131, 155

personality changes following stroke 170–71

return to public life and career after stroke 166–7, 169–70

speech therapy following stroke 153–62, 164, 165

stroke and recovery 131–41, 142–7, 150–52, 153–62, 184

surgery 138–9

The Night Digger 169–70

The Subject was Roses 167, 169

work for stroke rehabilitation 165

Newman, Paul 166

Osler, Sir William 190–92, 209

Parker, Professor Bill 12–13

Parris, Matthew 4

Phillips, Rodney 40, 190

Phipps, James 116

polio vaccine 118, 122–3

Pollinger, Murray 89

Rainsford Evans, Dr Phillip 99, 109

Ransohoff, Joseph 81–4, 85–6, 87–8

Rathbone, Basil 69

Repton School (Derbyshire) 15, 16, 26–7, 28, 112, 124

Richardson, Sir John 164

Ritchie, Dr Anne 165

Rogers, Ginger 69

Roosevelt, Eleanor 56, 69

Rudd, Professor Tony 163

Sabin, Albert 118

St Peter's School (Weston-Super-Mare) 16, 18, 25–6

Salk, Jonas 118

Saunders, Wally 68

Shine (Spina bifida, Hydrocephalus,

Information, Networking, Equality) 89

Shipman, Harold 209

Shulman, Kenneth 86, 87–8

Sinatra, Frank 153

Singer, Milton 81, 82

smallpox vaccination 106, 108

Smith, Dr Barry 119, 120–21

snakes

anti-venom treatments 32–3

featuring in Dahl's writing 29–30

snake injuries 30–32

venom-derived drugs 33

Solomon, Bruce 30

Solomon, Daisy 124

Solomon, Eva 124, 180

Solomon, Guy 30

Solomon, Leah 124

Solomon, Moses 3

Solomon, Rosie 124

Solomon, Tom 1–2, 124

'Hepatticus' column 51

as medical student in Thailand 30–33, 38–9

night-time discussions with RD in hospital ward 7–9, 28, 43

practice of keeping notes 43–4

research on brain infections 38

research on malaria 8, 39–42, 51, 190

surgical training 20–24

time in Mozambique 39–41, 45, 184

Steinbeck, John 61

Stephenson, William 56

Streule, Dr Michael 34, 186–7

stroke rehabilitation 147, 153–62, 164–73

Stroke Association 164

Volunteer Stroke Scheme 165

Sturrock, Donald 4, 62, 126, 203

Storyteller 60

subarachnoid haemorrhage 133

Charity Support

All of the author royalties from this book are being donated to charities working in areas that were of interest to Roald Dahl. The first five charities will receive ten per cent each, and the final one will receive fifty per cent.

The Encephalitis Society

Dahl's oldest daughter Olivia died from encephalitis (inflammation of the brain) caused by measles virus. The Encephalitis Society (Registered charity no: 1087843) improves the quality of life of all people affected directly and indirectly by encephalitis in the UK and internationally. It provides support to patients, their families and carers, raises awareness, and galvanises research into the condition. Tom Solomon chairs their Professional Advisory Panel.

www.encephalitis.info

Roald Dahl's Marvellous Children's Charity

Dahl went out of his way to help seriously ill children. Roald Dahl's Marvellous Children's Charity (Registered charity no: 1137409) helps to make life better for children with serious and rare conditions, and their families. The Roald Dahl specialist children's nurses support both children's medical and emotional needs. The charity believes every child has the right to a more marvellous life, no matter how ill they are, or how short their life may be.

www.roalddahlcharity.org

Shine
(Spina Bifida, Hydrocephalus, Information, Networking and Equality)

Dahl's son Theo had hydrocephalus, and he invented a valve to treat the condition. He joined meetings of parents whose children were similarly affected, the forerunner to The Association for Spina Bifida and Hydrocephalus (ASBAH), which recently became Shine (Registered charity no: 249338). Shine provides specialist support from before birth and throughout the life of anyone living with spina bifida and/ or hydrocephalus, as well as to parents, families, carers and professional care staff.

www.shinecharity.org.uk

The Stroke Association

When Dahl's first wife, Patricia Neal, had a stroke he devised a new innovative rehabilitation scheme, which was taken up by others and grew into a whole movement that was a key step in the formation of The Stroke Association. Today, the Stroke Association is the UK's leading charity dedicated to conquering stroke. It supports stroke survivors to make the best recovery they can, campaigns for better stroke care and funds research to develop new treatments and ways of preventing stroke (Registered charity nos: England and Wales 211015; Scotland SC037789; Northern Ireland XT33805; Isle of Man 945; Jersey NPO 369).

www.stroke.org.uk

The Walton Centre Charity

Dahl was intrigued by all manner of neurological conditions, believing his creative genius followed his own head injury, and spending time supporting both adults and children's neurology and neurosurgery services. The Walton Centre Charity (Registered charity no: 1050050) supports the work of The Walton Centre in Liverpool, where Tom Solomon is a consultant neurologist. It is the UK's only specialist neuroscience hospital trust dedicated to providing comprehensive neurology, neurosurgery, spinal and pain management services, treating over 100,000 patients a year with conditions including head and spinal trauma, stroke, tumours, epilepsy, and brain infections.

www.thewaltoncentre.nhs.uk/fundraising

The University of Liverpool, Institute of Infection and Global Health

Tom Solomon is Director of the Institute of Infection and Global Health at the University of Liverpool (Exempt charity no: X7758) and Heads the Liverpool Brain Infections Group. Established in 1998, the Group conducts research on encephalitis and other brain infections in the UK and globally. This includes vaccine preventable diseases, such as Japanese encephalitis, and other emerging brain infections. The Group also supports clinical service, training and capacity building.

www.liverpool.ac.uk/braininfections

'Somewhere inside all of us is the power to change the world'

– Matilda